# Paying for Progress in China

China's stunning record of economic development since the 1970s has been marred by an increasingly obvious gap between the country's "haves" and its "have-nots." While people living in some parts of the country have enjoyed dramatically improved conditions of life, those in other districts and regions have slipped ever further behind in terms of access to health, wealth, education, security and opportunity.

*Paying for Progress in China* is a collection of original essays which trace the causes of this growing inequality, using new data including surveys, interviews, newly available official statistics and in-depth fieldwork. Their findings expose the malfunctioning of China's "broken" intergovernmental fiscal system, which has exacerbated the disequalizing effects of emerging market forces. While the government's deliberately "pro-poor" development policies have in recent years sought to reduce the gap between rich and poor, both markets, and also state institutions and policies, are continuing to create perverse equity outcomes across the country, confounding hopes for better-balanced and more inclusive growth in China.

The interdisciplinary approach of this collection, incorporating work by economists, sociologists and political scientists, makes it a valuable resource for students of contemporary Chinese political economy and social development.

**Vivienne Shue** is the Leverhulme Professor and Director of the Contemporary China Studies Programme at Oxford University.

**Christine Wong** is the Henry M. Jackson Professor of International Studies at the University of Washington.

## Routledge Contemporary China Series

1 **Nationalism, Democracy and National Integration in China**
*Leong Liew and Wang Shaoguang*

2 **Hong Kong's Tortuous Democratization**
A comparative analysis
*Ming Sing*

3 **China's Business Reforms**
Institutional challenges in a globalised economy
*Edited by Russell Smyth and Cherrie Zhu*

4 **Challenges for China's Development**
An enterprise perspective
*Edited by David H. Brown and Alasdair MacBean*

5 **New Crime in China**
Public order and human rights
*Ron Keith and Zhiqiu Lin*

6 **Non-Governmental Organizations in Contemporary China**
Paving the way to civil society?
*Qiusha Ma*

7 **Globalization and the Chinese City**
*Fulong Wu*

8 **The Politics of China's Accession to the World Trade Organization**
The dragon goes global
*Hui Feng*

9 **Narrating China**
Jia Pingwa and his fictional world
*Yiyan Wang*

10 **Sex, Science and Morality in China**
*Joanne McMillan*

11 **Politics in China Since 1949**
Legitimizing authoritarian rule
*Robert Weatherley*

12 **International Human Resource Management in Chinese Multinationals**
*Jie Shen and Vincent Edwards*

13 **Unemployment in China**
Economy, human resources and labour markets
*Edited by Grace Lee and Malcolm Warner*

14 **China and Africa**
Engagement and compromise
*Ian Taylor*

15 **Gender and Education in China**
Gender discourses and women's schooling in the early twentieth century
*Paul J. Bailey*

16 **SARS**
Reception and interpretation in three Chinese cities
*Edited by Deborah Davis and Helen Siu*

17 **Human Security and the Chinese State**
Historical transformations and the modern quest for sovereignty
*Robert E. Bedeski*

18 **Gender and Work in Urban China**
Women workers of the unlucky generation
*Liu Jieyu*

19 **China's State Enterprise Reform**
From Marx to the market
*John Hassard, Jackie Sheehan, Meixiang Zhou, Jane Terpstra-Tong and Jonathan Morris*

20 **Cultural Heritage Management in China**
Preserving the cities of the Pearl River Delta
*Edited by Hilary du Cros and Yok-shiu F. Lee*

21 **Paying for Progress in China**
Public finance, human welfare and changing patterns of inequality
*Edited by Vivienne Shue and Christine Wong*

# Paying for Progress in China

## Public finance, human welfare and changing patterns of inequality

**Edited by Vivienne Shue and Christine Wong**

Routledge
Taylor & Francis Group
LONDON AND NEW YORK

First published 2007
by Routledge
2 Park Square, Milton Park, Abingdon, Oxon OX14 4RN

Simultaneously published in the USA and Canada
by Routledge
270 Madison Ave, New York, NY 10016

*Routledge is an imprint of the Taylor & Francis Group, an informa business*



Typeset in Times New Roman
by Keystroke, High Street, Tettenhall, Wolverhampton



*British Library Cataloguing in Publication Data*
A catalogue record for this book is available from the British Library

*Library of Congress Cataloging in Publication Data*
Shue, Vivienne
Paying for Progress in China: Public finance, human welfare and changing patterns of inequality/Vivienne Shue and Christine Wong
p.cm. – (Routledge contemporary China series)
Includes bibliographical references and index
1. China–Economic conditions–Regional disparities. 2. China–Social conditions–Regional disparities. I. Wong, Christine, 1950– II. Title
HC427.92.S5548 2007
330.951–dc22
2006035611

ISBN10: 0–415–42254–X (hbk)
ISBN10: 0–203–96197–8 (ebk)

ISBN13: 978–0–415–42254–3 (hbk)
ISBN13: 978–0–203–96197–1 (ebk)

*This volume is dedicated to Professor Dame Jessica Rawson, Warden of Merton College, Oxford, passionate student of the Chinese past and harbinger, in Oxford, for China's future*

# Contents

# Illustrations

## Figures



## Tables

## Box

# Contributors

**Jane Duckett** is Senior Lecturer in Politics at the University of Glasgow. She has published papers on Chinese local government, welfare, social security and urban health insurance. She is currently researching the impact of NGOs on health policy in China.

**Athar Hussain** is Acting Director of the Asia Research Centre at the London School of Economics. His research interests include social security, urban poverty and public finance.

**Liu Chengfang** is a doctoral candidate in the Department of Agricultural and Resource Economics at the University of California, Davis. Her research interests include public economics, labor economics and applied econometrics. Her current research work is mainly on public goods investment, land tenure, education, and gender.

**Liu Mingxing** is an Associate Professor in the School of Government at Peking University. His research interests cover a range of issues in contemporary China's local governance, including village elections, local public finance and fiscal decentralization.

**Luo Renfu** is a Postdoctoral Research Fellow at the Center for Chinese Agricultural Policy of the Chinese Academy of Sciences. His current research work is focused on rural fiscal systems, community governance and public goods investment.

**Rachel Murphy** is Senior Lecturer in East Asian Studies at Bristol University. Her publications include *How Migrant Labor is Changing Rural China* (2002), *Chinese Citizenship,* edited with V. L. Fong (2006), and papers on rural development, population, culture and communication technologies.

**Carl Riskin** is Distinguished Professor of Economics at Queens College, CUNY, and Senior Research Scholar at the Weatherhead East Asian Institute, Columbia University. He is the co-author (with A. R. Khan) of *Inequality and Poverty in China in the Age of Globalization* (2001).

**Scott Rozelle** holds the Helen Farnsworth Endowed Professorship at Stanford University and is Senior Fellow and Professor in the Shorenstein Asia-Pacific

Research Center, Freeman Spogli Institute of International Studies. His research is centered on agricultural policy, China's rural development and issues of resource and environment.

**Victor Shih** is Assistant Professor of Political Science at Northwestern University. His previous work focuses on the linkage between factional politics and financial policies, and his current research explores the links between authoritarian governance and fiscal policies.

**Vivienne Shue** is the Leverhulme Professor and Director of the Contemporary China Studies Programme at Oxford University and a Fellow of St Antony's College. She has published a number of books and papers on problems of local government and administration in China, taxation and public finance, public/private charity, and political legitimacy.

**Tao Ran** is the Shaw Research Fellow in the Economy of China at Oxford University. He is also affiliated with the Center for Chinese Agricultural Policy at the Chinese Academy of Sciences. His main area of research is local governance in transition, urbanization and labor market development in China.

**Christine Wong** holds the Henry M. Jackson Professorship in International Studies in the Henry M. Jackson School of International Studies, University of Washington. She was principal author of the World Bank report, *China: National Development and Subnational Finance, a Review of Provincial Expenditures* (2002). She is also editor and principal author of two previous books on China's public finance: *Financing Local Government in the People's Republic of China* (1997) and *Fiscal Management and Economic Reform in the People's Republic of China* (1995).

**Zhang Linxiu** is Professor and Deputy Director at the Center for Chinese Agricultural Policy of the Chinese Academy of Sciences. His current research is focused mainly in the areas of rural off-farm employment, poverty, land tenure and gender, community governance and public goods investment.

**Zhang Qi** is a doctoral candidate in the Department of Political Science at Northwestern University. He is also a consultant for the Center for Chinese Agricultural Policy at the Chinese Academy of Sciences.

# Introduction

## Is China moving to a more equitable development strategy?

*Vivienne Shue and Christine Wong*

Global opinion-leaders – some thinking they may need to find a way to beat it and others only wishing they could join it – are disposed these days to marvel at the miracle of China's swift and sustained economic growth and the brisk pace of its march toward technical modernization. Closer observers of Chinese affairs however, and the Chinese people themselves, know another side to this success story. China's recent stunning economic and technological developments have not benefited all of its people equally, and the Chinese social order has been marred by the appearance of increasingly stark divides between the country's "haves" and its "have nots."

At the time it began its transition to a market economy in the late 1970s, China already displayed certain peculiarly stark patterns of inequality in access to health, wealth, education, security and opportunity. By the mid- to late 1990s, despite a sharp general rise in the standard of living and impressive progress made along various other key dimensions of socio-economic development, the situation with respect to inequality had become strikingly worse. While people living in some parts of the country were manifestly enjoying dramatically improved conditions of life, those in other districts and regions were seen to be slipping ever further behind. With a Gini coefficient (measuring overall inequality) of 0.45 in the 1990s, China had fallen below most Asian countries in terms of equity – India for example has a Gini coefficient of 0.33, Indonesia 0.34, and Korea 0.32. Instead, it had joined the company of those Asian societies that are known to be more highly unequal – Thailand (0.43) and the Philippines (0.46). If this pace and direction of change continues, China may soon join the ranks of those Latin American countries such as Mexico (0.55) and Brazil (0.59), which are among the most inequitable societies on the globe.

The 1990s also witnessed, not coincidentally, a flood of angry public protests in various parts of the country that were being powered by poor people's frustrations – evermore bitterly voiced complaints of vulnerability, unfairness, and neglect. Although at first such protests went mostly unreported in the Chinese media, the public security apparatus accumulated records of hundreds, and then thousands, of demonstrations each year by people out of work, pensioners denied their allowances, desperately overburdened rural taxpayers, and parents who could not meet their children's school bills. After the 1999 Falun Gong demonstrations and the state's violent suppression of that movement highlighted just how many people, in the absence of adequate medical insurance coverage, had been turning to mystical religious practices in hope of curing disease and safeguarding their health, the painful gaps in China's public social service net and the human misery hidden in its hardening patterns of socio-economic inequality came to be linked more explicitly to concerns about the very maintenance of public calm, of nationwide political stability, and of popular support for the Party-state.

Toward the end of the 1990s the central government began to respond with new programs aimed at redressing the imbalances and patching up the social safety net, the most publicized of these being the Western Development Initiative in 1999. It seems possible, in fact, that inequalities in China may already have reached their peak in the late 1990s. The research reported by several of the contributors to this volume, when taken together (Wong, Zhang et al., Duckett, Hussain), suggests that a turning point may well have been reached around 1998/1999, when a number of central state programs were introduced in an effort to reverse existing inequities, strengthen social protection, and press for greater equalization in access to resources. The chapter prepared for this volume by Carl Riskin argues, furthermore, that the sheer unfolding of market forces may have been largely responsible for moderating the growth of inequality in China toward the end of the 1990s. His analysis, based on a well-designed 2002 household income survey, concludes that "at least in the period 1995 to 2002, poverty fell sharply and most dimensions of inequality held stable or fell." Thanks largely to the spread of wage employment in rural areas and to the phasing out of distorted public subsidies for housing in urban areas China, Riskin's data allow him to speculate, may now have passed "the maximum amount of inequality produced by its unbalanced development path."

The authors whose research is reported in this collection have each interrogated new data – gathered from surveys, statistical reports, fieldwork, and interviews – seeking to pinpoint and clarify the observable equity effects both of markets and of recent "pro-poor" state policies in China. The essays gathered here are notable for their empirical richness. The analyses in Chapter 2 by Carl Riskin and in Chapter 6 by Zhang Linxiu and his collaborators draw from large-scale surveys – covering 16,000 households in 21 provinces (Riskin) and nearly 2,500 villages scattered over 6 provinces (Zhang et al.). Rachel Murphy's chapter is based on three months of fieldwork plus an additional month-long follow-up study in rural Jiangxi, an area where she had previously spent over a year engaged in research. In Chapter 7, Victor Shih and Zhang Qi have made use of a national data-set from the Ministry of Finance, with detailed fiscal information for all of China's more than 2,000 counties. Liu Mingxing and Tao Ran have conducted extensive field-work and surveys of their own. The chapters by Christine Wong, Jane Duckett and Athar Hussain all draw upon official reports and Chinese government statistics, as well as fieldwork and interviews, mostly conducted in the course of multilateral and bilateral aid work in China. On the whole, these analysts' most up-to-date findings have not left them very sanguine about present trends. Their work reveals, rather, many reasons to conclude that *both* markets *and* state policies continue to create perverse equity outcomes across the country, largely confounding the hopes that have been raised for better balanced and more inclusive growth.

In Chapter 1, Christine Wong opens the discussion with a critical focus on China's fiscal system, the main instrument through which redistributions of resources to offset both regional and interpersonal inequalities might be effected in support of the government's new pro-poor policies. She emphasizes the extraordinary degree to which fiscal expenditures in China have become decentralized in the course of repeated waves of tax reform. As of 2004, the central government was allocating only about 30 percent of all budgetary expenditures while 70 percent of total budgeted spending was being carried out by local governments. This intergovernmental spending imbalance has come about because local authorities in China are burdened with responsibility for meeting the costs of such a large share of the nation's expensive public services, including the costs of basic public welfare, subsidies to pension schemes and unemployment insurance, as well as 70 percent of public spending on education and well over 50 percent of the costs of public health. Since 1994 the fiscal system has not provided adequate resources, on average, for local governments to finance the costs of their responsibilities. The intergovernmental fiscal transfers, which could and should be used to assist poorer localities in meeting these public responsibilities, Wong explains further, have actually been heavily assigned through mechanisms such as earmarked subsidies and tax rebates, which are regressive and disequalizing. "By leaving so many costly but important responsibilities at the local level and providing no support to their financing, [during the 1990s] the national government [had] essentially abrogated its responsibility to the poor regions," she concludes.

In more recent years however – even before the announcement of its new, more balanced, development paradigm – the central state had begun to make amends. Starting from 1998/1999, resource transfers to poorer inland provinces were increased sharply, with some improvements in equalization. Viewed overall however, China's budgetary spending on public services such as health and education remained just too low – in the region of 2 to 2.5 percent of gross domestic product (GDP) on education, and under 2 percent on health. Moreover, the majority of these increased central subsidies were going to bailing out underfunded local social security schemes, filling other funding gaps, and paying for the mandated wage increases of civil servants at local levels. Draining off central funds to put out local fires like these has limited the overall allocative strength of central authorities, since too little discretionary funding has remained with which the center might actually press forward on new and more effective pro-poor programs and investments. Wong describes the current intergovernmental fiscal system as "broken" and concludes that, until there is a "fundamental reform" of that system, central policymakers will continue to be very largely frustrated in their attempts to effect a significant reversal of China's troubling trends toward evermore gross inequalities.

In Chapter 2, "Has China reached the top of the Kuznets Curve?," Carl Riskin provides a detailed analysis of the 2002 round of an ongoing nationwide survey of households in both rural and urban China that has, in the past, found income inequality to be more serious and growing faster than the government acknowledged. Comparing levels and patterns of inequality between 1995 and 2002, he finds that inequality (as measured by the Gini ratio) declined by 10 percent among the rural households, and by 4.2 percent among the urban households in the sample. Within both rural and urban sectors, Riskin finds that regional inequality also declined.

The major factor behind the decline in rural income inequality during that period was the growth of wage income and its spread into inland provinces. Examining the different components of rural income, Riskin discovers an extraordinary growth in the spread of wage income throughout rural China. While in 1995 only 5 percent of rural households reported having off-farm earnings from wage employment, this proportion was seen to have risen to over 27 percent by 2002. Moreover, the biggest increases occurred in the provinces with the lowest percentage of wage recipients in 1995 – Yunnan went from nearly 0 percent in 1995 to 15 percent in 2002, Jiangxi from 1 to 34 percent, and Guizhou from 1 to 24 percent. These trends led the share of wages in overall rural income to grow from 22 to 29 percent, and for its distribution to be 38 percent less unequal.

The "Kuznets Curve" derives from a hypothesis advanced by Simon Kuznets in the 1950s that the change in inequality over time follows an inverted U shape, i.e. inequality increases during the initial phase of industrialization, then stabilizes and eventually decreases as modern economic growth spreads more widely throughout the economy and society. The decline Riskin observes in regional inequality and the role wage income plays in the rural story are both consistent with a turnaround in the Kuznets Curve. That is, both an increase in the share of wage income and a decline in its concentration ratio are consistent with a story of geographic and sectoral spread of wage employment that reduces the extreme advantage of the early developing localities and sectors.

Could we now be looking forward to a long period during which the benefits of development will spread more equally across the country and be enjoyed by more and more of China's people? Perhaps. However, Riskin cautions that it may in reality be "too early to predict that China is becoming a more egalitarian society" since the "forces impeding that evolution are still very strong." For starters, in contrast to the Kuznets story about the beneficent effects that flow from the development of market forces, the urban picture Riskin observes is rather different. While urban areas did also see a decline in inequality between 1995 and 2002, this was mainly due to policy factors: the introduction of new safety net measures that propped up incomes for the poorest, and the phasing out of housing subsidies that had been highly disequalizing. These trends point to the important role played by government policy in shaping distributional outcomes. Furthermore, according to Riskin's analysis, overall income inequality remained virtually unchanged for the nation as a whole between 1995 and 2002 because of the continued increase in the average gap between urban and rural incomes. These findings run counter to the expectation that fuller development of market forces will be sufficient to turn around the recent very sharp trends towards inequality in China.

Chapters 3, 4, and 5 look in much greater depth at the forms and the extent of inequalities in access to three fundamental categories of public goods: health services, education, and social security (or basic welfare) services. Jane Duckett draws on a large number of official reports and scholarly studies to analyze changing patterns in unequal access to health services in both rural and urban China since the 1980s. The picture she paints is a nuanced, yet unequivocally dismal one. The already gaping urban–rural differential in access to health care that had characterized the Mao period remains in place. Superimposed upon that critical divide now, as a result of all the recent piecemeal restructurings in health finance and the spread of private health care, are some radically new patterns of interpersonal and inter-household inequality as well.

The expansion of private health services, for example, has brought new practitioners and better technology to wealthier areas, even as it has drawn doctors and nurses looking for higher incomes away from poorer towns and counties. "Since ill-health is likely to be more prevalent among the poor, the fact that health service provision is weakest in areas where risk of poverty is highest means that the present pattern of provision is particularly inequitable," Duckett observes.

Since the mid-1990s, as Duckett documents, some efforts have been made to re-establish voluntary, cooperative, risk-pooling systems to finance rural health provision. In urban areas, compulsory basic social health insurance schemes have been launched with risk-pooling at city level and contributions from employers and employees. In both rural and urban areas, some medical financial assistance programs to help the very poor and those out of work meet medical costs have also been set up. But most of these programs are not yet functioning well and they remain very far from reaching all who need them. Such glaring inequalities in access to health services are "unlikely to be challenged in the near future" she concludes, unless the prevailing basic systems of health finance and administration are comprehensively addressed. "Central investment needs to be increased and better targeted, while local governments need to be given more incentives to prioritize health."

Rachel Murphy comes to parallel conclusions where patterns of unequal access to good quality primary and secondary education are concerned. China's public investment in education has been low by comparison with other developing countries, and per student investment is much lower in rural than in urban areas. Under the present highly decentralized fiscal system, school funding at local levels has depended heavily on the general affluence, or poverty, of different communities and jurisdictions. Citing a 2001 study conducted by Chinese scholars, Murphy notes that in the case of Jiangxi province a full 78 percent of public spending on education has been coming from township-level resources, 20 percent from county- and provincial-levels together, and a mere 2 percent from the center. To raise the required funds to pay teachers, maintain school buildings and buy equipment, then, local authorities have had little alternative but to resort to levying numerous special taxes and surcharges on rural residents. In poorer villages and towns, however, there have been very sharp limits on how much money can be raised this way: teachers have frequently gone unpaid, and the quality of the classrooms, accommodations, and services delivered to children and their parents have been compromised.

When local fiscal resources are limited by poverty, and government support is chronically inadequate, schools themselves are frequently forced into raising some of their own funds. Some have tried running small businesses on the side to bring in cash, with children sometimes pressed into service as workers in these enterprises. Virtually all schools are compelled to charge fees now for attendance – fees that are proportionately much steeper and harder for poor rural families to meet than those collected from more comfortably off urban residents when they enrol their children in city public schools. Based on her fieldwork and interviews, Murphy argues that the comparatively high costs of keeping children in school, and the generally lower quality of the education they receive in poorer communities, are leading large numbers of children in poor areas to drop out well before graduation. Furthermore, senior high schools charging higher and higher enrolment fees, "school selection fees," and "top-up fees" can also be seen, in the current environment, as contributing to a corrosive culture of "commercialization" in secondary education, and to the gradual conversion of open access to non-compulsory education from a universal right into a privilege realistically available only to those who can afford it.

Murphy finds also that the nationwide "fees-for-tax" reform, implemented in 2004, appears only to have worsened the situation in poor regions. Intended to relieve the heavy tax burden on farmers by abolishing informal local levies and *ad hoc* fees, replacing these with a single fixed-rate tax and transfers to compensate for funding shortfalls, the immediate effect of the reform has been instead to exacerbate the capital shortage in rural schools. The transfers delivered – in Murphy's fieldwork site, just 30 yuan per student per semester for junior high school and 12 yuan per student per semester for senior high school – have been "far from adequate and many county and township governments and schools in agricultural localities were forced into debt." Murphy, like Duckett, finds little reason to look for any broad improvement in the situation unless certain fundamental systemic changes can be brought about. Ensuring fairer access to basic education in China's poor rural communities will ultimately depend on raising central investments, targeting them more sensitively, and giving local authorities the effective incentives they need to prioritize the achievement of universal primary and secondary school attendance.

In Chapter 5, Athar Hussain presents a comprehensive overview of China's social security system and of how it has been changing gradually – all too gradually – when observed against the backdrop of a number of epochal social transitions that have also been taking place over the past 25 years: transitions such as the very rapid aging of the population, the massive shift of labor out of agriculture and into industry and services, the decline of state sector employment generally, and the increasing privatization of assets. His account makes it clear that while the transition to a market economy has brought dramatic improvements to the well-being of the Chinese populace, it has also exposed many to new risks and economic insecurities that call for stronger safety nets. The government's response to this particular challenge of the transition has been piecemeal, fragmentary, inadequate, and powerfully urban-biased.

According to Hussain, reform of the social security regime and "particularly of the schemes covering the urban population" has been a policy strand running steadily through the transition period since 1978. This is because the market reforms very quickly began to erode the "three pillars" upon which the old socialist urban social security system had rested. The first of these pillars was what Hussain calls "a planned economy version of 'welfare through work'" – the requirement that all able-bodied members of society contribute to it through work, coupled with the "government's obligation to provide them with a job." The second pillar of the regime was the extended social welfare roles that were assumed by urban work units (*danwei*), including the enterprise-based system of Labor Insurance that covered disability pay and retirement pensions. The third pillar was the confident expectation each worker could have of life-long tenure as a member of the *danwei*. The relentless crumbling of these three pillars during the reform period brought great hardship to many, eventually forcing the government to fund bailouts for faltering Labor Insurance schemes and to start looking for alternative schemes better suited to the changing socio-economy.

In the rural sector under market reforms, poverty has demonstrably fallen dramatically. However, the dissolution of the old agricultural collectives brought with it also the near total collapse of local cooperative health insurance schemes, leaving hundreds of millions of farmers with no alternative but to pay out-of-pocket for health care, and thus exposing them to financial risks, as Jane Duckett pointedly details in Chapter 3. The large-scale movement of younger rural laborers into urban employment increased rural incomes, to be sure, but it often also left elderly family members alone in the villages without the necessary support of kin in times of illness or other crises. Changes such as these, which have created new and sometimes greater needs, have prompted experimentation with novel forms of welfare assistance in the villages.

Still, Hussain notes that the government's efforts to build a new social security system have focused overwhelmingly on the urban population, and the result has been to leave "glaring" differences in safety net coverage for the urban and rural populations. The new system of Social Insurance, which replaced the Labor Insurance scheme, currently covers 43 percent of the urban labor force. In contrast, few among the rural population enjoy old-age pensions. Those rural pension schemes that do exist are very small-scale; they cover only 11 percent of the rural labor force and promise to provide only a very modest percentage of what is judged to be minimum subsistence. Nor is it only those actually engaged in farming who are not covered by currently existing Social Insurance schemes. Excluded also are most rural migrants living and working in cities and towns and rural employees in township and village enterprises, who are also not covered for unemployment. The clear result at present, as Hussain explains, is that (at least on paper) China's "urban population enjoys a comparatively high level of social security by the standards of developing economies" while, in stark contrast, all existing schemes covering rural people "fall under the category of 'social assistance', aimed at relieving severe poverty only."

Chapters 6 and 7 examine in much greater depth two key components of China's economic strategy for the alleviation of poverty and promotion of greater equity: its rural investments program and its system for allocating fiscal subsidies and transfers. The research team of Zhang Linxiu, Luo Renfu, Liu Chengfang and Scott Rozelle present statistics from a 1998–2003 six province, 36 county, data-set on the sources and types of investments that were then being made in China's rural villages. Their data is unusually interesting in that it is based on information collected from village-level representatives themselves, rather than from higher level authorities and other aggregate sources. Their findings are also, overall, rather more positive than previous studies would have led us to expect.

First, they find that during those five years there was a "surprising level of investment activity in rural China" – some 9,138 investment projects in their total of 2,459 sample villages. They are also able to show that a very considerable proportion of this investment – that is, *most* of it, counting that which came both from higher levels of the state and that which was raised by villagers themselves – was being devoted to public goods projects. Roads, bridges, irrigation and drainage projects, drinking water, schools, and environmental protection forestry investments were most common. They find evidence, also, that the quality of the projects undertaken was improving over those carried out in earlier years.

In measuring the proportion of funding coming from higher state levels into the villages, Zhang and his co-authors found also that public goods investments were being targeted at especially poor villages and at villages inhabited by ethnic minorities. "The results," they observe, "show that officials are channelling funds to smaller, more remote and mountainous villages with little irrigated area." And this leads them to the view that state officials in China have now moved to a "progressive or pro-poor, ethnically sensitive and environmentally oriented" strategy of rural investment.

These signs of significant progress over the patterns that prevailed in earlier years are then put into comparative perspective. The amounts being invested now in China are found, for example, to be larger, by comparison, than those invested in many other developing countries. When compared to other East Asian nations during their take-off periods, however, the picture darkens. "While China currently is only investing between 40 to 50 US dollars per capita into rural areas, Japan during the 1950s and 1960s was spending about 400 US dollars per capita." The comparable figure for South Korea during the 1970s and 1980s was over 200 US dollars. Thus the authors conclude, from the rich evidence they were able to gather, that there is indeed reason to believe that we are now witnessing in China a shift away from net taxation to net investment in rural areas. The magnitude of this shift, however, is so far "not sufficient to push the nation decisively toward rural modernization."

In Chapter 7, Victor Shih and Zhang Qi investigate the workings of China's system of redistribution through subsidies and fiscal transfers. Using a Ministry of Finance data-set that covers every county-level unit in the country in both 1995 and 2000, their study aims to clarify the factors that have driven the distribution of subsidies from higher levels to counties. They seek to understand whether, following the centralizing 1994 tax reforms, the center's ability to allocate to poor regions was, as claimed, actually improved. Their analysis and findings, interestingly, suggest just "the opposite." In large part this, they argue, is due to the fact, already highlighted by Wong, that programs of earmarked subsidies and subsidies granted in the form of tax rebates are inherently regressive rather than equalizing. Still, the clearest result that emerges from the authors' analysis of factors, for both 1995 and 2000, is not about the disequalizing effects of tax rebates but about the high correlation that exists between the number of county-level personnel (payment of whose salaries is dependent on fiscal allocations) on the payroll in a county, and the total amount of subsidies per capita that the county has received.

On the basis of this strong correlation, Shih and Zhang conclude that their "data do not suggest that concerns of economic equity underlie the allocation of subsidies to counties" after 1994. On the contrary, it is anxiety about being unable to meet the wage bill for county-level personnel (and the political instability that might cause) that is seen as driving choices about the allocation of transfers. Shih and Zhang argue that the Chinese fiscal system, through the device of transfers, has rewarded counties that have managed to find ways to increase their payroll demands rather than allocating resources specifically to needy localities. Their analysis helps in understanding why China's local governments have continued to expand the size of their personnel despite the fact that they lack the revenue to pay for wages. Expanding payroll has amounted to a nearly sure way for them to increase the remittance of higher level subsidies to their localities. The transfer system, therefore, is revealed to have been largely self-defeating: turning a nearly blind eye to the actual needs of poor communities and creating, instead, perverse incentives for local officials to pad their staffs rather than to pursue more efficient uses of available resources.

The final chapter, by Liu Mingxing and Tao Ran, takes a closer look at what the authors call the "logic of local governance" – the complex set of administrative institutions and practices that condition the investment priorities and the political tactics of local-level officials with responsibility for delivering public goods. They point out that, while economic and fiscal decentralization have indeed gone very far in China, the system of administrative appointments and political accountability remains a highly unified and centralized one. All local government officials are assigned to the posts they hold – and all can be obliged to transfer to different posts – by Party-state authorities who are situated at superior levels of the bureaucracy. The performance of all local government officials is, furthermore, continuously monitored from above. The economic, social, environmental and other policy targets (or "mandates") they are required to meet are also all set at higher levels. And their individual performances in their posts are evaluated according to goals and criteria which are stipulated in detail by higher authorities.

Under such a centralized target-setting and monitoring system, it may be imagined that fairly consistent levels of local government competence and efficiency should be maintained across regions. In fact, however, the quality of leadership provided and services delivered by local officials varies notoriously from place to place in China today. Liu and Tao, using data they gathered in a survey conducted in 12 counties across nine provinces – some of which are economically highly developed localities, some middling, and some less-developed – seek to account for the wide variation that is to be found in local public services. They compare levels of labor and capital mobility as well as the relative degrees of priority given to different policy targets in township and village cadre evaluation exercises. They find that it is relatively much easier for local officials in more developed areas to meet or exceed the policy targets on which their own performance will be measured and their suitability for career advancement judged. In such fortunate circumstances, they find it possible, indeed desirable, to bend their efforts to better provision of public services that will both satisfy local residents and attract new business and investment. In less developed regions the reverse obtains: local cadres are compelled to press residents hard for tax payments to meet their revenue targets, resort to levying extra fees to meet their economic growth and social control targets, and scheme about how to secure central subsidies to cover shortfalls and provide what public goods they can.

"All in all," Liu and Tao conclude then, "in more developed regions, the increasingly intensive interregional competition that has resulted from the much higher mobility of labor and capital, together with what are in effect proportionately lower policy burdens from above, have worked well to curb predatory and excessively regulatory government behaviour and to make local government officials relatively adept at adjusting irrational policies to better meet local realities and relatively quick to compete in providing better services. However, in less developed regions, lower factor mobility, together with higher dependence on upper-level transfers and the relatively tougher-to-meet central development mandates work systematically to distort local government behavior and draw local governments in these regions into unhealthy competition for upper-level transfers and a style of political performance that caters to higher levels of government instead of local people." Thus, Liu and Tao argue that the current fiscal system – when combined with policy mandates that have given high priority to rapid growth and to social control, and with the competitive top-down, single yardstick cadre evaluation system – has "significantly impaired" the capacity of local governments in poorer areas to respond to local needs and demands for decent public goods.

Like so many of the other authors in this volume, Liu and Tao see a need for thoroughgoing reform in both the fiscal system and the broader system of public administration. Local officials in poor and backward regions, they conclude, should not be tasked with trying to create economic growth itself but, rather, with delivering the kinds of improved public goods and services to local people that will permit them, in the longer run, to generate that growth themselves. "Only when unreasonable policy burdens are downgraded and cadre evaluation criteria are reoriented to providing public goods that are more closely related to local needs can the conditions for downsizing excessive local bureaucracies be created and the role of healthy regional competition be strengthened to contain local misbehavior."

When read together, the chapters in this volume clearly raise a number of common themes. First, they document an urgent need to put far greater resources into the effort to achieve better equity as China continues to develop. But second, they point out that simply pumping more resources through China's "broken" fiscal system cannot and will not deliver the desired results. Fixing that system must be addressed very early on if a more equitable development strategy is to be achieved. This could well entail making primary and secondary education, basic health protection, and provision of a minimum social welfare net into national or provincial, not locally bounded, responsibilities. At whichever levels it is determined comprehensive responsibility should lie, the task of assuring adequate public goods provision in an economy and society as large and as diverse as that in China is going to require also a redesign of key mechanisms and a recalibration of incentives throughout the entire hierarchy of the nation's public administration. These are giant tasks, to be sure, but ones that arguably have already been postponed too long.

Systemic and institutional inadequacies are surely at the root of many of the problems brought to light in the research reported here. The decentralized fiscal system, in particular, allowed the central government, for too long, to ignore the appalling state of public services in poor localities or blame the onerous burden of fees on local mismanagement or malfeasance. But our authors also note certain discursive elements – motifs and themes that have been injected into China's official public discourse on the market, modernity, and markers of national progress – that have been heavily implicated in concealing, even condoning, certain forms of suffering and social inequality that might otherwise have been alleviated. An excessively aggressive culture of "competition" that sets the conditions in which individual and social choices must be made is noted by several contributors to this collection. Certain public discourses on poverty and individual responsibility promote attitudes that have plainly worked to exclude, rather than include, those who are entering the headlong race toward the glittering rewards of affluent modernity from positions of disadvantage. A redesign of the official public discourse on poverty and vulnerability in China, and a recalibration of the proper norms of social responsibility may be just as much requisites for achieving a more equitable development strategy as are redesigning institutional mechanisms and recalibrating administrative incentives.

The title of this volume, *Paying for Progress in China*, has been intended to be read as a *double entendre*. We hope that the essays included here will encourage all who look at them to ask better questions not only about how the goods and services that go with social and economic progress can and should be paid for in China, but also about who exactly has been paying the price for progress up until now, and why, and how that human cost could be reduced.

# 1 Can the retreat from equality be reversed?

## An assessment of redistributive fiscal policies from Deng Xiaoping to Wen Jiabao

*Christine Wong*

In recent years China has acquired a reputation as a country that has abandoned its socialist past and embraced a particularly virulent form of capitalism. There is plenty of evidence to buttress this reputation, including a rapid rise in interpersonal income inequalities as measured by Gini coefficients; an urban–rural income gap that is among the biggest in the world and continuing to grow; an ever-increasing divide between coastal and inland provinces; a third-to-last place ranking by the World Health Organization on the fairness of health-care provision for its citizens; a residency permit system (*hukou*) that imposes a caste-like divide between urban and rural populations, denies rural migrants access to social services and exposes them to exploitation by employers; and a National Land Law that ensures that farmers cannot reap the benefits of rising land prices even while urbanization gobbles up their farmland.[1]

In short, the picture is that of a society that is unjust and unfeeling. Although this makes China perhaps not unlike many other poor countries in the world, this picture is noteworthy because: (1) China is still ruled by a Communist Party that espouses socialist principles of equality and inclusiveness. (2) China is perceived to have a stable political order and a government that has substantial capacity for economic management.[2] (3) The country has achieved phenomenal growth over the past 25 years and the big cities along the coast are quite prosperous, with a burgeoning middle class that is embracing all the values typical of modern consumer societies. The overwhelming emphasis on growth and scant attention to social justice in China (at least until recently) stand in especially sharp contrast to neighboring Vietnam, which has followed China's footsteps in liberalizing government control, privatizing agriculture and many industries, and pursuing policies to promote exports and attract foreign investment. Yet the official rhetoric in Vietnam puts great emphasis on the need to protect the poor and other vulnerable groups in the process of change, and the government has promulgated many measures designed to provide social safety nets for the poor and minority groups including government-sponsored health insurance for the poorest residents.[3]

It is commonly assumed that China's "retreat from equality"[4] began with Deng Xiaoping's call, at the outset of reform, for "letting some people [regions] get rich first." The logic behind the call appeared to be that, if market reform brought with it rising inequality, it was the price to pay for faster growth, to lift the country out of abject poverty. Given the spectacular growth brought by market reforms, it is hardly surprising that Deng's call remained the ruling paradigm for so long. It was not until 2003 that the paradigm appeared to change under the new administration of Hu Jintao and Wen Jiabao. Beginning with the communiqué of the 16th Party Congress (November 2002), the government has called for emphasizing the *quality* of growth that includes balanced, sustainable, people-centered development, rather than quantitative growth targets. Premier Wen Jiabao, in particular, has called for redressing the current inequalities by tilting toward the rural sector through promulgating his *sannong* policies.[5]

This chapter assesses the effect of fiscal policies in shaping income distribution through 25 years of China's transition to a market economy, and asks whether the government will be able to reverse the trend toward growing inequality under the new paradigm. While government has only a limited, mostly indirect, effect on the distribution of income, fiscal policies are the primary instrument for government in implementing the new paradigm. As China changed from a planned economy to an increasingly decentralized, market-oriented economy, fiscal policy – how government is financed and how it spends public monies – increasingly became the key instrument for allocating resources.

In assessing the role of fiscal policy, we will focus especially on the intergovernmental fiscal system – the arrangements for the sharing of responsibilities and resources across levels of government down the hierarchy from the central government, provinces, all the way to the townships and villages. Under China's highly decentralized fiscal system, local governments play a key role in implementing national policies. The bulk of the critical public goods that touch people's lives – social security, health care, education and public safety, are delivered by local governments at the municipal, county and township levels. The intergovernmental fiscal system not only assigns responsibilities to these levels of local government but also channels resources and shapes incentives for local governments to perform their assigned functions. In this chapter, I will show that the intergovernmental system was undermined by the piecemeal reforms applied to the fiscal system during the 1980s and especially the 1990s, which eroded the ability of local governments to perform many of their assigned functions. The damage was extensive and deep-rooted, and fixing the system will require fundamental reforms. Until these fundamental reforms are undertaken, increasing transfers from the central government will have limited effect on outcomes in poor regions, and the intergovernmental system will continue to be a bottleneck to the implementation of the national development agenda.

The chapter is organized as follows: Part one begins by discussing the effect of market reforms on government revenues and how the steep fiscal decline shaped intergovernmental fiscal relations during 1980–93 and beyond. This provides the background to the introduction of the Tax Sharing System in 1994. Part two analyzes the effects of the 1994 reform as strongly disequalizing and extremely harmful to the local public finance system. As the reform cut funding for local governments, it allowed them to seek off-budget revenues to fill fiscal gaps; this trade-off further contributed to eroding the integrity of the public finance system. Part three explains how the current intergovernmental system shapes distributional outcomes. Part four concludes by emphasizing the structural/systemic obstacles to implementing Wen Jiabao's promise to redress the balance by "tilting" toward the poor under the *sannong* policies.

## Decline of the budget: 1978–93

Market reform brought a rapid and dramatic erosion in the traditional tax base of the planned economy – state-owned enterprise profits, and revenue collection declined steeply. Central revenues were especially hard-hit as local governments in rich regions often shielded local enterprises from taxation to avoid sharing revenues with the central government.[6] Faced with a steep fiscal decline and lacking the capacity to monitor tax effort at the provinces, the central government retreated to a system of fiscal contracts in 1988 in an attempt to revive revenue collection – by offering better incentives to local governments to boost revenues, as well as ensure stable receipts at the center. The contracts stipulated a lump-sum remittance (or subsidy) for each province, to increase annually by an agreed rate, with all the rest accruing to the province. In return, provinces accepted responsibility for meeting their expenditure requirements from retained revenues. This marked a fundamental change that had gone largely unnoticed – by de-linking revenue-sharing from expenditure needs, the fiscal contracts put local governments on a self-financing basis for the first time – a de facto devolution of responsibilities that was later codified in the Budget Law (1994).

Fiscal contracts did not solve the central government's financial problems, though, as revenues continued to decline due to continuing problems of state-owned enterprise (SOE) profitability and persistent credibility problems of the central government (Figure 1.1) (Wong et al. 1995). Moreover, as the generous terms of the contracts gave local governments a disproportionate share of new revenues, the central share of revenues fell rapidly, to just over 20 percent in 1993.[7] The extent to which the funding crisis dominated thinking at the center can be glimpsed in Figures 1.2 and 1.3. At the nadir, the central government allocated only 3 percent of GDP, with no end in sight to the decline.

This desperate situation spurred the government to push through a drastic reform, with two paramount objectives – stemming the decline of revenues and clawing back a majority share for the central government – "raising the two ratios."[8] This background helps to explain the final design of the Tax Sharing System in 1994 that swept aside all earlier concerns about the disequalizing effect of the tax assignment system, in an all-out effort to win a quick agreement from the (rich) provinces.[9]

---

*Figure 1.1* (opposite) The long decline

*Figure 1.2* (opposite) Decline of the "two ratios"

*Figure 1.3* (opposite) Resources under central government allocation

*1.1*

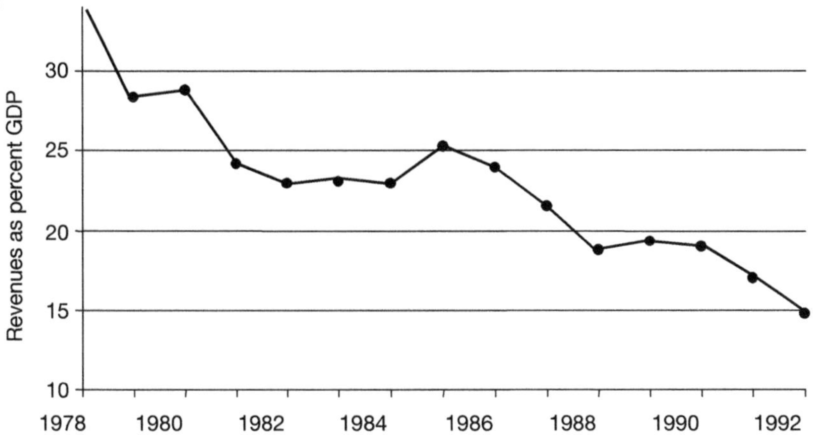
Revenues as percent GDP
30
25
20
15
10
1978
1980
1982
1984
1986
1988
1990
1992

*1.2*

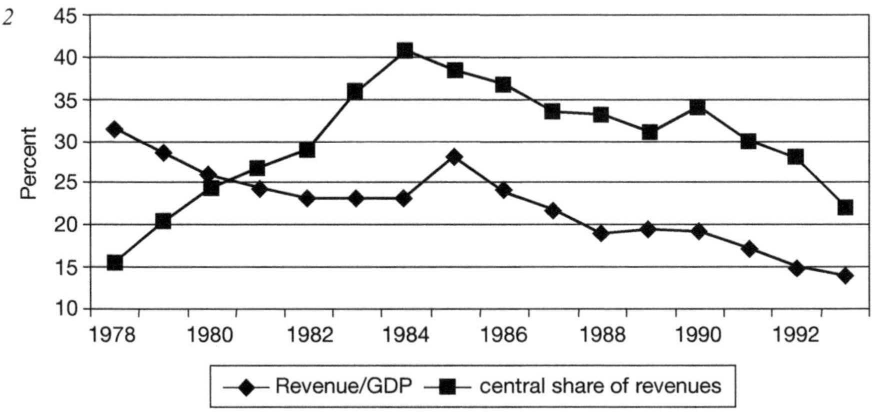
Percent
45
40
35
30
25
20
15
10
1978
1980
1982
1984
1986
1988
1990
1992
Revenue/GDP
central share of revenues

*1.3*

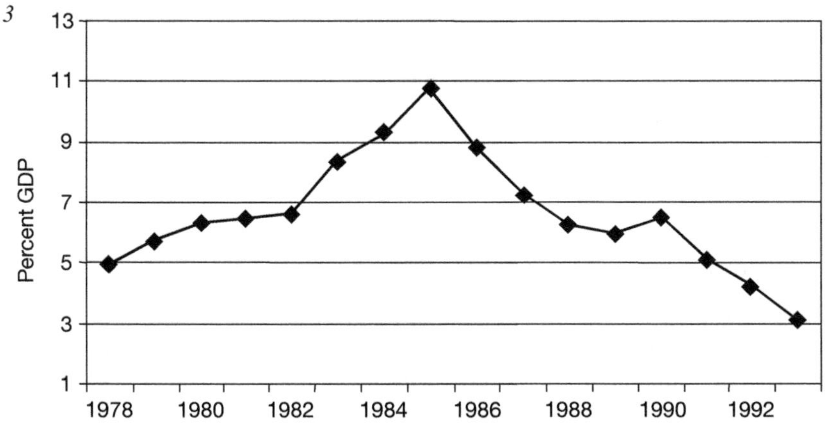
Percent GDP
13
11
9
7
5
3
1
1978
1980
1982
1984
1986
1988
1990
1992

## The Tax Sharing System: 1994 to present

The fiscal reform package that was introduced in 1994 had three components. The most visible and controversial was the Tax Sharing System (*fenshuizhi*) (hereafter TSS), which fundamentally changed the way revenues are shared between the central and provincial governments, by shifting from a negotiated system of general revenue sharing to a mix of tax assignments and tax sharing. The other components are equally significant, but have attracted less attention: tax modernization and tax administration reform. Under the TSS, taxes are assigned to central government, local government, or shared (see Table 1.1). By assigning the biggest tax, the value-added tax (VAT), as a shared tax and claiming 75 percent of its receipts, the central government reclaimed a majority portion of total revenues.[10]

However, this recentralization hurt mainly the poor regions, since the TSS had made the system much more favorable to rich localities. By sharing VAT revenues with local governments at a flat rate by origin, the TSS introduced a highly disequalizing feature to revenue sharing, ensuring that revenue-rich regions keep more of the revenues. Under the TSS, coastal provinces have gained revenue shares relative to inland provinces. During 1993–8, the ratio of provincial per capita fiscal expenditures to the national average grew from 2.8 to 4.5 in Shanghai, from 2.0 to 3.0 in Beijing, and from 0.66 to 0.74 in Jiangsu. In contrast, in Hebei the ratio fell from 0.57 to 0.24, in Gansu from 0.76 to 0.61, and in Hunan from 0.60 to 0.52 (World Bank 2002: Table 2.5).

Because the TSS had recentralized revenues but left expenditure assignments unchanged, it created a huge fiscal gap for local governments (see Figure 1.4). Unlike the previous regime, under which only poor provinces received transfers, under TSS all provincial units including Shanghai and Beijing are now dependent on central transfers to finance expenditures.[11] In the aggregate provinces are now dependent on transfers to finance nearly half of their expenditures (Figure 1.5). How these transfers are designed would thus have a great impact on the distributional outcomes. Even though the central government had promised to roll out a formula-based equalization transfer system to counter the regressive effects of the TSS, this did not happen. A "transitional intergovernmental transfer" was introduced in 1995, but the scheme was so grossly underfunded that throughout the 1990s it never accounted for more than 1–2 percent of total transfers. Instead, under the TSS, transfers have been dominated by tax rebates that also favor the rich, reinforcing the disequalizing character of the tax sharing system itself (see Figures 1.6 and 1.7).[12]

## The current intergovernmental system

An intergovernmental fiscal system has three components: expenditure assignments, revenue assignments, and transfers; and they are interrelated.[13] The choices made for each component are governed by economic, political and historical considerations that differ from country to country. Bahl (2000) argues that an ideal

*Table 1.1* Revenue assignments under the Tax Sharing System (*c*. 1994)

I Taxes exclusively assigned to the central government

1 Excise (consumption) taxes
2 Taxes collected from the Ministry of Railroads and from the headquarters of banks and insurance companies
3 Income taxes, sales taxes and royalties from offshore oil activities of foreign companies and joint ventures
4 Energy and transportation fund contributions
5 Seventy percent of the three sales taxes collected from enterprises owned by the Ministry of Industry, the Ministry of Power, SINOPEC (petrochemicals), and the China nonferrous metals companies
6 All customs duty, VAT and excise taxes on imports
7 Enterprise income tax collected from banks and other financial institutions

II Taxes shared between the central and local governments

1 Value-added tax (75 percent central, 25 percent local)
2 Natural resource taxes (coal, gas, oil, and other minerals if the enterprises are fully Chinese owned)
3 Construction tax on the cost of construction of buildings that are outside the plan and financed from retained earnings
4 Salt tax
5 Industrial and commercial tax, and income tax levied on foreign and joint venture enterprises

III Taxes exclusively assigned to local governments

1 Business (gross receipts) tax falling on sectors not covered by VAT (transportation and communications, construction, finance and insurance, post and telecommunications, culture and sports, entertainment, hotels and restaurants, and other)
2 Rural market (stall rental) trading tax
3 The urban maintenance and construction tax (a surcharge on the tax liability of enterprises for business tax, consumption tax, and VAT)
4 The urban land use tax
5 Vehicle and vessel utilization tax
6 Thirty percent of the product and VAT revenues collected from enterprises owned by the Ministry of Industry, Ministry of Power, SINOPEC, and the China nonferrous metals companies
7 Value-added tax on land
8 Education surtax
9 Entertainment and slaughter taxes
10 Property tax
11 Surtax on collective enterprises
12 Resources tax
13 Fixed asset investment tax (discontinued in 1999)
14 Fines for delinquent taxes

Source: adapted from World Bank (2002: Table 4.1)

Note: Since the introduction of TSS in 1994, the central government has changed revenue assignments – the earliest was moving the securities trading tax from local to shared taxes and changing the sharing rate several times. More recently the central government has revised assignments for the enterprise and personal incomes taxes to take 60 percent of revenues. New taxes have also been introduced, invariably central (e.g. the vehicle purchase tax).

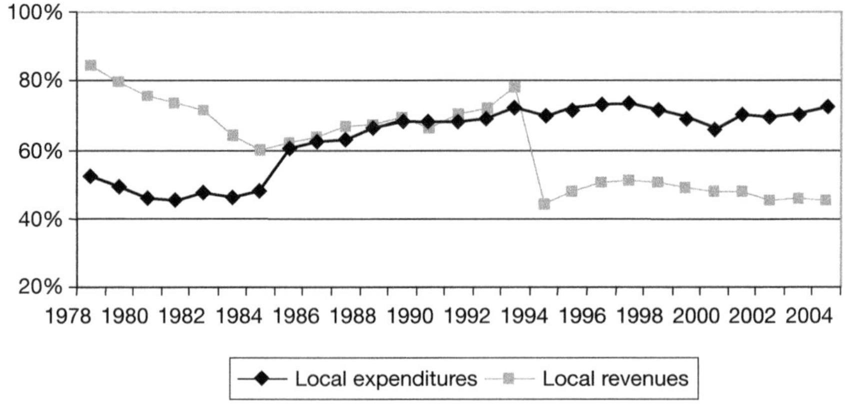


*Figure 1.4* Fiscal balance at the subnational level

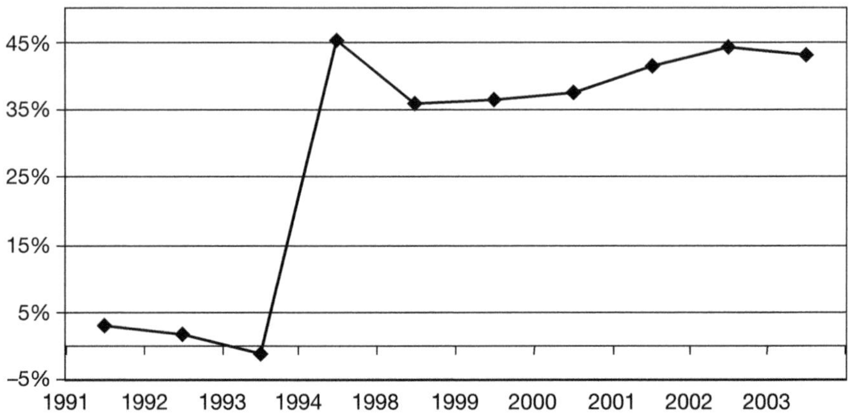


*Figure 1.5* Transfers as percentage of local expenditures

intergovernmental system should start by assigning responsibilities to each level of government to best satisfy society's demands for responsiveness and accountability in the delivery of public services, subject to meeting minimum requirements for efficiency. Once these expenditure assignments are set, revenues would be assigned to each level of government in a way that meets two conditions: (1) the assignments would be efficient and nondistortionary for tax policy and tax administration, and (2) they provide sufficient revenues for local governments, on average, to finance their expenditure responsibilities. Finally, transfers are designed to help meet the financing gap for local governments in poorer regions – i.e. to meet the equalization objectives of society. This scenario assumes that local governments are more likely to use revenues efficiently when they are responsible for raising them, and thus Bahl advocates giving significant taxing power to local governments to minimize the vertical fiscal gap as much as possible. In this view,

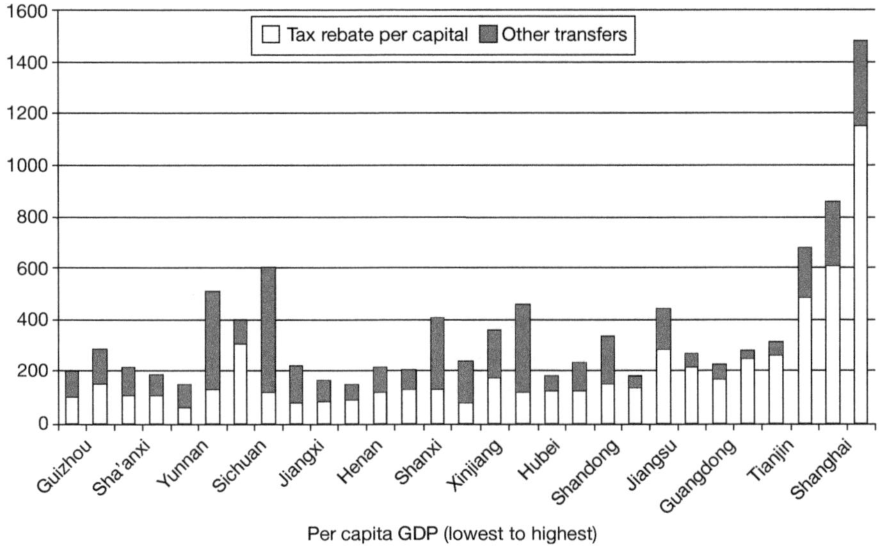


*Figure 1.6* Per capita transfers, 1998

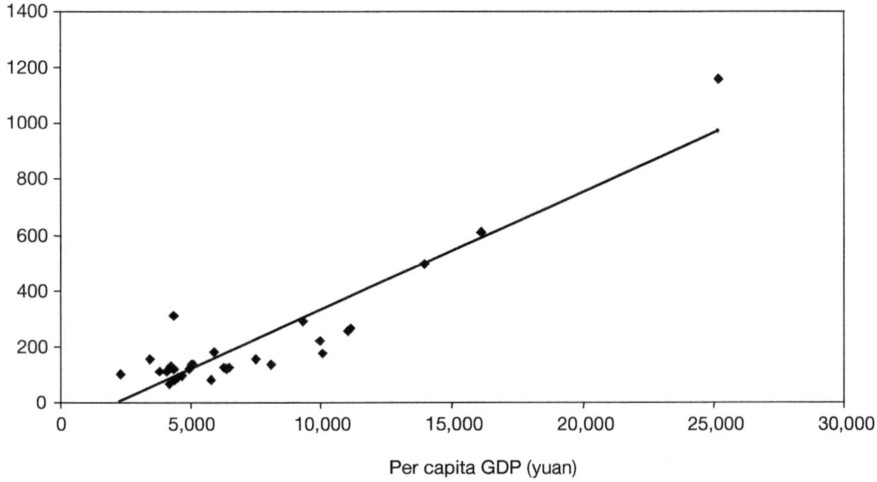


*Figure 1.7* Per capita tax rebates, 1998

transfers would be needed mainly for equalization purposes. Richard Bird (2003) has argued that, in reality, revenues are usually much more centralized than expenditures in developing countries. In such countries (including China post-1993), transfers play a dual role of financing a vertical fiscal gap as well as meeting equalization objectives. In either case, the choices are linked among the three components of the intergovernmental system, and decentralization works best when the choices are coherent.[14] At any given level of decentralization (usually measured in terms of subnational expenditure shares), a low proportion of revenues assigned to local governments requires high transfers, and vice versa.

The intergovernmental fiscal arrangements were quite unique in the Soviet-type economies. Under their highly centralized fiscal systems, the three components of the intergovernmental system were less clearly defined, and more *ad hoc* and fluid. Under the centrally planned economy, responsibilities for day-to-day public administration and social services such as education (except universities), public safety, health care, social security, housing, and other local and urban services were assigned to local governments. When measured in terms of the share of budgetary expenditures accounted for by subnational governments, these economies looked highly decentralized. However, these were *delegated* functions whose norms (or service standards) were often set by the central government, and the services were delivered by local governments acting as *agents* of the central government. Revenues were collected by local governments and remitted upward. Revenue assignments were ex post, negotiated annually, and adjusted to finance the delegated functions. In this system, the line between transfers and revenue assignments was fluid, and most of what would be considered "transfers" in Western systems was hidden: strictly speaking, all local expenditures were financed with central transfers. In other words, even though big cities such as Moscow and Shanghai were allowed to retain only a small fraction of the revenues they collected, they were actually receiving per capita transfers that were much higher than the national averages, as evidenced by their higher per capita fiscal spending. Instead, what were called "transfers" were only the additional injections that were necessary for those benighted provinces that could not meet expenditure needs even after being assigned 100 percent of their own collected revenues. This was essentially the system operating in China at the outset of market reforms.

Throughout the transition period in China, the coherence of this intergovernmental fiscal system was steadily chipped away by the piecemeal, incremental reforms applied. While the Soviet-type system was conducive to neither efficiency nor growth, it had built-in mechanisms for adjusting revenue assignments and transfers to expenditure needs. During the 1980s, amidst the steep fiscal decline, attention was focused on how to resuscitate revenue collection. Reforms of the intergovernmental system were designed to stimulate tax effort by local governments, and virtually no attention was paid to issues of expenditure assignments. Equally little attention was paid to transfers, which were increasingly driven by dwindling central resources (Wong 1997). This continued into the 1990s, when the TSS again paid no attention to expenditure assignments, and little to transfers. Through these changes, expenditure assignments have remained remarkably unaltered. By changing only one component of the intergovernmental system – revenue assignments – and delinking them from expenditure needs, the reforms have left local governments saddled with unusually heavy and unsustainable expenditure assignments, especially at low levels of government: social security and pensions are the responsibility of cities and counties, basic education and health care are primarily the responsibilities of city districts and townships (until

2001). These are costly responsibilities that are elsewhere in the world usually *financed* by the central (or federal) and provincial governments, although often with local governments acting as *providers*.

With the built-in adjustment mechanisms eliminated in the 1980s,[15] but the government slow to reform the system of transfers, many local governments have been unable to perform their assigned functions, especially in poorer regions. As economic growth also became more concentrated in coastal regions during the 1990s, income disparities accelerated, and the fiscal system provided no palliative. The outcome was a sharp rise in interregional disparities in fiscal spending dating from 1994 (World Bank 2002). By the mid-1990s fiscal problems were very serious in poor regions. There were even reports of deterioration in public services provided in the inland provinces. Heberer (2001) reports that in the Liangshan Yi Autonomous Prefecture in Sichuan province fiscal problems led to the elimination of free medical care and epidemic prevention programs, free films and cultural activities. Many clinics and health stations closed. Epidemic diseases thought to have been wiped out reappeared. In 1996 only 40 percent of Yi children attended school, a figure that dropped to 10 percent in the poorer villages.

These outcomes were highly regressive, where governments in poor regions were providing fewer and lower quality services and passing along a higher proportion of the costs to their constituents. By leaving so many costly but important responsibilities at the local level and providing no support to their financing, the national government essentially abrogated its social responsibility to the poor regions.

From the national perspective, the intergovernmental system increasingly became a bottleneck to policy implementation. With local funding problems limiting services, the national government has been unable to deliver on some priority programs such as universal basic education – China is still years away from providing nine years of free education to all children that was targeted for the year 2000. In spite of repeated pledges by the State Council to increase investment in human development, budgetary spending on education remained stagnant at about 2–2.5 percent of GDP during 1978–99, half the level called for in the 1985 Education Law, and well below the levels of spending in neighboring East Asian economies. Similarly in health care public spending was low, also less than 2 percent of GDP.[16]

### *The growing reliance on off-budget finance*

Another aspect of the breakdown of the intergovernmental fiscal system is the growth of off-budget financing of government, especially at the local levels (Wong 1998; Fan 1998; Wong and Bird forthcoming). The rapid growth of extra-budgetary funds during the 1990s was linked to the recentralization of revenues under the TSS; allowing local governments to tap off-budget revenues was at least in part designed to avoid hampering economic growth by enabling local governments to find supplementary funds to carry out their assigned functions. In addition to the well-known "fees and levies," at present many other implicit and hidden revenues, transfers, and expenditures pervade the system, driven in part by the lack of any good formal taxes that local governments control, and facilitated by the continuing obscurity of the line between "government" and "business" at the local level. In the aggregate, in the late 1990s off-budget resources used by government and public agencies may have amounted to as much as 19–27 percent of GDP (in addition to the formal budget).[17] Reforms in the past few years have abolished many fees and levies – including, most famously, all rural levies under the Rural Fee Reform; others have been brought into the budget.[18] As fees and levies are abolished, however, local governments have grown increasingly dependent on revenues from land development, and these revenues are reported in neither budgetary nor extrabudgetary accounts. Since off-budget resources are generally more plentiful in rich regions than poor ones, be they "management fees" collected on gross turnover or on profits, or land sales and revenues from user charges, this reliance on off-budget finance probably exacerbates regional disparities since, unlike budgetary revenues, they are not subject to redistribution through the intergovernmental fiscal system.

## The prospects for reversing inequalities

Some attempt to reverse this appalling "retreat from equality" had already begun under the Zhu Rongji administration. Beginning around 1998 the government began to redirect fiscal resources toward equalization, including the "Go West" development strategy launched in 1999. Some evidence of improvement can be seen in Box 1.1.

From the late 1990s, the Ministry of Finance also began to revise the system of transfers to significantly reduce the dominance of tax rebates, intended to improve equalization (see Figure 1.8). An especially important boost was given by the change in 2002 to shift the enterprise income tax and the personal income tax from local taxes to shared taxes. To make the shift more acceptable to local governments, the central government committed to retaining only 20 percent of the total receipts from these taxes, its share prior to 2002, and to put all additional receipts into equalization under the "transitional transfer." In 2003 this added about 14 billion yuan to equalization.[19]

In the absence of government statements, we cannot know exactly what motivated this change in policy. Partly the government might have been responding to the mounting evidence of inequalities and the growing divide between coastal and inland regions.[20] I believe that perhaps more directly relevant were the increased resources that became available for central government allocation around the late 1990s. The upturn in revenue-GDP ratio seemed finally to have taken hold (Figure 1.1). In 1998 the government launched the first Fiscal Stimulus package to ward off contagion from the Asian financial crisis. The RMB 100 billion yuan bond issue produced additional *new* resources to be allocated, and the decision was clearly taken to "tilt" toward inland provinces and pro-poor projects (World Bank 1999).

A third and very important explanation is that the intergovernmental fiscal system is failing, and has required increasing central government bailouts in

**Box 1.1 Comparing the distribution of per capita transfers across provinces (yuan)**

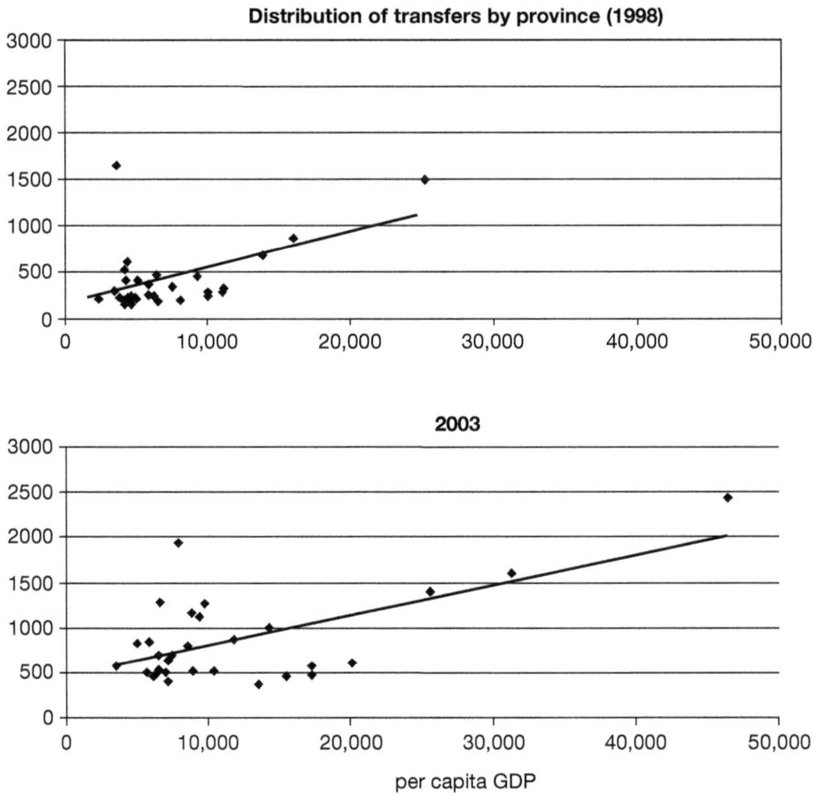


response to emerging problems in pension arrears, arrears or defaults on living stipend support for laid-off workers, problems of financing rural basic education, and so on. The costs of these bailouts have risen rapidly since 1998.

- Subsidies to local social security schemes rose from zero to RMB 10 billion in 2000, RMB 34.9 billion in 2001, and RMB 51.2 billion in the 2002 budget.
- Subsidies for living stipends to laid-off workers from state-owned enterprises continue to be substantial though they are scattered in different categories and difficult to count. (In the 2004 budget the total of pension and living stipends for laid-off workers and their re-employment training appeared to total RMB 86 billion.)
- Subsidies to local minimum living stipend schemes rose from zero to RMB 2.3 billion in 2001, and RMB 4.6 billion in the 2002 budget. By 2004 it was RMB 17.7 billion.

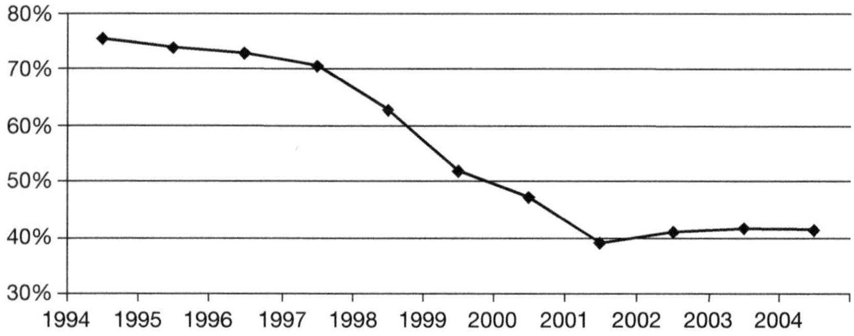


*Figure 1.8* Tax rebates as share of total transfers

While all these figures above demonstrate changes moving generally in the right direction, they also show that China is still a long, long way from having a fiscal system that equalizes. They also demonstrate some major problems for the prospects for implementing Wen Jiabao's laudable program to "tilt" toward the rural sector.

Starting from the current situation where tax rebates remain 40 percent of the total, the amount of change necessary just to neutralize their disequalizing effect is far too huge to be politically feasible, and would face enormous resistance from the rich provinces.

*Table 1.2* The size of central transfers

| | *2003* | *2004* |
|---|---|---|
| Total (billions yuan) | 826.1 | 1037.88 |
| Tax rebates | 342.5 | 405.1 |

As shown above, the "wrong" assignment of responsibilities has forced the central government to subsidize local expenditures. While these have mostly gone to inland provinces, they are all urban, and SOE related, and are not well targeted to reach the poorest population. More importantly, paying for the civil service wage increases introduced since 1999 has absorbed a growing portion of central transfers and squeezed out other needed subsidies: by comparison, subsidies for rural fee reform are far smaller.

Moreover, the government's tax capacity remains weak – even though revenues have recovered significantly, and currently account for about 20 percent of GDP, the central government still allocates only about 10 percent – a relatively low figure for a large and diversified country that faces many large expenditure needs in continuing SOE reform, recapitalization of the banking sector, pension reform, and so on.

Finally, the decades of piecemeal changes to the intergovernmental system have created many distortions, so that local government is extremely inefficient, and

*Table 1.3* The growing share of wage increase subsidies in central transfers (unit: billions yuan)

| | *1999* | *2000* | *2001* | *2002* | *2003* | *2004* |
|---|---|---|---|---|---|---|
| **Transfers for wage adjustments** | 10.8 | 21.7 | 62.3 | 80.7 | 89.1 | 99.4 |
| As share of total transfers | 2.6% | 4.6% | 10.4% | 11.0% | 10.8% | 9.6% |
| As share of transfers net of tax rebates | 5.5% | 8.8% | 16.8% | 18.5% | 18.4% | 15.9% |
| **Subsidies for rural fee reform** | | 2 | 3.3 | 24.5 | 30.5 | 52.4 |
| As share of total transfers | | 0.4% | 0.5% | 3.3% | 3.7% | 5.0% |
| As share of transfers net of tax rebates | | 0.8% | 0.9% | 5.6% | 6.3% | 8.3% |

Sources: Zhang and Martinez (2002), budget speeches and speeches on government work reports at the National People's Congress, and author interviews

increased transfers from the center do not translate straightforwardly into better services at the periphery.[21] The single biggest distortion is that of civil service wages. First, over the years, everyone has come to understand that the Ministry of Finance intervenes whenever necessary to preserve social stability, and will provide injections of funds to pay off wage arrears but not to ensure public services are available. This translates into civil servants being free goods to local governments. Second, the nationally unified civil service scale for basic wages translates into salaries that are very high relative to local incomes in poor regions. This gap has grown even greater as civil service wages have more than doubled since 1998. The result is that local governments are adding staff at alarming rates during the period when Zhu Rongji was trying to impose a draconian program to downsize the civil service. This makes it more difficult to "tilt" toward the rural sector. In one extremely poor rural county I visited in early 2004, what we found was that in spite of increased transfers from higher levels, because the county has been adding staff at an accelerating rate, there is no money for non-personnel recurrent expenses in any department, from schools to agricultural stations to government departments, to provide any services to residents.

To effect a significant reversal of inequalities that reaches the people, then, China needs a fundamental reform in the fiscal system, starting with the intergovernmental components. Otherwise, the recently introduced rural reforms will not be sustainable, and Premier Wen Jiabao faces an uphill struggle to redirect resources to the rural sector.

## Notes

1 The National Land Law pegs the compensation for requisitioned farmland at 6–10 times the average annual output value for the three preceding years. The additional resettlement subsidy is pegged at 4–6 times the average output value. In cases where

this creates financial difficulties for the families to be resettled, the subsidy can be negotiated, but "not to exceed 15 times" (Article 47, Land Administration Law of the People's Republic of China, August 29, 1998).

2 This is shown by the impressive investments in infrastructure that have taken place all over China at all levels of government. For multilateral aid institutions, China is considered an outstanding borrower because it is able to implement development projects quickly.

3 See, for examples, World Bank 2003 and forthcoming.

4 This phrase is borrowed from the book, *China's Retreat from Equality: Income Distribution and Economic Transition* (Carl Riskin et al. 2001).

5 See, for example, Wen Jiabao's Report on the Work of the Government, delivered on March 5, 2005, to the Third Session of the Tenth National People's Congress. *Sannong* refers broadly to the rural sector: agricultural production, farmers, and rural villages.

6 For example, under the planned economy Shanghai remitted more than 80 percent of its revenues to the central government. This high "tax" on Shanghai revenues created incentives for collusion between the municipal government and its subordinate enterprises and the potential for informally sharing the "saved revenues" within Shanghai. For analyses of this evolution, see Oksenberg and Tong (1991); Wong (1991) and (1992).

7 This was largely because the contracts had failed to anticipate the high inflation rates through the late 1980s and early 1990s, when revenues grew at an annual rate of 12 percent from 1987 to 1993, while remittances grew at low single-digit rates.

8 As shown in Figure 1.2, the "two ratios" refer to the ratio of budgetary revenues to GDP, and the central government's share of total revenues. Aside from raising the two ratios, the Tax Sharing System reform had several important objectives including reforming the system of taxes and tax administration, to meet the needs of the decentralized, diversified economy that China was fast becoming. For a discussion of these other aspects, see Wong and Bird (forthcoming).

9 See, for example, Zhao (2003). Zhao described the desperate situation where, in addition to the funding crisis, the central leadership was also discovering that they had lost control over tax collection at the local levels. In the course of introducing the VAT, for example, they discovered that Beijing Municipality had under-reported 9.8 billion yuan in revenues.

10 The VAT accounts for nearly half of all tax revenues in China. It is also a reliable tax whose revenues go up with GDP regardless of profitability, and thus is less cyclical than income or profit taxes.

11 In this essay, "(intergovernmental) transfer" refers to all monies distributed to local governments outside of the revenue assignment system, whose amounts are decided by the central government; it includes tax rebates (*shuishou fanhuan*). The inclusion of tax rebates as one component of transfers is consistent with Chinese official treatment until about 2003. Since then, official statements from the Ministry of Finance have distinguished between "transfer payments" (*zhuanyi zhufu*) and tax rebates. However, in statistical reports, tax rebates remain lumped together with other transfers. In any case, tax rebates fit the definition of a transfer in that the central (provincial) government decides on the amount to be distributed to the local governments.

12 As a concession to gain support for the TSS from the coastal provinces, the government committed to returning to provinces a portion of the "growth" in VAT and excise taxes, also by origin, in tax rebates. Tax rebates accounted for three quarters of central transfers to the provinces in the mid-1990s, while equalization transfers were only 1–2 percent (World Bank 2002).

13 A fourth aspect of the intergovernmental system, local borrowing, is being omitted since it is not relevant to this discussion.

14 See Mountfield and Wong (2004) for a discussion of the East Asian experiences in decentralization.

15 As explained earlier, the linkage between revenue assignments and expenditure needs was severed by the fiscal contracting system in 1988.
16 What public spending there is is highly concentrated in the civil service medical insurance system and in urban hospitals, and little trickles down to the rural sector. The *World Health Report 2000* ranked China 144th for the overall performance of the health system out of 191 countries, but 188th in terms of fairness in financial contribution. See also Chapters 3 and 4 by Duckett and Murphy in this volume.
17 The nature and size of extrabudgetary funds are explored in Wong (1999).
18 Reported extrabudgetary revenues have fallen to just 3.4 percent of GDP in 2003.
19 Interview with officials at Ministry of Finance, February 2004.
20 Studies such as World Bank (1997), and works such as Khan and Riskin (2001), and Riskin, Zhao and Li (2001) were coming out around this time and generating a good deal of interest and discussion in policy circles.
21 See also Chapter 8 by Liu and Tao in this volume.

## References

Bahl, Roy (2000) "Intergovernmental Transfers in Developing and Transition Countries: Principles and Practice," in Urban and Local Government Background Series, World Bank, Report No. 21097; available online at <http://www1.worldbank.org/publicsector/decentralization/cd/ITFPrinciples.pdf>.

Bird, Richard (2003) "Local and Regional Revenues: Realities and Prospects," in R. M. Bird and F. Vaillancourt (eds.) *Perspectives on Fiscal Federalism*, WBI Learning Resources Series, Washington: World Bank, 2006, pp. 177–96.

Fan Gang (1998) "Market-oriented Economic Reform and the Growth of Off-budget Local Public Finance," in D. Brean (ed.) *Taxation in Modern China*, London and New York: Routledge.

Heberer, Thomas (2001) "Nationalities Conflict and Ethnicity in the People's Republic of China, with Special Reference to the Yi," in S. Harrell (ed.) *Perspectives on the Yi of Southwest China*, Berkeley: University of California Press.

Khan, A. R. and Riskin, C. (2001) *Inequality and Poverty in China in the Age of Globalization*, New York: Oxford University Press.

Mountfield, Edward, and Wong, Christine (2004) "Public Expenditure on the Frontline: Towards Effective Management of Public Expenditure by Subnational Governments in East Asia," draft paper prepared for the East Asia Regional Flagship Study on Decentralization, World Bank.

Oksenberg, Michel and Tong, James (1991) "The Evolution of Central-provincial Fiscal Relations in China, 1953–1983: the Formal System," *China Quarterly*, March, 125: 1–32.

Riskin, Carl, Zhao Renwei and Li Shi (eds.) (2001) *China's Retreat From Equality: Income Distribution and Economic Transition*, Armonk, New York: M. E. Sharpe.

Wong, Christine (1991) "Central-local Relations in an Era of Fiscal Decline: The Paradox of Fiscal Decentralization in Post-Mao China," *China Quarterly*, 128 (December): 691–715.

Wong, Christine (1992) "Fiscal Reform and Local Industrialization: The Problematic Sequencing of Reform in Post-Mao China," *Modern China*, 18 (2) (April): 197–227.

Wong, Christine (1998) "Fiscal Dualism in China: Gradualist Reform and the Growth of Off-budget Finance," in D. J. S. Brean (ed.) *Taxation in Modern China*, New York and London: Routledge.

Wong, Christine (1999) "Converting Fees into Taxes: Reform of Extrabudgetary Funds and Intergovernmental Fiscal Relations in China, 1999 and Beyond," paper presented at the Annual Meetings of the Association for Asian Studies, Boston, Massachusetts.

Wong, Christine (ed.) (1997) *Financing Local Government in the People's Republic of China*, Hong Kong: Oxford University Press.

Wong, Christine, and Bird, Richard (forthcoming) "China's Public Finance, a Work in Progress," in L. Brandt and T. Rawski (eds.) *China's Great Transformation*, New York: Cambridge University Press.

Wong, Christine, Heady, Christopher and Woo, Wing Thye (1995) *Fiscal Management and Economic Reform in the People's Republic of China*, Hong Kong: Oxford University Press.

World Bank (1997) *Sharing Rising Incomes*, vol. 5 of *China 2020: Development Challenges in the New Century*, Washington: World Bank.

World Bank (1999) *China: Weathering the Storm and Learning the Lessons*, Country Economic Memorandum, Washington: World Bank.

World Bank (2000) *China: Managing Public Expenditures for Better Results*, Country Economic Memorandum, Washington: World Bank.

World Bank (2002) *China: National Development and Subnational Finance, a Review of Provincial Expenditures*, April, Washington: World Bank.

World Bank (2003) *Vietnam: Delivering on Its Promise*, Development Report No. 25050–VN, Washington: World Bank.

World Bank (2004) *World Development Report: Making Services Serve Poor People*, available online at <http://www.worldbank.org/reference>.

World Bank (2005) *Vietnam: Public Expenditure Review*, Washington: World Bank.

Zhang Zhihua and Martinez-Vazquez, Jorge (2002) "The System of Equalization Transfers in China," International Studies Program Working Paper, Andrew Young School of Policy Studies, Georgia State University.

Zhao Yining (2003) "Replaying the Strategic Background to the Tax Sharing System Reform," *Liaowang News Weekly*, September 15, no. 37.

# 2 Has China reached the top of the Kuznets Curve?

*Carl Riskin*

In 2003, China's economy grew by 9.1 percent. Yet the number of rural poor officially increased by 800,000, the first such officially announced increase in the past quarter century of reform and transition (see Xinhua News Agency 2004). The correspondence of rapid growth and increased poverty strongly suggests that inequality, as measured by the Gini coefficient, increased in 2003.[1] Yet findings from household income surveys carried out for 1995 and 2002 indicate that income inequality actually declined between those two years. The apparently contrary data for 2003 raise questions about the causes and sustainability of that decline, and that is the subject of this chapter.

China has become franker about the phenomenon of rural poverty. The new leaders have adopted a populist stance of listening to the poor and taking their problems seriously. Publication in 2003 of *Zhongguo Nongmin Diaocha* (Investigation of China's Villagers),[2] by Chen Guidi and Wu Chuntao created a great splash in China with its exposure of widespread rural hardship, local corruption, and exploitation and mistreatment of the rural population – before the book was banned in mid-2004. Indeed, the situation described by this book and other studies,[3] and the attention given to rural hardship and poverty by Zhu Rongji and later Wen Jiabao, all leave the distinct impression that poverty in the countryside remains a much bigger problem than is implied by the very low official poverty rates.

We have suggested in the past, based on analysis of independent surveys of household income in both rural and urban China, that poverty was in fact more widespread and was disappearing less rapidly than the government acknowledged, and that inequality was more serious and growing faster (Khan and Riskin 1998, 2001). The unprecedented acknowledgement of an increase in rural poverty in 2003 would seem to be consistent with our past conclusions. However, it should also be seen against the background of our analysis of the most recent household income survey, for 2002, indicating that at least in the period 1995 to 2002, poverty fell sharply and most dimensions of inequality held stable or fell.

The 2002 household income survey was the latest round of an ongoing series of surveys of household income designed by an international team of scholars under the auspices of the Chinese Academy of Social Sciences (CASS). The rural component covered 9,200 households in 21 provinces and the urban survey 6,835 households in eleven provinces.[4] The average per capita disposable income for the rural sample was 3,302.43 yuan and the Gini ratio for its distribution was 0.375, a 10 percent *decline* from its 1995 value of 0.416. This decline reversed just over half of the increase in the Gini from 1988 to 1995. For the urban sample, the average per capita disposable income was 9,766 yuan and its Gini ratio was 0.318, a 4.2 percent decline from 1995 (0.332). Because of continued increase in the average gap between urban and rural incomes, however, the overall national Gini coefficient remained virtually unchanged at 0.45.[5]

This result has been greeted with some skepticism. It runs up against a general sense that inequality continues to be serious and troublesome in both urban and rural China and that there is little if any perception that it is improving. Moreover, at least one other study of a similar time frame comes to a different conclusion.[6] However, the CASS study has the advantage of being able to use a broader definition of income that is more consistent with international practice than is official data, and the added advantage of the use of household and individual level data rather than the grouped data released annually by the National Bureau of Statistics (NBS). It is precisely the elements of income omitted by the NBS, such as rental value of owned housing and housing subsidy in kind, that bear a large degree of responsibility for our findings of reduced inequality in urban China, for instance. We shall therefore treat our results as real, always subject of course to new information.

What is the significance of this apparent improvement? Might it signify that China has reached or is approaching the top of its Kuznets Curve, the maximum amount of inequality produced by its unbalanced development path, and has entered an equalization phase in which development spreads more evenly through the territory and population?

## The Kuznets Curve

The Kuznets Curve derives from a half-century old hypothesis advanced by Simon Kuznets (Kuznets 1955) that the change in inequality over time follows an inverted U shape, i.e. that inequality increases during the initial phase of industrialization, then stabilizes and eventually decreases as modern economic growth spreads more widely throughout the economy and society. Although just stated in temporal terms, the Kuznets Curve hypothesis has often been tested in cross-sectional terms, to see whether a firm statistical relation can be established among countries as between GDP per capita and some measure of inequality.[7] While much evidence supports such a relationship, there is also great variability of national experience around it.[8] Deaton (2005: 396) states that recent work has produced a "professional consensus" that "contrary to Kuznets's hypothesis, and contrary to beliefs in the 1970s, there is no *general* relationship between inequality and growth, and certainly not one in which growth systematically widens inequality." Moreover, no relationship has been found between *rate* of growth and inequality and so there is no basis for arguing that higher growth requires sacrificing equity goals.[9] On balance, it seems evident that market forces do give rise to both disequalizing and equalizing tendencies at different stages of development but that no given level of inequality can be regarded as "inevitable" and beyond the purview of enlightened economic policy.

Indeed, the role of public policy in explaining the changes in income inequality over time or the differences between countries of different income levels is easy to ignore in Kuznets Curve discussions. At its most elemental, the Kuznets Curve hypothesis appears to be describing pure market forces responding to changing cost relations. It is also possible, of course, that changing levels of income go hand in hand with social, political and ideological changes that result in the adoption of redistributive policies to achieve more equitable and inclusive forms of development. In this case, which was explicitly recognized by Simon Kuznets himself, predicting future changes in income inequality becomes a highly complex task.[10] Despite modern skepticism about the very existence of a Kuznets Curve, the concept is retained here as a convenient heuristic representation of the effects of market forces on income distribution.

## Regional inequality

The first dimension of inequality we examine is that of regional (inter-provincial) inequality, an issue that has been of much concern to the Chinese government and various international agencies throughout the reform period. Kuznets' hypothesis rested partly on the reasonable supposition that what he called modern economic growth had to start somewhere, and that when it did, it would quickly widen inequality between those initially industrializing localities and elsewhere. Eventually, market forces such as rising costs in the early developing localities would promote the spread of the process more broadly through the country, causing inequality to level off and then fall.

In post-1949 China, the history of regional inequality up to the start of the reform period was one of absolute divergence but relative convergence among the provinces. For example, between 1952 and 1979 the ratio of the most industrialized province to the least industrialized province in absolute per capita industrial output tripled, but the coefficient of variation of provincial industrial output per capita fell by about 20 percent (Riskin 1987). The latter development stemmed not only from the extremely small base from which the least industrialized provinces began, which made high relative growth rates easy to achieve, but also from conscious government efforts to bring about greater geographic balance in industrialization, promoted in part by highly redistributive central plans and fiscal policies. The widening of absolute inequality in this period despite fairly strenuous efforts to reduce it was consistent with Kuznets' expectations.

For the post-reform era, there seems to have been convergence in provincial GDP per capita until 1990 and divergence thereafter, although not enough divergence to prevent a one-third decline in the coefficient of variation overall. The prior convergence is somewhat suspect because the use of province-specific price deflators removes much of it (Naughton 2002). Moreover, personal income showed no convergence, evidently widening steadily at least until the mid-1990s.

Our own surveys indicate that inequality in personal disposable income widened from 1988 to 1995 and then declined up to 2002. For the former period, the coefficient of variation of *rural* provincial per capita disposable income grew by two thirds, but for the latter period it fell by about 11 percent. For *urban* per capita disposable income, the coefficient of variation of provincial averages increased by 24 percent during the first period and fell by 20 percent during the second. This striking change in development pattern helped to prompt the question that forms the title of this essay and constitutes an important component of the overall drop in rural and urban inequality, taken separately. For the rural population, the decline in regional inequality was matched by falling inequality within 14 of the 19 provinces that made up our sample. However, 8 of the 11 provinces in the *urban* sample actually experienced an increase in inequality, which implies that it was declining regional inequality that was largely responsible for the fall in the urban Gini ratio (Khan and Riskin 2005).

## Rural inequality

The reduction in overall rural income inequality revealed by our surveys between 1995 and 2002 was caused by improved distribution of two components of rural income, farm income and wages, and by the reduced regressiveness of net taxes.[11] Together, the change in distribution of these three sources account for a reduction of 6.9 points in the Gini, substantially more than its total decline (4.1 points), implying that other income sources became more unequal. Indeed, all other enumerated sources of rural income became more unequal in distribution, notably family income from non-farm activities and the imputed rental value of private housing.

Thus, inequality increased for some components of rural income and decreased for others, with the decreases out-weighing the increases. Of the components on the decrease side of the ledger, net taxes (a negative component) were largely a product of policy,[12] rather than of equalizing forces intrinsic to China's growth path.

The Kuznets Curve story implies rising income shares and falling concentration ratios for income components like wages, whose geographic and sectoral spread is necessarily disequalizing at first. The reduced contribution of family farm income to the Gini came from a small decrease in the concentration ratio of this component (from 0.238 to 0.202) plus a somewhat larger decline in its share of total income (from 46.4 percent of the total to 39 percent), by which the concentration ratio is weighted in calculating its contribution to the Gini. Farm income was already distributed very equally (more so than any other component of rural income); a further decline in its concentration ratio does not seem to be part of a coherent development story consistent with a turnaround of the Kuznets Curve. Of course, a declining share of farm income in total income *is* implicit in the normal growth experience, but in China farm income is the most equally distributed income component. Its importance to the decline in China's Gini from 1995 to 2002 is an ironic arithmetical result of the size of farm income. However

*Table 2.1* Sources of reduced inequality of rural income

| | *Percent of income* | | *Gini/concentration ratio*[a] | | *Gini points contributed by* | | *Reduction in contribution to Gini/ concentration ratio* |
|---|---|---|---|---|---|---|---|
| | *1995* | *2002* | *1995* | *2002* | *1995* | *2002* | |
| All income | 100 | 100 | 0.416 | 0.375 | 41.6 | 37.5 | 4.1 |
| Net farm income | 46.44 | 38.97 | 0.238 | 0.202 | 11.1 | 7.9 | 3.2 |
| Individual wages | 22.38 | 29.46 | 0.738 | 0.455 | 16.5 | 13.4 | 3.1 |
| Net transfer from/to state & collective[b] | –0.48 | –2.62 | –1.759 | 0.106 | 0.8 | 0.3 | 0.5 |

Source: Khan and Riskin (2005: Table 6)

Notes:

a The numbers in these columns are for the Gini in the case of all income, and for the concentration ratio in the case of individual components of income.

b The negative sign for the "net transfer" percentages indicates subtractions from income (net tax). A negative value for the concentration ratio of net taxes indicates that the poor paid more than the rich.

low its concentration ratio, the share of farm income is still very large, hence it continues to have a big impact on the Gini, so that its decline, *ceteris paribus*, will reduce the Gini.

The *ceteris paribus* condition relates particularly to the question of which income component(s) expand(s) to "take the place of" farm income as the latter contracts relative to total income. The answer is that most of the contraction of farm income (seven percentage points in toto) is made up by the expansion of wage income (five points) and the rest by family non-farming activities (two points). The latter increased its share of rural income (from 9.7 percent to 11.8 percent) and its distribution also became more unequal from 1995 to 2002. Both of these changes are to be expected in the course of early economic development, but are more consistent with the early, rising phase of the Kuznets Curve than with its later falling phase.

As for wage income, it is indeed far more unequally distributed than farm income, and is a disequalizing source of rural income in the sense that its concentration ratio is higher than the rural Gini in both 1995 and 2002. Had this ratio remained constant between those years, the increase in wage income's share of total income to replace the diminishing share of farm income would not have resulted in a reduced overall rural Gini. However, wage income's concentration ratio did not stay constant, but rather diminished very sharply between 1995 and 2002 (from 0.74 to 0.45). This decline in its inequality of distribution overwhelmed the rise in its share of rural income, so the net effect was a fall in the rural Gini.

The role that wage income plays in this story seems consistent with a turnaround in the Kuznets Curve. That is, both an increase in the share of wage income and a decline in its concentration ratio are consistent with a story of geographic and sectoral spread of wage employment that reduces the extreme advantage of the early localities and sectors. But did that process proceed far enough to bring China's countryside onto the declining portion of the putative Kuznets Curve? True, wage income increased very rapidly, moving from 22 to 29 percent of total rural income in seven years, growing by an annual rate of 8.9 percent and accounting for more than half of the total increase in rural income over that period. However, how do we explain the sharp fall in inequality of wages, amounting to a 38 percent drop in their concentration ratio?

An examination of rural wages reported in 1995 and 2002 and shown in Table 2.2 provides at least a good part of the answer. The table reveals an extraordinary growth in the prevalence of wage income throughout rural China. In 1995 only 5 percent of rural respondents reported having any wage income, and if one leaves out the three most developed provinces in the sample – Beijing, Jiangsu and Zhejiang – the percentage would fall to only about 2 percent. By 2002, however, over 27 percent of rural respondents reported wage income, an almost five-fold increase. Moreover, while the rise was ubiquitous, the biggest increases occurred in the provinces with the lowest percentage of wage recipients in 1995. For example, Yunnan went from close to 0 percent wage earners in 1995 to 15 percent in 2002, Jiangxi from 1 to 34 percent, Guizhou from 1 to 24 percent; while Beijing

*Table 2.2* Change in rural wage situation, by province, 1995 to 2002

| | *Mean annual rural wage per province sample* | | *Change* | *Mean annual rural wage per worker* | | *% of province sample with wage income* | | *Change* |
|---|---|---|---|---|---|---|---|---|
| | *1995* | *2002* | *2002/1995* | *1995* | *2002* | *1995* | *2002* | *2002/1995* |
| Beijing | 1801.2 | 3642.2 | 2.0 | 5947 | 8137 | 30 | 45 | 1.5 |
| Hebei | 158.4 | 1177.1 | 7.4 | 4363 | 4408 | 4 | 27 | 6.8 |
| Shanxi | 108 | 908.6 | 8.4 | 5168 | 3239 | 2 | 28 | 14.0 |
| Liaoning | 304.8 | 788.2 | 2.6 | 8048 | 3409 | 4 | 23 | 5.8 |
| Jilin | 252 | 483.4 | 1.9 | 18800 | 2310 | 1 | 21 | 21.0 |
| Jiangsu | 782.4 | 2342.6 | 3.0 | 5375 | 5829 | 15 | 40 | 2.7 |
| Zhejiang | 1029.6 | 3361.3 | 3.3 | 7115 | 7649 | 14 | 44 | 3.1 |
| Anhui | 141.6 | 738.6 | 5.2 | 6048 | 2449 | 2 | 30 | 15.0 |
| Jiangxi | 132 | 833.1 | 6.3 | 9480 | 2425 | 1 | 34 | 34.0 |
| Shandong | 852 | 1105.9 | 1.3 | 11676 | 3816 | 7 | 29 | 4.1 |
| Henan | 169.2 | 614.1 | 3.6 | 4331 | 2469 | 4 | 25 | 6.3 |
| Hubei | 158.4 | 588 | 3.7 | 7118 | 2930 | 2 | 20 | 10.0 |
| Hunan | 72 | 942.7 | 3.1 | 8393 | 3370 | 1 | 28 | 28.0 |
| Guangdong | 690 | 1982.4 | 2.9 | 10669 | 6047 | 6 | 33 | 5.5 |
| Sichuan* | 162 | 825.1 | 5.1 | 9469 | 2546 | 2 | 32 | 16.0 |
| Guizhou | 56.4 | 400.8 | 7.1 | 10326 | 1659 | 1 | 24 | 24.0 |
| Yunnan | 84 | 230.3 | 2.7 | 17542 | 1534 | 0 | 15 | 37.0 |
| Shaanxi | 360 | 523.6 | 1.5 | 19088 | 2329 | 2 | 22 | 11.0 |
| Gansu | 90 | 559 | 6.2 | 6078 | 2454 | 1 | 23 | 23.0 |
| Guangxi | | 755.1 | | | 2761 | | | |
| Xinjiang | | 166.3 | | | 1608 | | | |
| MEAN | 389.68 | 1160.4 | 4.6 | 9212.3 | 3632.1 | 5.21 | 28.58 | 14.1 |
| St Dev | 453.20 | 972.41 | | 4519.8 | 1878.0 | 7.31 | 8.02 | |
| CV | 116.30 | 83.80 | | 49.1 | 51.7 | 140.4 | 28.07 | |

Notes:
* Sichuan is a weighted average of wages of Sichuan and Chongqing, with the weights being the respective proportions of the combined sample.
Guangxi and Xinjiang are omitted from the summary statistics in 2002 for greater comparability with the 1995 sample, which excluded these two provinces.

advanced only from 30 to 45 percent. Thus, the coefficient of variation for percentage of wage earners by province fell from 140 to 28, showing that wage employment became much more evenly distributed among provinces. The coefficient of variation (CV) of average provincial per capita wages also falls by 28 percent, despite the fact that the CV of average provincial per-*worker* wages remains basically unchanged. This contrast is explained by the rise in per capita wage income in provinces that reported little of it in 1995.

The increase in wage recipients reported in the surveys is higher than that indicated by available national statistics on rural wage earners. The latter show rural non-farm wage employment rising from 133.3 million in 1995 (27 percent of the rural labor force) to 147 million (30 percent of the rural labor force) in 2002, an increase of 10 percent. Moreover, the orders of magnitude of wage earners are different for 1995: 15.5 percent of the rural population (official statistics) versus only 5 percent (survey). Different definitions may help explain these differences. For example, the CASS results cited here refer only to the primary job of wage earners. It is also possible that the official statistics enumerated as wage earners what the CASS survey enumerated as migrants. On the other hand, de Brauw et al. (2002), who do include migrant workers and migrant self-employed in "off-farm wage employment," report that 43 percent of rural residents participated in such employment in 2000, an increase of 34 percent over the 32 percent of rural residents who engaged in it in 1995. Their results indicate that 200 million rural dwellers worked off-farm in 2000.[13] Clearly, differences in the definition and degree of inclusiveness of rural wage employment, and especially the treatment of rural–urban migrants, account for these differences in extent and growth of rural wage employment. However, all estimates agree that it was growing and spreading rapidly.

While wage earning was becoming far more common over the seven years between 1995 and 2002, the average rural wage was falling. In 1995, the small number of rural wage recipients reported an annual average rural wage of 7,872 yuan; by 2002 the much larger number of wage earners reported an average wage of 3,709 yuan, some 53 percent lower. This suggests that early wage recipients in the rural population tended to be highly paid government and collective officials, administrators, technicians, or skilled workers and that wage employment has spread rapidly downward to unskilled workers and farmers. The narrowing of variation of wages and their downward convergence also suggests that developing rural labor markets were exerting increasing influence on wage levels.

Table 2.3 presents the breakdown by occupation of those rural workers reporting wage income for their primary job in 1995 and 2002. In addition to the large increase in the number of wage earners, there is a sharp change in their occupational structure. In 1995 almost half of wage earners were "ordinary workers" but this category claimed less than 17 percent in 2002. "Ordinary workers" is a category generally applied to unskilled workers in state enterprises. On the other hand, between these years the number of temporary or contract workers more than doubled from 10 percent to 23 percent and there was a huge increase in workers or owners of individual enterprises – from only 1.5 percent to 23 percent. Two

*Table 2.3* Occupations of rural workers reporting wage income, 1995 and 2002

| | *1995* | | *2002* | |
|---|---|---|---|---|
| | *Frequency* | *Percentage* | *Frequency* | *Percentage* |
| Farm labor | 69 | 4.6 | 790 | 8.1 |
| Ordinary worker | 733 | 48.8 | 1634 | 16.8 |
| Skilled worker | 98 | 6.5 | 425 | 4.4 |
| Professional or technical worker | 60 | 4.0 | 194 | 2.0 |
| Enterprise owner or manager | 16 | 1.1 | 62 | 0.6 |
| Township/ Village cadre* | 15 | 1.0 | 751 | 7.7 |
| Official of party or government office/institution | 171 | 11.4 | 71 | 0.7 |
| Ordinary enterprise cadre | 50 | 3.3 | 50 | 0.5 |
| Temporary/contract worker | 152 | 10.1 | 2223 | 22.9 |
| Non-agricultural individual enterprise (e.g. retailer, driver, etc.)** | 19 | 1.3 | 1788 | 18.4 |
| Other | 120 | 8.0 | 1740 | 17.9 |
| Total | 1503 | 100.0 | 9728 | 100.0 |

Notes:
* In 1995 only one category (*xiangcun*) of cadre was asked for. In 2002 this question was broken down into village/team (*cunzu*) cadre and town (*xiangzhen*) cadre, the results of both of which are combined in this row.
** In 1995 no distinction was made between owners and workers in individual enterprises. The separate figures for these categories in 2002 therefore have been pooled.

categories associated with the "old" economy – party/government officials and enterprise cadres – declined as percentages of the workforce. These officials and cadres are paid on a national civil service salary scale that is "very high relative to local incomes in poor regions," and this gap grew substantially in the late 1990s (Wong 2005: 18). Yet the decline in their share of wage earners as wage employment spread and became more common, lowered the average wage. Skilled, professional and technical workers and enterprise owners/managers also all declined as a share of wage earners.[14] These changes are all consistent with a story of wage employment spreading more widely through the countryside, labor markets developing and average wage falling toward the rural income level. In short, this is a story that Simon Kuznets would have understood.

Sharp changes also occurred in the ownership structure of wage earners' work units (Table 2.4). The majority of wage earners (55 percent) in 1995 worked in township/village enterprises; by 2002 this category of employer had declined to less than 8 percent. The same story holds for state enterprises/institutions, which fell from a quarter of all work units to under 6 percent. However, private enterprises (including small ones denoted as "individual" in China) employed over 43 percent of all rural wage earners in 2002, as compared to only 5.4 percent in

*Table 2.4* Distribution of rural wage earners by ownership of work unit, 1995 and 2002 (%)

| | *1995* | *2002* |
|---|---|---|
| Farm household | 7.5 | 7.4 |
| Private enterprise | 4.3 | 29.5 |
| Non-farm individual enterprise | 1.1 | 14.0 |
| TVEs or other collective enterprises | 55.2 | 7.7 |
| State-owned enterprise or institution | 24.7 | 5.7 |
| Sino-foreign joint venture | 1.9 | 1.8 |
| Foreign owned enterprise | 0.3 | 1.2 |
| Other | 5.0 | 32.6 |
| TOTAL | 100.0 | 100.0 |

1995. And the catchall category of "Other," fairly insignificant in 1995, captured almost a third of all workers in 2002. This category is probably largely comprised of various forms of partnerships, joint ventures and ill-defined arrangements that embody both private and collective entrepreneurship.

By 2002, fully two thirds of all rural wage earners were working outside their home village (Table 2.5) and one third worked outside their home county. This information is not available for 1995, but in that year only 3 percent of rural wage earners worked outside their home province, whereas some 18 percent did in 2002. These changes paint a picture of substantial and rapidly increasing labor mobility.

Consistent with this picture is the information about living arrangements of rural wage earners in 2002 (Table 2.6). Fully 43 percent did not live at home in that year, but rather in workplace dormitories (19.3 percent), construction sites (9.5 percent) and rented housing (9.2 percent). This is quite close to the percentage of wage earners shown in Table 2.5 who worked outside their home township (45.1 percent), and thus at some distance from their homes.

Thus, the surveys reveal not only a rapid spread of wage employment among the rural population between 1995 and 2002, but also big increases in private sector employment, employment in the vague and nebulous "Other" category and a sharp decline in state sector employment. The data on place of work and living arrangements indicate a huge rise in labor mobility, while the big decline in the average wage suggests the spread of a genuine rural labor market that made labor available at wages much closer to the theoretical entry level implied by the average rural income from household production of 1,645 yuan. Indeed, the average rural wage in 2002 was 2.25 times the average per capita income from household farm and non-farm production. In 1995 it was 6.1 times that income. It seems that the rapid geographic and sectoral spread of wage employment mediated through vigorously growing labor markets had an equalizing impact on rural income distribution, following the path that Kuznets had anticipated.

The third cause of reduced inequality of rural income was a reduction in inequality of net taxes, which accounted for a decline of 0.5 points in the overall

*Table 2.5* Distribution of rural wage earners by location of workplace, 2002 (%)

| | *Percentage* |
|---|---|
| Within home village | 33.1 |
| Out of village, within township | 21.8 |
| Out of township, within county | 12.1 |
| Out of county, within province | 15.1 |
| Out of province | 17.9 |
| All of above | 100.0 |

*Table 2.6* Living arrangements of rural wage earners, 2002 (%)

| | |
|---|---|
| Living at home | 57.1 |
| Living in dormitory | 19.3 |
| Shed in construction site | 9.5 |
| Rented housing | 9.2 |
| Other | 4.8 |
| TOTAL | 100.0 |

rural Gini ratio (see Table 2.1). In both 1995 and 2002 the value of "net subsidies from the state/collective" to rural residents was negative, indicating that on average they paid net taxes. Both equity and equality considerations would require that such taxes be distributed *more unequally* than income, i.e. that the upper income groups pay a higher share of taxes than their share of income. In 1995 the "concentration ratio" of net taxes paid by the rural population (the "pseudo-Gini" ratio measuring the distribution of net taxes over all income recipients) was negative, indicating not only that this condition was not met, but that low income households actually paid more than the total of net taxes while high income households received net subsidies. In 2002, on the other hand, the concentration ratio had become positive while remaining well below the overall Gini ratio for income. Thus, while low income households were no longer paying more than the total of net taxes, they were still paying more than their share of income in a highly regressive manner. As we have seen, however, the decline in the regressiveness of net taxes helps to explain the decline in the overall Gini.

We cannot rule out the possibility that far more taxes were reported in 2002 than in 1995 (net taxes rose from 0.48 percent to 2.62 percent of per capita income) and that this caused the rise in concentration ratio. Assuming the latter was real, however, it represents a somewhat less regressive fiscal approach by the state, which is an important story but not a Kuznets-type one. Developments in China since the late 1990s, when government statements began expressing serious concern about regional inequalities and rural disadvantages, support this view. The spending program undertaken in 1998 to offset reduced foreign demand because of the Asian economic crisis, and the concomitant Western Region Development program injected large amounts of infrastructure development spending into poorer interior provinces. Christine Wong (2005) has documented a proliferation of miscellaneous grants going principally to poorer provinces and a decline in the regressiveness of per capita fiscal transfers between 1998 and 2002. She finds the coefficient of variation of provincial per capita budgetary expenditures falling by 9 percent between 1998 and 2002. Thus, improvements in the progressivity of various aspects of fiscal policy may help to explain the fall in rural inequality that we observed from 1995 to 2002. By the same token, however, they may also be a large factor in our other principal story – the spread of wage employment – by creating many wage earning jobs in infrastructure projects in poorer interior parts of the country.

## Urban inequality

We have already seen that the decline in urban inequality was due principally to falling regional differences rather than to declines in inequality within individual provinces. From the perspective of income sources, there were sharp changes in the distribution of several types of income (Table 2.7). Wages continued their trend of increasing inequality but there was a sharp decline in housing subsidy in kind. This is the difference between the rent actually paid by residents and the estimated market value of their housing. Because of the housing reform, this form of income fell from almost 10 percent of total income in 1995 to less than 2 percent in 2002. In addition, its concentration ratio fell by almost 40 percent. In 1995 this subsidy was disproportionately appropriated by high income groups and its targeting was much improved in 2002. The imputed rental value of owned housing was also largely appropriated by high income residents: it had a concentration ratio in 1995 of 0.64 and fully three fifths of it went to the richest decile of the urban population (Khan and Riskin 2001). This reflected the extremely inequitable early implementation of the housing reform. As reform spread more broadly through the urban population (the share of income coming from this income source rose from 11.5 percent in 1995 to 17.7 percent in 2002) imputed rental income became a far less disequalizing income source, its concentration ratio falling almost by half.

*Table 2.7* Urban concentration ratios of selected income sources

| | *Percentage of income* | | *Concentration ratio* | | *Percentage of Gini contributed by* | |
|---|---|---|---|---|---|---|
| | *1995* | *2002* | *1995* | *2002* | *1995* | *2002* |
| Wages | 61.3 | 59.5 | 0.25 | 0.32 | 45.6 | 59.0 |
| Housing subsidy in kind | 9.7 | 1.9 | 0.52 | 0.32 | 15.1 | 1.9 |
| Rental value of housing | 11.4 | 17.7 | 0.64 | 0.38 | 21.9 | 21.0 |
| Other net subsidies | 1.3 | 0.1 | 0.30 | –2.16 | 1.1 | –0.5 |

Source: Khan and Riskin (2005: Table 12)

Other net subsidies,[15] while declining to a negligibly small fraction of income, became much better targeted at the poor. The negative sign on the concentration ratio indicates that low income groups received more than the total of all net subsidies while higher income groups paid net tax. This is most likely the outcome of government efforts to shore up local social security funds, finance both compensation payments to laid-off state workers and the growing unemployment insurance fund, and increase funding for the new Minimum Living Standard schemes to help poor urban households. Wong (2005) shows that subsidies to local social security programs grew from 15 billion yuan in 1998 to 51.2 billion yuan in 2002; subsidies for laid-off workers' stipends grew from 7.6 billion yuan in 1998 to 12.7 billion in 2001 and urban minimum living stipends, which did not exist in 1998, reached 4.6 billion yuan in 2002.

These changes reflect important developments in the nature and function of social benefits to the urban population during the reform period. Over the period as a whole there has been a notable decline in the proportion of social benefit income to total household income. In 1988 it accounted for around 46 percent of urban income and by 2002 this had declined to 28 percent (Gao 2005). Moreover, as argued above, by the mid-1990s at least elements of the benefits package, notably housing subsidy, were very regressively distributed. In 2002, however, Gao (2005) finds that remaining and new programs together had a degree of progressivity. The bottom decile of the population depended upon benefits for fully 80 percent of their total income (Table 2.8) and a large share of that took the form of cash transfers. Gao shows that the sub-category of cash transfers made up of traditional supplementary income programs (one-child subsidy, price and regional subsidies, etc.) had faded away by 2002 to be replaced by social insurance and public assistance programs of the kind detailed above.[16]

Government policy that more proactively promotes human development and corrects for excessive inequality is what many international agencies, such as the

*Table 2.8* Share of social benefits in total income, by decile, urban China, 2002 (%)

| *Decile* | *Total social benefits* | *Of which, cash transfers* |
|---|---|---|
| 1 | 80.29 | 69.43 |
| 2 | 44.14 | 30.95 |
| 3 | 29.70 | 17.35 |
| 4 | 25.52 | 14.08 |
| 5 | 21.85 | 11.00 |
| 6 | 19.63 | 9.60 |
| 7 | 17.01 | 7.51 |
| 8 | 15.73 | 7.09 |
| 9 | 15.82 | 5.14 |
| 10 | 11.86 | 3.40 |
| Total | 27.76 | 17.19 |

Source: Gao (2005)

United Nations Development Programme (UNDP) and the World Bank, have been advocating for years. Comparative international experience shows that such policies can profoundly affect the welfare outcomes of economic growth and indeed have a favorable impact on growth itself (UNDP 2004). However, this is different from the kind of market-driven equalization that characterizes the right half of the putative Kuznets Curve. Moreover, it is questionable whether the more inclusive development strategy suggested by the changes since the late 1990s can be more fully implemented. In urban China, the appearance of large-scale unemployment and poverty in China's cities with the transition to a market economy presented an emergency. The maintenance of social stability required forceful steps to replace vanishing social benefits with new social insurance programs and public assistance, and to provide enough funding to make these programs credible. In other important components of the social benefits package, such as education and housing, however, Gao (2005) shows that progressivity is conspicuously lacking. The re-design of the approach to social welfare provision in general along progressive lines will require a reform of the public finance system along the lines described by Wong (2005). Indeed, Wong makes a compelling case that a more equitable development strategy will not be achievable absent a "fundamental reform of the intergovernmental fiscal system" (2005: 18). The current system, unique to China, of assigning pensions, social welfare and unemployment insurance, as well as basic education and public health exclusively to local governments without giving them the means to finance these responsibilities, is incompatible with a more "people-centered" and equitable development strategy.

## Conclusion

Decreasing inequality in urban and rural income distributions, taken separately, was an unexpected result of the 2002 CASS household income survey. Decreasing inequality in personal disposable income within urban and rural China from 1995 to 2002 was the result of various forces. One was the rapid spread of wage employment in rural areas. Another was the evolution of the housing reform into a far less regressive program than when it began. A third was the significant reduction in the regressiveness of net taxes (subsidies) paid (received) by urban and rural residents and the adoption of a less regressive fiscal policy by the government. A fourth was the emergence of social insurance and public assistance programs that began to make large proportional contributions to the incomes of poor urban (but not rural) residents. In both rural and especially in urban China, these changes took in part a regional form, in that inter-provincial disparities in income fell over the period. There were countervailing tendencies, as well. In particular, urban wages continued to become more unequally distributed. Most conspicuously, China's already huge urban–rural divide widened still further, despite rapid increases in labor mobility and the beginnings of the existence of a national labor market.

Among these forces, the spread of rural wage employment is the one most supportive of a simple Kuznets Curve story. But even that may have been due to some degree to employment opportunities created by government spending programs beginning in the late 1990s to counter the effects of the Asian Crisis and begin addressing China's burgeoning east-west disparity. If one takes a less mechanical view of the Kuznets Curve and recognizes that the *mode* of development, as influenced by public policy, has a large impact on the nature of the development paradigm (UNDP 2004), then the answer to the title question of this chapter depends upon coming to grips with the full complexity of China's present and future political economy – a tall order, indeed! In short, it is far too early to predict that China is becoming a more egalitarian society. The forces impeding that evolution are still very strong. Yet it is noteworthy that factors promoting less inequality are present in enough strength to have produced the declines we observed between 1995 and 2002. If one rejects a simple Kuznets Curve story as vague and speculative and turns to macro- and sectoral policy changes for an explanation, it would perhaps be even more remarkable that a fiscally weakened central government could have stemmed the tide of relentlessly increasing inequality, at least for a while. Yet the acknowledged increase in poverty in 2003 symbolizes the difficulty China faces in trying to sustain that success.

## Notes

1 This suggestion is not quite an implication since it is possible for poverty to have risen without the Gini rising if the Lorenz curve shifted in such a way as to intersect the original curve. In this case the increase in poor people would be offset by a rise in middle income recipients relative to high income recipients. This is unlikely, however.
2 English has no word that exactly renders "*nongmin*" and the usual "peasantry" is unsatisfactory for well-known reasons.
3 See especially Bernstein and Lü (2003).
4 For details of the samples, see Khan and Riskin (2001) and Khan and Riskin (2005).
5 See Khan and Riskin (2005). The figure is for national income inequality when migrants are excluded from the calculation (no income data for migrants are available for 1995). Including migrants in the 2002 data causes the Gini to fall slightly to 0.448 (ibid.).
6 Wu and Perloff (2004), using different data and a different methodology, find measures of inequality to have increased for both urban and rural populations between 1995 and 2001.
7 For discussion of the Kuznets Curve and literature about it see Meier (1989) and Jha (1996).
8 For instance, in the study by Jha (1996), the $R^2$s are 0.324 or below.
9 A recent empirical discussion of the links between growth, poverty and inequality in Asia can be found in Pasha and Palanivel (2004).
10 Kuznets in his original 1955 article referred to the "vital force that would operate in democratic societies" constituted by changing views about the desirability of large income inequalities, and the resulting "increasing pressure of legal and political decisions on upper-income shares – increasing as a country moves to higher income levels" (1955: 9). Thus, the treatment in this chapter of the Kuznets Curve dynamic as an exclusively market-driven phenomenon is really something of a caricature of the more sophisticated argument originally put forward by Kuznets.
11 "Net transfer from/to state and collective" in Table 2.1 is the difference between any direct subsidies and transfers received by households, on the one hand, and taxes and

fees paid by households, on the other. A negative sign indicates a net tax (taxes larger than subsidies) and a positive sign indicates a net subsidy.

12 It is possible, but in our judgment unlikely, that the concentration ratio for net taxes fell because incomes of poor residents rose sharply relative to taxes they paid and/or the opposite happened for rich residents.

13 De Brauw et al. (2002) include migrant workers and migrant self-employed in off-farm rural employment.

14 The significance of the apparent increase in numbers of local cadres is uncertain because the category may not be comparable between 1995 and 2002. See notes to Table 2.3.

15 Net of taxes paid. See note 11.

16 Further analysis indicates, however, that of the various categories of social benefits that can be tracked, only housing subsidy and public assistance were substantially more progressive in 2002 than in 1995. See Gao and Riskin (2006).

## References

Bernstein, Thomas P. and Lü Xiabo (2003) *Taxation Without Representation in Contemporary Rural China*, New York and Cambridge: Cambridge University Press.

Chen Guidi and Wu Chuntao (2003) *Zhongguo Nongmin Diaocha*, Beijing: People's Culture Publishing House; translated by Zhu Hong as "Will the Boat Sink the Water? The Life of China's Peasants" with an introduction by John Pomfret (PublicAffairs).

De Brauw, Alan, Huang Jikun, Rozelle, Scott, Zhang Linxiu and Zhang Yigang (2002) "The Evolution of China's Rural Labor Markets during the Reforms," Working Paper 02–003, University of California at Davis.

Deaton, Angus (2005) "Measuring Poverty in a Growing World (or Measuring Growth in a Poor World)," *Review of Economics and Statistics*, 87 (1) February: 1–19.

Gao Qin (2005) "The Redistributive Mechanism of Social Benefits in Urban China From 1988 to 2002," New York, unpublished manuscript.

Gao Qin and Riskin, Carl (2006) "Explaining China's Changing Income Inequality: Market vs. Social Benefits," in D. Davis and F. Wang, (eds.) *Creating Wealth and Poverty in China*, forthcoming 2007.

Jha, Sailesh K. (1996) "The Kuznets Curve: A Reassessment," *World Development*, 24 (4): 773–80.

Khan, Azizur Rahman and Riskin, Carl (2005) "China's Household Income and its Distribution, 1995 and 2002," *China Quarterly*, 182, June: 356–84.

Khan, Azizur Rahman and Riskin, Carl (2001) *Inequality and Poverty in China in the Age of Globalization*, Oxford and New York: Oxford University Press.

Khan, Azizur Rahman and Riskin, Carl (1998) "Income and Inequality in China: Composition, Distribution and Growth of Household Income, 1988 to 1995," *China Quarterly,* 154, June: 221–53.

Kuznets, Simon (1955) "Economic Growth and Income Inequality," *American Economic Review*, 45 (1): 1–28.

Meier, Gerald M. (1989) *Leading Issues in Economic Development*, New York and Oxford: Oxford University Press.

Naughton, Barry (2002) "Provincial Economic Growth in China: Causes and Consequences of Regional Differentiation," in M.-F. Renard et al. (ed.) *China and its Regions*, Northampton, MA: Edward Elgar.

Pasha, Hafiz A. and Palanivel, T. (2004) *Pro-Poor Growth and Policies: The Asian Experience*, New York: UNDP.

Riskin, Carl (1987) *China's Political Economy: The Quest for Development since 1949*, Oxford and New York: Oxford University Press.

UNDP (2004) *The Macroeconomics of Poverty Reduction: The Case of China*, Beijing: United Nations Development Programme.

Wong, Christine (2005) "Can China Change Development Paradigm for the 21st Century? Fiscal Policy Options for Hu Jintao and Wen Jiabao after Two Decades of Muddling Through", paper for the Stiftung Wissenschaft und Politik, Berlin, Germany, January 2005; available online at <http://www.swp-berlin.org/common/get_document.php?id=1248&PHPSESSID=82c3a943f90732e6d4637eb8981c355d> (accessed 7 December 2006).

Wu Ximing and Perloff, Jeffrey M. (2004) "China's Income Distribution over Time: Reasons for Rising Inequality," Econometric Society 2004 Summer Meetings.

Xinhua News Agency (2004) "800,000 More Chinese Live in Poverty in 2003," *China Daily*; available online at <http://www.chinadaily.com.cn/english/doc/2004–07/20/content_350069.htm> (accessed 7 December 2006).

# 3 Local governance, health financing, and changing patterns of inequality in access to health care[1]

*Jane Duckett*

## Introduction

This chapter examines how changing systems and practices of local governance and health financing in China have influenced patterns of inequality in access to health services.[2] These patterns of inequality are important because they can be closely connected to the patterns of income inequality discussed in other chapters in this volume, as well as to experiences of poverty and social inequality, and to health inequalities.[3] First, for example, in health financing systems like China's today, where health insurance participation is low and most people have to pay directly for health services, patterns of inequality in access map onto patterns of income inequality. In turn, people – particularly those with low incomes – who do not have health insurance are vulnerable to impoverishment due to ill health, so that inequalities in access may contribute to rising poverty and income inequalities. Second, where access to care is dependent on ability to pay, those on low incomes may be unable to afford the medical treatment they need, meaning that in China as elsewhere "unequal legitimate claims upon a health system, and unequal experiences of seeking care are important elements of poverty and inequality in people's experience" (Mackintosh 2001: 175). Third, inequalities in access to health services can interact with factors such as age, socio-economic differences or diet to contribute to increasing or reducing health inequalities (Peter and Evans 2001).

The chapter is divided into four main sections. Section 1 looks at institutions of local governance and their relationship with the provision and financing of health, and particular patterns of inequality in access to health services in the late 1970s, while Section 2 examines how changing institutions of governance and health financing produced substantially re-shaped patterns of inequality in the 1980s–1990s. Section 3 considers how reforms since the late 1990s are affecting the patterns of inequality that emerged that decade. The concluding section discusses how evolving patterns of unequal access to health services relate to income, social and health inequalities in China, and what changes in wider systems of governance and public finance would be needed to provide health services and medical treatment more equally.

The chapter argues that in the late Mao era systems of health financing (state budgetary investment, cooperative medical systems (CMS) in rural areas, and employer-financed health insurance in the cities) were tied closely to systems and practices of local governance (notably state planning, rural communes, and the urban work unit) and produced patterns of inequality characterized by a rural–urban divide, with the main differences in the countryside between localities and in the cities between work units. Since the late 1970s, rural–urban differential access has increased and neither health financing nor governance reforms have significantly challenged this divide. In the countryside, changes to systems and practices of local rural governance, notably the end of the commune system and fiscal decentralization, led to changes in health financing and re-patterned inequality in financial access to health care so that interpersonal inequalities now overlie inter-local ones. In the context of continued fiscal decentralization, attempts to re-establish cooperative systems of health financing since the late 1980s have had limited success in most parts of the country, although there has perhaps been more progress in wealthier rural areas. Unless fundamental financing and governance problems are tackled, progress with this reform and rural medical finance assistance (MFA) will be slow, and both interpersonal and location-based inequalities in access are unlikely to be fundamentally challenged in the near future.

In urban China, some changes in health financing (such as allowing health service providers to earn income from sales of medicine) preceded and contributed to changes in governance institutions (especially the erosion of the work unit system) in the 1980s and 1990s by pushing up health costs for both government and enterprise work units. As work units reneged on health insurance payments, made workers redundant, and went bankrupt, growing numbers of urban dwellers had to pay directly for their own medical treatment. This transformed patterns of inequality in access to health care from mainly employment-based ones determined by work unit to interpersonal (or household) ones based on ability to pay. Compulsory basic social health insurance (BSHI) introduced across urban China since the late 1990s involves risk-pooling at the city level and so reduces some of the interpersonal inequalities in financial access among those who participate. A shift to location-based differentials in access is now emerging, though the differences between cities are limited by a national framework of provision. BSHI also involves an important change in systems and practices of local governance because along with urban MFA for the poorest, it has shifted responsibility for provision from employers to the local government. However, some continuities in wider governance practices mean that many working in the private sector, or informally in the state sector, as well as the non-working population, are excluded, leaving them and their families vulnerable to impoverishment due to illness. Although MFA is now being extended, it is not yet adequately financed and administered and so remains an unreliable safety net for the poor. The chapter concludes that contemporary patterns of inequality in access can be tackled by reforms of financing systems as well as improvements in local government capacity in the health sector.

## Late Mao local governance, financing, and inter-local and inter-work unit patterns of inequality in access

By the late 1970s, health service provision and financing in China was linked to wider systems and practices of governance in at least two important ways. First, the organization of health services was mapped onto structures of local government administration, economic production, and social control. Health services were organized and administered by local government health departments and the key organizations of rural and urban governance, the commune and the work unit. Second, health was financed through a combination of local government budgetary investment, rural collective funds, and urban employers, in line with the wider planning and fiscal practices of the command economy. In both cities and countryside, local governments allocated parts of their budgets to capital investment, preventive public health programs, and the running costs of hospitals, including salaries. This helped extend health services across China from the 1950s, improving the availability of at least basic services. A World Bank study has noted that by 1975 "almost all the urban population and 85 percent of the rural" had insurance or CMS, and this provided people with "access to cost-effective preventive and curative health services and some sharing of the risks of medically caused financial misfortune" (World Bank 1997: 2). The system is generally credited with contributing to significant gains in health and life expectancy (World Bank 1992).

### *Rural governance, health financing and inter-local patterns of inequality*

In the countryside, a three-tier system of counties, communes, and production brigades administered and delivered health services and programs (World Bank 1983). There were hospitals at county level, communes would have a health center that provided referral services and supervised preventive work, and many villages (or production brigades) had a health station staffed by "barefoot doctors" (Bloom and Gu 1997b). Commune health centers were administered by the local commune management committee and party committee. They were supervised and supported technologically by the county-level general hospital, maternal and child health hospital, and anti-epidemic station. These three county health care institutions were in turn administered by the county health bureau. This brought a network of health services to many rural areas that had not had them before.

During the late 1960s and 1970s, within governance structures shaped by the commune system, some form of CMS was established in most villages.[4] As some authors have noted, this system of health financing "was an integrated part of the overall system of collective agriculture production and social services" (Liu et al. 1999: 1354). Although CMS schemes were sometimes subsidised by government budgets, especially for vaccines and contraceptives, health campaign materials, and training of local medical personnel,[5] they were mainly funded by households, brigades and commune welfare funds so that in effect rural communities financed most of their own health services, especially curative care (Huang 1988; Kan 1990: 42).

In terms of the three-tier system of health service providers, this meant that there was more state financing for county and sometimes commune level, but little for the level below that. County-level service providers were funded entirely from the state budget, while commune health centers, often small hospitals, were funded from a combination of "contributions from the commune welfare fund, transfers of funds from the cooperative medical funds of the brigades under its jurisdiction, cost-sharing with users, and subsidies from the county and provincial government" (World Bank 1983: 49).[6] Brigade medical stations were financed cooperatively by premiums from members of the production brigade and contributions from the brigade's welfare fund, as well as user fees, income from sales of medicinal herbs, and "various subsidies from the commune, county, province and state" (World Bank 1983: 49).

As a result of tying health service provision to a penetrative government administrative system, physical access to health services was improved for many rural dwellers in the late Mao era. However, for people living in mountainous areas or those without good transport connections, the nearest hospital could be beyond easy reach. Inequality in financial access to health services was also patterned primarily on an inter-local basis. While risk-pooling at brigade level ensured that its members probably had relatively equal access to basic outpatient medical treatment, the quality and range of treatments available were dependent on the amount of money raised by members of the production brigade and the amount that the brigade, commune and county were able and willing to subsidize the cooperative funds. "The more affluent communities can afford to subsidize health care costs, invest more to increase the quantity and raise the quality of their health personnel, and enjoy easier access to better health care, relative to the less affluent communities," whereas "some of the poorest brigades and teams hav[e] reportedly cut back their provision of services in recent years" (World Bank 1983: 50, 9).

### *Urban governance, health financing and work unit-based patterns of inequality*

Urban health services were provided through hospitals and clinics beneath the Ministry of Health and its municipal and district health bureaux, and separately through the military, some large state enterprises, and public institutions such as universities, which often had their own clinics and hospitals that provided health services directly to their personnel and dependants (World Bank 1983). Within the Ministry of Health system there were, in addition to municipal and district hospitals, small neighbourhood hospitals or health "stations," which were relatively autonomous during the Cultural Revolution. Finally, there were health stations organized around resident committee organizations and staffed by supervised paramedics called "red medical workers" who assisted with neighbourhood preventive work and offered some very simple diagnostic and curative services (Sidel and Sidel 1982). Local governments (cities and districts) funded Ministry of Health system hospitals while military and work unit hospitals were funded through budgets for their own systems (*xitong*), all within the wider planning and budgetary arrangements of the command economy.

In addition to municipal and district government financing of health service provision within state plans, from the 1950s many urban dwellers' medical expenses, paid for by employers, or "work units" (*danwei*), formed another important source of investment. Work units were state or collective sector employers that provided for urban workers and delivered urban public goods, while at the same time they were a mechanism for their control and a cornerstone of structures and practices of urban governance (Lü and Perry 1997). There were two programs of work-unit-financed medical care: one for workers in enterprises (mainly state and collective enterprises) under "labor insurance" (*laodong baoxian*, hereafter LI) and one for government and public sector employees (such as officials, teachers, doctors, students) under "publicly financed health insurance" (*gongfei yiliao baoxian*, hereafter PHI). LI was financed by enterprises, though of course within the planning system, so that expenditures on employees' medical treatment were factored into enterprise plans under soft budget constraints. PHI was financed directly from the budgets of the relevant level of government, so that for example central government financed the payments of public sector institutions at the center. Neither LI nor PHI involved individual employees making contributions or significant co-payments,[7] and patients usually received treatment free at the point of delivery, paying only a nominal registration fee on arrival at a clinic or hospital (Yin 1997). Additionally, enterprise work units paid half the medical expenses of their employees' dependants.

Patterns of financial inequality in access to urban health services in the late 1970s were thus based mainly on employer and employment status, and tied to the fundamental institution of urban governance, the work unit. The generosity of health insurance varied, and was influenced by a work unit's administrative level as well as individual factors such as an employee's rank, contract type, or political label.[8] Thus those with access to the best curative services free at the point of delivery were central government officials and workers in central government-level state enterprises, while local officials and workers in small urban government collectives received less generous assistance.[9] And provision was better for employees with high rank and/or permanent posts than for lower-ranking officials, workers with temporary contracts and rural migrants to the cities, while political 'rightists' were deprived altogether of any entitlements.[10]

### *Overlapping and intersecting patterns of inequality*

As well as the intra-rural and intra-urban inequalities in access to health care discussed above, there were also in the late Mao era significant inequalities in access between urban and rural areas. Cities received a greater share of government investment in health, resulting in more hospital beds and doctors per head of population and meaning better *physical* access for urban dwellers (World Bank 1983). In 1975, for example, there were 4.6 hospital beds per thousand people in the cities, but only 1.2 per thousand in rural counties, and 2.7 doctors per thousand in the cities but only 0.7 per thousand in the countryside (Ministry of Health 2000: 426). Both this and rural–urban inequalities in *financial* access to health services were due to high levels of funding for LI and PHI by enterprises and the state, while in rural areas CMS was self-funded and much less generous. In terms of health expenditures, in 1980, 34 percent of health spending was on urban PHI and LI alone, when China's urban population was only 19 percent of the total (Hossain 1997; State Statistical Bureau of China 1992). In addition, central and local government budgetary spending on health (excluding PHI and LI), which was about 25 percent of total health spending, will have been disproportionately targeted at urban areas (Hossain 1997). Studies in the early 1980s showed that total urban per capita expenditure on health was three times that in rural areas (Liu et al. 1995).

Overlapping patterns of inequality in access between and within countryside and city arise from unequal government budgetary spending. But differences in local and work unit resource endowments will also have contributed to other still poorly understood intersecting patterns of inequality caused by factors such as age and gender discrimination in employment. For example, because higher ranking (often heavy industrial) work units tended to employ men, while less well-resourced urban local government collectives tended to employ women, women were less likely to be directly entitled to better quality health care.[11] Indeed, access to health care for many women (as well as children) will have been through their status as dependants of male workers. And the fact that enterprises usually paid for only half the medical costs of dependants can be expected to have had real effects on their abilities to seek treatment.[12]

## Local governance and health finance in the era of market reform: growing individual inequalities in access

As is well known, key features of the late Mao systems and practices of local governance underpinning health service provision and finance were transformed with the turn to market-led economic growth in the 1980s. The system of rural governance based on the communes was dismantled as townships replaced the communes and agricultural production was devolved to rural households. Urban governance practices centered on the work unit eroded over this period as state and collective enterprises were encouraged to become more efficient and competitive while growing numbers of urban dwellers worked in the private sector.[13] Underpinning all this was the introduction of market mechanisms to replace planning ones in the allocation of goods and resources, and fiscal decentralization that increased local government autonomy and reduced the state's redistributive capacity (Naughton 1996; Park et al. 1996).

These transformations in wider systems and practices of governance had direct and dramatic effects on the provision and financing of health services. Dismantling rural communes led to a collapse in CMS, while market competition meant that poorly performing enterprise work units were no longer able to afford generous health provision for their workers. At the same time, fiscal decentralization caused budgetary investment in health services to become less redistributive so that many hospitals were short of finance and increasingly reliant on generating their own income. The decentralization of government responsibilities for hospitals that accompanied fiscal decentralization has also contributed to problems regulating them. These changes together with the growth of private practice have raised the costs of health care and resulted in increased inequalities in patterns of provision as well as increased and re-shaped patterns of inequality in financial access. The transformations in health services provision and financing and their effects on access are set out in more detail below.

### *The collapse of CMS*

The abolition of communes and introduction of household farming in the late 1970s and early 1980s led to the collapse of cooperative health financing in many parts of rural China. The share of villages with CMS fell from an estimated 90 percent in the late 1970s to less than 5 percent by 1984 (Carrin et al. 1999; Feng et al. 1995: 1112; Grogan 1995). This had an enormous impact on patterns of inequality in financial access to health services because it meant that in most villages risk-pooling and collective cover ended as CMS funds ceased to exist.[14] Individuals and households increasingly had to pay for their own curative treatment, and often even for preventive services such as vaccinations and immunizations. In 1980, individual patient fees were 23 percent of total health spending, but the share had risen to 39 percent in 1991 (Hossain 1997). On one mid-1990s' analysis, approximately 95 percent of rural residents were paying for their own care (Grogan 1995). Where CMS funds could no longer pay village health workers (formerly "barefoot doctors"), they could be forced to charge fees, sell medicines, be driven out of medical practice, or have to move to other areas (Feng et al. 1995: 1113). As a result there was a decline in the number of village health stations, and rural health services had lost 3.7 million employees by the late 1980s (Hillier and Jie 1996; Hillier and Zheng 1991).

### *Uneven urban work unit health finance and provision*

In the cities, the key institution of local governance, the work unit, was not suddenly dismantled, but eroded more gradually, in part due to the growing burden of the health benefits it provided. From the late 1980s, as urban industrial reforms began to encourage greater competition among enterprises, the numbers of employees entitled to benefits increased (particularly in older enterprises with larger numbers of retired workers), and as medical costs rose (due to policies discussed below), health financing began to feel more burdensome for employers.[15] As a result, they increasingly either reneged completely on their commitment to pay for their employees' health treatment, introduced patient co-payments, or simply paid small annual or monthly lump sums to employees for health care regardless of their actual health care needs. As cities, government administrative systems (*xitong*), and employers across the country experimented with different arrangements, work unit provision began to vary, and increasingly employees found that they had to pay directly for their own curative care. The likelihood of this grew during the 1990s as more and more people became self-employed or shifted to private sector or informal employment, where they were much less likely to have work unit assistance with their medical costs.[16] The 1993 and 1998 National Health Services Surveys revealed that the percentage of urban dwellers without health insurance had increased from 27 to 44 percent between the two survey years (Liu et al. 2002).[17] And by the 1990s, whether someone had LI or PHI (or assistance with medical costs of any kind) was still dependent on whether or not they had work and their employer provided such benefits. Those most likely to have good access were still higher-ranking officials and people in public institutions, as well as workers in state enterprises that continued to do well (Tang and Parish 2000).

### *Decentralization and the emergence of private practice*

In addition to these changes to rural collective and urban work unit sources of finance for health, a number of other transformations to health system finance also affected provision of, and access to, health services. First, fiscal decentralization in the health sector meant that budgetary finance for health came from local government coffers, so that for example, in rural areas township hospitals were no longer subsidized by counties and the task of handling local health policy at sub-county level was left to township officials who did not understand it well.[18] Second, because local government officials were given incentives to prioritize economic growth through the inclusion of economic indicators in their performance targets, spending on health was relatively neglected (Edin 2003; Park et al. 1996). Third, another series of policies has increased all state (including township) hospitals' autonomy and financial self-reliance. In 1983 a State Council circular began the practice of permitting hospital staff to earn bonuses for extra work and hospitals to retain profits for reinvestment (Hillier and Jie 1996: 261). This resulted in incentives for them to provide unnecessary diagnostic tests, medicine and curative care, as well as meaning that patients became prey to unethical treatment by medical professionals. Together, all these factors contributed to hospitals receiving a declining share of state budgetary support, so that by the early 1990s only about 20–25 percent of hospital expenditures were financed in this way (Hsiao and Liu 1996).[19] In some areas, health centers closed, with the total number of township health centers falling by 14 percent between 1980 and 1990, probably reducing the availability of health services for some rural dwellers, especially those in poorer areas (Feng et al. 1995).

Further changes resulted from allowing private doctors to practice and the private ownership of health facilities (Hsiao 1995).[20] Village (formerly brigade) health stations, previously run and financed through CMS, were often sold off to private practitioners, and medical personnel were permitted to provide private services outside their state hospital shifts (Ho 1995). Between 1980 and 1995 the share of the medical personnel in private practice grew from 0 to 5 percent, though private hospital numbers have grown much more slowly (Hindle 2000). The result of the expansion of private services has been that in wealthier areas provision has increased, and better technology has been available, while in poorer areas, where medical practice incomes are lower, practitioners have financial problems, and so have been leaving for wealthier areas where they can make a better living (Feng et al. 1995). There has also been a decline in preventive programs in some rural areas (Bloom and Gu 1997a).

### *Changing patterns of unequal access*

These fundamental transformations to rural communes and the urban work unit, along with the decentralization of health service finance and permission for private practice, reconfigured locality- and work unit-based patterns of unequal access to health services in the 1980s and 1990s. Locality still affected the quality of services available, and differences between localities in the quality and quantity of provision increased, widening the rural–urban divide.[21] But an interpersonal pattern of inequality in financial access to health care had begun to overlie those based on locality and work unit. For the many no longer participating in CMS or protected by work unit provision, access was dependent on individual (or household) ability to pay, and individuals and families on low incomes were more likely to defer care or leave their illnesses untreated. Gu and Tang (1995) report that the 1988 National Household Survey showed 25 percent of the rural population referred to hospital were unable to attend for treatment because they could not afford it. Similarly the 1993 National Health Services Survey found that almost 40 percent of the urban population reported that they could not afford the medical treatment they had been diagnosed as needing (Liu et al. 1999). And there had been little improvement towards the end of the decade, with research in 1998 finding that among poor urban households between 50 and 70 percent could not afford medical treatment.[22] Another study has shown that those with government or labor insurance were more likely to seek medical treatment, and twice as likely to receive hospital treatment (Grogan 1995).

These emergent patterns of interpersonal inequalities in access may have overlapped with and reinforced growing income inequalities that are often themselves influenced by interactions among household registration, gender and employment status.[23] For example Grogan (1995) shows how in urban China in the market reform period those with the highest wages receive the best benefits, while the growing numbers of people with agricultural household registration working in the cities on low incomes are unlikely to be given assistance (Solinger 1999). And women were more likely to be employed in low-paying urban collectives that found it harder to provide assistance with medical treatment costs. Those without work and income, particularly the long-term unemployed, were increasingly likely to have no health insurance, while middle-aged men and especially women were disproportionately represented among urban unemployed and laid-off workers, and usually among the first to lose their jobs when enterprises retrenched.

They were therefore less likely overall to be receiving work unit assistance with health care.

## The limits of reform to health system financing and new patterns of unequal access

This section examines attempts in the late 1990s to reform the system of health financing and their outcomes in terms of inequality in access to health services. In rural areas since the mid-1990s, reforms have focused on the re-establishment of cooperative, risk-pooling financing based on voluntary payments by rural dwellers.[24] In urban areas, LI and PHI are being replaced by a single basic compulsory social health insurance system for people in work, with risk-pooling at city level, and contributions made by employers and employees. In both countryside and cities, medical financial assistance (*yiliao jiuzhu*) programs have begun to be introduced to help the poor with their medical costs. While indicating that collective (redistributory, risk-pooling) solutions have not entirely been abandoned, these reforms are all encountering problems so that interpersonal inequalities remain significant.

### *Attempts to re-establish CMS, continuing patterns of inequality, and local governance problems*

Since 1993 the Chinese central government has attempted several times to re-establish some form of CMS in rural areas, but to little effect. In 1994, in conjunction with the World Health Organization (WHO), trials were initiated in 14 counties across seven provinces,[25] and efforts were again renewed in 1997, when a target was set of extending the system to most of the rural population by 2000 (Shi 2004; Xinhua (Anhui) 2002). Despite this, the second National Health Services Survey in 1998 found that only about 7 percent of rural dwellers were participating in CMS, and thereafter the trials received little publicity (Liu et al. 2002). In May 2001, a State Council document on rural reform and development mentioned CMS, but without setting targets or prioritizing it (State Council System Reform Office et al. 2001).

From 2002 there was renewed central policy emphasis on re-establishing CMS. In October that year the Party Central Committee and State Council issued a "Decision" on improving rural health work that instructed all areas to set up CMS pilots and gradually promote "new-type" CMS with the target of "basically covering rural dwellers" by 2010 (Central Committee of the Chinese Communist Party and State Council 2002). Since then, there have been concerted efforts to make progress with these trials (Ministry of Health et al. 2003; Ministry of Health Office 2003; State Council 2003), and the importance of the CMS work has been reiterated by then Vice-Premier and Minister of Health, Wu Yi, and Deputy Minister Gao Qiang (Gao 2004; Wu 2004). Although these speeches and documents reveal that there have already been problems, particularly with local governments overstating participation in the pilots, and in August 2003 they were narrowed to four provinces, CMS does now seem to be a priority for the State Council and the Ministry of Health. By June 2004, 69 million rural residents were reported as participating in "new-type CMS" trials, equivalent to just under 9 percent of the 768.5 million rural population (State Council 2004).

MFA schemes aimed at improving access to health care for the poorest were piloted in rural areas from 1998 through World Bank and UK government-funded programs in conjunction with the Chinese Ministry of Health, and in 2002 were introduced as national policy. Those eligible for MFA are the poorest households, including but not limited to families receiving poverty relief (*wubaohu*). MFA can take the form of direct assistance with health expenses for preventive as well as hospital treatment costs, or assistance to allow households to participate in CMS. Although local governments are required to help fund MFA, from 2003 the central government announced that it would contribute 10 yuan per CMS participant in China's middle and western regions (Central Committee of the Chinese Communist Party and State Council 2002). In November 2003 it was announced that the MFA system should be set up by 2005, beginning with 2–3 pilots in each province (Ministry of Civil Affairs et al. 2003). While it is a significant step towards tackling inequalities in access to health care and improving the access for poor rural dwellers, because MFA pays only a share of expenses it does not protect the poorest, and may not be affordable for governments in the poorest localities where it is most needed. By 1999 the Ministry of Health was still reporting that 23 percent of the rural population had to forego hospital treatment because they could not afford it (Liu et al. 2002).

With less than 10 percent of the rural population participating in CMS, patterns of inequality in financial access to health services in rural areas that appeared after the abolition of the communes remain, and are still mainly interpersonal or inter-household and closely connected with income inequalities.[26] While some rural dwellers participate in collective systems and have access to MFA or may be able to afford to take out private insurance, most must still pay directly for their own medical treatment and risk impoverishment from serious illness. Since CMS and MFA are most likely in the wealthiest areas, inter-local inequalities underlie interpersonal ones.

Problems in establishing some form of CMS (as well as institutionalizing MFA) are due in part to the fact that structures and practices of local governance that resulted in the initial collapse of cooperative medical systems are still in place: notably decentralized production and local government finance. When coupled with prioritization of economic growth throughout the political system and use of economic indicators to evaluate officials' performance, there is a local unwillingness to subsidize CMS or raise investment in the health system. At the same time, these governance structures and practices have led to problems of predatory local government and low levels of trust in it. Thus attempts to establish CMS are met with suspicion from farmers who see it as yet another means to extract income from them.[27] Indeed, central policies to tackle the problem of farmers being burdened with local taxes and fees have also damaged efforts to re-establish CMS (Liu et al. 2002).[28]

Recent developments indicate that top leaders, particularly Vice-premier Wu Yi, formerly Minister of Health, seem to be pushing for real progress in the implementation of CMS and MFA. Importantly for local-level prioritization of and investment in health, the Party Central Committee and State Council have issued a decision that instructs city and county people's congresses to make achieving targets in establishing CMS and reducing the numbers of people impoverished by ill health "an important part" of local leaders' performance assessment (*zhengji kaohe*) (Central Committee of the Chinese Communist Party and State Council 2002). Moreover, central policy documents on CMS have recently begun to argue against the view that CMS contributions are unreasonable fees that increase farmers' burden, pointing out that in fact they can reduce farmers' vulnerability to impoverishment through ill-health (Ministry of Health et al. 2003). Despite this, the obstacles to establishing CMS (and MFA) nationwide are still enormous. Participation remains voluntary and so CMS continues to be undermined by lack of trust in local government as well as problems created by weaknesses in the health system, such as poor or costly provision.[29] Local government mismanagement of funds and over-reporting of participation (so as to obtain higher level subsidies) has been reported even in pilot schemes in 2003, indicating that the goal of establishing CMS nationwide will be difficult to attain (Gao 2004).

### *Urban employee Basic Social Health Insurance, inequality and local governance*

Experimentation with new programs of urban health insurance began in the early 1990s and resulted in the introduction of a new compulsory national framework for urban BSHI in December 1998 (State Council 1999). This framework stipulates that city governments must establish social health insurance funds into which employers and employees contribute a share of their wage bill and wages respectively. Some of the contributions are channeled into individual health accounts for participating employees. The insurance fund and the health accounts are then used to finance outpatient and inpatient treatment, with patients making co-payments (either from their accounts or out of their own pockets) alongside those from the fund. Gradually since 1999 cities across the country have begun implementing the framework.[30]

The new framework is designed to include employees not only in public institutions and the state and collective sectors (that is those who formerly participated in PHI and LI), but also private and foreign-invested enterprises, and the self-employed. For those in work, therefore, there is now in principle a single system that delivers the same benefits for uniform contribution rates (though officials receive some enhanced provisions). This means that the late Mao intra-urban pattern of work-unit-based inequality in access within cities has been tackled. Moreover, where the framework is implemented fully, city-level risk-pooling limits the interpersonal inequalities in financial access of the post-Mao period, since some employees whose employers had not been paying for their health care are now participating in the schemes and so once again have insurance (Duckett 2004).[31]

However, there are limits to the redistribution involved in BSHI. First, with risk-pooling at city level, there are still differences in provision between cities. Although central policy is to establish province-wide risk-pooling, this does not seem likely in the short term. Second, individual health accounts institutionalize some interpersonal inequalities in financial access because employees with higher salaries will accumulate more in them. Third, significant interpersonal inequalities in financial access will remain due to the exclusion from the new system of the non-working population, notably the long-term unemployed and dependants. Although a safety net, Minimum Living Security, has been established in China's cities to provide low-level, means-tested, income support to the poorest urban dwellers, in most cities it includes only a very small nominal standard amount for health expenses. And although some cities have now also established MFA to assist the poor that mitigates some interpersonal inequalities,[32] it still leaves some vulnerable to impoverishment or at risk of going untreated because there are upper limits on the amounts awarded to individuals and co-payments are required.[33] As in rural areas, continued local fiscal decentralization and prioritization of economic growth means that local governments are unwilling to commit themselves to funding means-tested provisions for the poor. However, recent announcements of central government financial assistance of 300 million yuan per year for urban MFA does signal that central government is beginning to give financial backing to support, and that there is therefore also likely to be improvement in implementation of this policy.[34]

Fourth, the national framework for BSHI is not always fully implemented, and in practice many enterprises, particularly urban collective and private ones, do not participate in the schemes – either because they cannot afford to or because participation would increase their expenditures on health or reduce the quality of their own employees' health provision (Duckett 2001). Moreover, despite the growth of rural–urban migration, there is still inequality in access based on household registration. Although in principle the new BSHI allows the employees of urban enterprises who have agricultural registration and long-term (more than one year) contracts to join the scheme, there is as yet little evidence that they are participating in significant numbers.[35] Inequalities based on household registration are in part due to fiscal decentralization, which means that local governments are unwilling to finance provisions to people from outside their own administrative jurisdictions. The result is a mix of eroded or modified late Mao and reform era arrangements that co-exist to create a very varied picture across China in which, because many individuals do not participate in BSHI, there are still significant intra-local inequalities in access. Still, the trend has been strongly towards extending the program to include more urban residents. Nationally, participation in BSHI has increased rapidly from just under 19 million in 1998 to 109 million at the end of 2003, about 21 percent of the urban population and 42 percent of the urban working population (Ministry of Labor and Social Security 2003; State Council 2004).[36] The challenge now is to sustain the improvement in participation so that those in collective and private employment are also included.

Although (enterprise) work units are still the main source of finance for urban social health insurance, it is no longer organized, administered and delivered by them. These tasks have been transferred to urban government social health insurance agencies (part of the new Ministry of Labor and Social Security system) which are responsible for administering the new social health insurance funds, collecting contributions to them and organizing payments to health service providers. (This involves selecting hospitals and clinics as well as arranging and overseeing payment mechanisms.) Thus the creation of urban basic social health insurance has involved transforming institutions and practices of local governance in a way that CMS reform attempts have not. First, responsibility for administering the financing and delivery of social insurance benefits has been transferred from work units to local governments, which along with other measures such as those to halt the provision of work-unit housing, constitutes a deliberate move towards abandoning the work unit as an institution of governance. This transformation entails a concomitant increase in government responsibility for provision although there has been a lag in establishing the mechanisms that enable social health insurance agencies to enforce employer participation in BSHI and deal effectively with the hospitals to which they now channel finance.

## Concluding remarks

### *Inequalities in access to health services: relationships with income inequality, health inequalities, and experiences of poverty and social inequality*

Attempts throughout the 1990s to re-establish some form of rural CMS, urban BSHI, and MFA show that redistributive, collective solutions have not entirely been abandoned. But governance problems are undermining their implementation and reducing the amounts of finance available to them. As a result, direct payments "out-of pocket" for health care had risen to 61 percent of spending in 2000, something that has contributed significantly in highly unequal access to health services (Ministry of Health 2002). It is because of this that in 2000 the WHO ranked China only 188th out of 191 countries in terms of the fairness of its health financing system (World Health Organization 2000). The primary patterns of inequality are still those between countryside and city, and within these sectors between localities and individuals. As discussed above, these patterns may also – through social institutions such as household and workplace – interact with and reinforce inequalities due to gender or age.

Inequalities in access to health care are also connected to other dimensions of inequality, notably those in income and health, as well as contributing to experiences of social inequality and poverty. Interpersonal inequalities in access to health care due to the absence of risk-pooling CMS or insurance are closely related to income inequalities and may contribute to their increase, while illness can also increase poverty. Gu and Tang (1995) cite a 1991 study of 60 poor families in Yuhan county in Zhejiang which found that 47 percent said family members' medical care had forced them into poverty. According to other sources, 30–50 percent of rural households living beneath the poverty line had become impoverished due to illness (Liu et al. 1999). In urban areas, too, declining participation in labor insurance means that risk of impoverishment due to ill health increased in the 1990s.

Local and individual inequalities in access to health services in China may also have contributed to growing health inequalities. Despite limited data on the health status of the Chinese population in the late Mao era, we know that there were significant health inequalities. For example, the World Bank in 1981 reported higher mortality rates and poorer nutrition in the countryside than in urban areas (Hillier and Jie 1996: 263). However, there are some indications that despite sustained growth in China's economy, health inequalities have on some indicators increased since then. Data on inter-provincial and rural–urban differences, for example, indicate increases for indicators such as life expectancy and infant mortality (Hossain 1997; Liu et al. 1999).[37] Although health inequalities are caused by a combination of many factors including age, diet, access to clean water, as well as housing conditions, working conditions and perhaps social status and social inequalities, inequalities in access to health services are likely to have had an influence. Since ill-health is likely to be more prevalent among the poor, the fact that health service provision is weakest in areas where risk of poverty is highest means that provision is particularly inequitable. And since ill-health may also increase the risk of poverty, inequalities in health service provision may be contributing to a vicious circle of deepening poverty and ill-health.

Finally, since those on the lowest incomes in China are the least likely to have adequate health protection, poor access to both preventive services and especially medical treatment has added a new dimension to experiences of poverty in China. Being poor now means being more vulnerable to disease, having to suffer illness without access to many medicines and treatments or only to very low quality services in often unsanitary conditions, and so living with the fear of serious disease and ill-health.

### *Health financing, local governance and the prospects for improving access to health services*

The national policy initiatives since 2003 may indicate a new political will among leaders at the center to prioritize health. The SARS outbreak that year, as well as China's low WHO ranking for the fairness of its health system in 2000, and the spread of the HIV/AIDS epidemic have focused more attention on the health system, and apparently created a determination to push things forward, not only in relation to HIV/AIDS and other communicable disease prevention, but also with improving access to health services through "new-type" CMS and MFA. Central government budgetary investment has increased in support of these policies.

However, improving access to health services in China requires more than political will at the top, new policy initiatives, and the allocation of *ad hoc* ear-marked central government investment. Although these are all important, access is significantly influenced by modes of health financing and provision that are closely tied into wider local governance systems and practices. The commune, work unit, and planning system that contributed to more equitable access in the past are no longer functioning, while new systems and practices in the era of market reform, such as fiscal decentralization, local government administration of social insurance, and the prioritization of economic growth through new incentive systems for officials, create new obstacles to rebuilding CMS and extending urban BSHI.[38] Perhaps the most important steps towards tackling the problem would be those in the sphere of health financing to deal with the negative consequences of fiscal decentralization, and those in the sphere of local governance to improve the capacity of the new social insurance and other government agencies.

In terms of health financing, first, there is a need for more central government financial intervention. As Wong notes in Chapter 1, central government transfers back to the provinces have shifted significantly away from disequalizing tax rebates towards a greater share of more redistributive earmarked grants.[39] However, these earmarked grants need to be reviewed, rationalized and better targeted, and they need to operate alongside more and better local health financing (World Bank 2002). Second, to tackle the problem of disincentives for local governments to invest in health (both in services and health protection systems for their populations) that has been created by fiscal decentralization, governance reforms are important. Decentralization hinders the creation of a nationwide (even province-wide) health insurance system and a more equitable health system. Central co-ordination of health planning and resource allocation, including prioritization of redistribution within the health system could contribute to tackling this problem, but both local investment in health and the implementation of urban social health insurance could be improved by making them an important component of local leaders' performance targets.[40]

However, simply increasing finance alone will not tackle some of the most serious obstacles to improving access. To ensure that government investment is used effectively and more efficiently, certain local governance systems and practices need to be improved. Two issues are central here: first, delineation of responsibilities need to be clearer. For example, in the countryside CMS work needs to be better integrated into county and township administration. Second, administrative capacities of new government agencies could be improved. For example, the capacity of new urban social health insurance departments to monitor employers and ensure all their employees participate in BSHI would increase participation in this scheme. At present, departments are better at ensuring the participation of state enterprises (though they do not always ensure that all their employees participate) than private sector businesses. Social health insurance departments, as "third party payers" of patients' medical expenses, could, through better systems for monitoring and paying health service providers, strengthen their capacity to tackle the incentives to over-prescribe medicines, provide unnecessary diagnostic tests and require informal payments. At present they lack experience in dealing with providers, and while participation in BSHI is low, they are not major purchasers of health services and so lack influence. Thus improving participation in BSHI can help increase departments' capacity to deal with service providers.

Should these and the recommendations for improving the quality of basic health services be implemented, the prospects for reducing interpersonal inequalities through re-establishing CMS and extending BSHI would be significantly improved, though the re-establishment of CMS may also require tackling the wider lack of trust in rural government,[41] while extending BSHI to urban dwellers without work would require substantial state investment. This would in itself be a major accomplishment, even though it would neither tackle the entrenched rural–urban inequalities in the system nor the new and growing inequalities in the cities. China's rural dwellers continue to be those to whom progress comes most slowly and with least state budgetary support, though there is now a growing urban underclass that is little better off.

## Notes

1 This chapter has benefited from discussions with Lesley Doyal, Marianne Hester and Randall Smith, as well as from the comments of participants at the workshop "Paying for Progress" held at the University of Oxford in May 2004, notably Athar Hussain, Vivienne Shue, Christine Wong, Carl Riskin and Tao Ran.

2 Financial access relates to how financing arrangements affect ability to utilize health services. Physical access relates to how location or proximity of health service providers may affect utilization. This chapter concentrates on financial access, but its discussion of local differences in health service provision helps understand changing patterns of physical access.

3 Health inequalities are inequalities in health status as evidenced by for example differential life expectancy or experience of ill health.

4 The first CMS-type schemes were introduced experimentally from 1955 in Henan and Shanxi. They were established more widely from the late 1960s. By the mid-1970s more than 90 percent of brigades are thought to have had such a scheme (Feng et al. 1995; Kan 1990).

5 There was also effectively government subsidy for western drugs because their prices were set artificially low (World Bank 1983).

6 There was, however, great variety in the detail of local funding arrangements. For example, higher levels might fund all the salaries of the commune hospital, or only some of them.

7 Co-payments refer to direct out-of-pocket payments by patients alongside those made by the insurer.

8 Negative political labels (such as "rightist" or "capitalist roader") assigned to individuals in the leftist Mao era were often accompanied by sanctions and persecution ranging from social exclusion through withdrawal of entitlements to imprisonment.

9 On how state enterprise employees get "more extensive benefits," including health care, in terms of both quantity and quality, than collective sector employees, see Whyte and Parish (1984), and Davis (1988).

10 See Duckett (2004), drawing for this information on Dixon (1981).

11 Bauer et al. (1992) report that a survey in 1987 found that women were only a third of employees in state enterprises, but almost half of those in urban collective enterprises. They also found men to be more concentrated in higher-paying industrial sectors and to be a large proportion of employees in government and party organizations.

12 See for example Östlin et al. (2001) on how a range of intra-household and other factors can limit women's access to health services.

13 Most private sector employers do not provide the same range of benefits as state and collective work units once did (though for a discussion of some exceptions see Francis 1996).

14 Rural cooperative health funds accounted for 17 percent of total health spending nationally in 1980 but had declined to less than 6 percent in 1983 (Hossain 1997).

15 Total expenditures on labor and government employee health insurance had risen almost five times between 1980 and 1990, from 670 million yuan to 3,236 million yuan (at 1980 prices) (Gu and Tang 1995).

16 The numbers employed in state work units (*guoyou danwei*) declined from a peak of 112 million in 1995 to 76 million at the end of 2001, and the number in urban collective enterprises declined from 36 million in 1991 to 13 million at the end of 2001. Meanwhile the number employed in private enterprises rose from 0.7 million in 1991 to 15 million at the end of 2001, and the numbers of self-employed rose from 7 million to 21 million over the same period (State Statistical Bureau of China 2001, 1996). The registered unemployed, who are entitled to unemployment benefits, should also have their medical costs paid, but only during the period they are entitled to benefits, a maximum of two years. Many of the unemployed are not actually registered as such.

17 And a restricted access official source noted from a survey of 11 cities in the late 1990s found only 14 percent of urban dwellers to have health insurance (cited in Duckett 2004). Only 3.17 percent of urban dwellers and 1.4 percent of rural dwellers had private health insurance in 1998 (Liu 2002).

18 Similar decentralization has taken place in urban areas, but there are no accounts of the effects in terms of management capacity and investment of urban districts.

19 Overall there was, as a result, a decline in the government budgetary share of spending on health as a percentage of total health spending from 36 percent in 1980 to 15 percent in 2002 (Ministry of Health 2004). Central government funding of health care had fallen to less than 1 percent by the early 1990s (Hesketh and Zhu 1997).

20 Doctors were encouraged to set up private practices from 1980 (Ho 1995).

21 The World Bank reports that in 1993, average health spending per capita was four times higher in urban than in rural areas and "the poorest quarter of the rural population accounted for only about 5 percent of all health spending" that year (World Bank 1997: 3). This source also notes that although the urban PHI and LI systems covered only 15 percent of the population, they accounted for "two-thirds of public spending on health and 36 percent of all health spending" (ibid.).

22 The figure was 50 percent in Shanghai, and 70 percent in Tianjin (see Cui 2004 citing Tang 2002). Note, however, that according to the Ministry of Health in 1999, 20 percent of the urban population went without hospital treatment because they could not afford it (Liu et al. 2002).

23 "Household registration" refers to the system by which everyone in China is assigned at birth either "agricultural" or "non-agricultural" registration that entitles them to different public goods and benefits. The urban "non-agricultural" registration brings better entitlements.

24 There have also been attempts to establish "prepaid prevention programs," but there is not the space to discuss them here. See Liu et al. (2002).

25 These experiments included some county and/or township government budgetary contribution, with different arrangements in different localities.

26 Note that there may be inequalities based on employment status even where CMS is implemented. According to Carrin et al. (1999) some of the 1994 county-level experiments established separate funds for farmers and rural enterprise employees. Since enterprise employees paid more into the funds their reimbursement rates were higher.

27 Author's interview, Shanghai, 2001.

28 According to Liu et al. (2002), in some areas, CMS contributions were included in lists of illegal fees that local governments were no longer permitted to levy on villagers.

29 Farmers are unwilling to contribute to CMS if they think it entitles them to only poor quality services; or if it is insufficient to pay for their health expenses. See discussion in Liu et al. (2002).

30 For a discussion of local pilots and the 1998 programme see Duckett (2001), Liu (2002), and Duckett (2004).

31 The inclusion of rural enterprise employees (92 million people, 30 percent of the rural labor force (Hussain 2000)) in urban BSHI means that, in principle at least, participation in urban health systems for those with rural agricultural registration has been accepted, an important step (though it might reduce the viability of CMS schemes).

32 The State Council in January 2002 announced that medical treatment assistance for the poor was a priority and since then urban governments have been instructed to develop this. Author's interview, Ministry of Civil Affairs, 2002.

33 The upper limit was, for example, 10,000 yuan in Chengdu and Beijing in mid-2004 (*Renmin ribao*, 4 February 2002, *Sichuan Daily* website, *Sichuan lianbo*, at <http://sichuan.scol.com.cn> accessed 24 August 2004, and the China National Population and Family Planning Commission website, *Zhongguo renkou wang*, at <http://www.chinapop.gov.cn> accessed 25 September 2004).

34 *Taiyuan Daily* website, 13 September 2004.

35 Shanghai and Chengdu are reported to have launched a social security scheme, including medical insurance, for migrant workers, in late 2002 and early 2004 respectively (*Xinhuanet* 23 February 2003, 26 March 2004). Zhejiang is reported to have introduced MFA for both urban and rural dwellers (Ministry of Civil Affairs website, at <http://www.mca.gov.cn> 20 September 2004, accessed on 25 September 2004).

36 Population data for 2003 from the State Statistical Bureau (State Statistical Bureau 2004).

37 In 2001, for example, the infant mortality rate in Beijing was six per thousand live births, while that of Ningxia was 33 per thousand. There was also a gap in maternal mortality rates, with Beijing reporting a rate of 12 per 100,000 live births while Ningxia reported 73 per 100,000 (Ministry of Health 2002).

38 I assume here that a first practical step towards equalizing access would be to fully implement CMS and BSHI so that most of the population has some health protection, though this would not in itself tackle the problem of the rural–urban divide. Nor would it provide for urban dwellers without work, who are not eligible to participate in BSHI. Numerous other recommendations relating to improvement of health service provision, especially in rural areas, are given by the World Bank (2002) and Liu et al. (2002). I deal here with those that are most fundamental to the issue of equality, financing, and local governance.

39 See also a report by the World Bank (2002: 19) that shows tax rebates to have fallen from 72 percent of central transfers in 1996 to 45 percent in 2001.

40 In 2002 the central party and government announced that health targets would be included in the performance targets of officials (Bloom and Fang 2003). And this has been reiterated more recently. Much depends on how this is done – which officials' targets include health, and how important those targets are in performance evaluations.

41 While village elections have been introduced in part to try to deal with such problems, there is as yet no evidence that they result in the development of collective mechanisms for financing health or the provision of other public goods.

## References

Bauer, J., Wang Feng , Nancy E. Riley and Zhao Xiaohua (1992) "Gender Inequality in Urban China: Education and Employment," *Modern China*, 18 (3): 333–70.

Bloom, Gerald and Fang Jing (2003) "China's Rural Health System in Changing Institutional Context" in *IDS Working Paper* 194, Brighton: Institute of Development Studies.

Bloom, Gerald and Gu Xingyuan (1997a) "Health Sector Reforms: Lessons From China," *Social Science and Medicine*, 45 (3): 351–60.

Bloom, Gerald and Gu Xingyuan (1997b) "Introduction to Health Sector Reform in China," *IDS Bulletin*, 28 (1): 1–11.

Carrin, Guy, Aviva, Ron, Yang, Hui, Wang Hong, Zhang Tuohong, Zhang Licheng, Zhang Shuo, Ye Yide, Chen Jiaying, Jiang Qicheng, Zhang Zhaoyang, Yu Jun, Li Xuesheng (1999) "The Reform of the Rural Cooperative Medical System in the People's Republic of China: Interim Experience in 14 Pilot Countries," *Social Science and Medicine*, 48 (7): 961–72.

Central Committee of the Chinese Communist Party and State Council (2002) "Guanyu jin yi bu jiaqiang nongcun weisheng gongzuo de jueding" (Decision concerning further strengthening rural health work), *Zhongfa* (2002) 13, Beijing.

Cui Feng (2004) "Chengshi pinkun renkou de yiliao kunjing ji qi zhengce xuanze" (The health problems of the urban poor population and policy choices)" CASS, Social Policy Center; available online at <www.social-policy.info/884.htm> (accessed 24 September 2004).

Davis, Deborah (1988) "Unequal Chances, Unequal Outcomes: Pension Reform and Urban Inequality," *China Quarterly*, 114: 223–42.

Dixon, John (1981) *The Chinese Welfare System, 1949–1979*, New York: Praeger.

Duckett, Jane (2001) "Political Interests and the Implementation of China's Urban Health Insurance Reform," *Social Policy and Administration*, 35 (3 July): 290–306.

Duckett, Jane (2004) "State, Collectivism and Worker Privilege: A Study of Urban Health Insurance," *China Quarterly* 177: 155–73.

Edin, Maria (2003) "State Capacity and Local Agent Control in China: CCP Cadre Management from a Township Perspective," *China Quarterly*, 173: 35–52.

Feng Xue-Shan, Tang, Sheng-lan, Bloom, Gerald, Segall, Malcolm and Gu Xingyuan (1995) "Cooperative Medical Schemes in Contemprary Rural China," *Social Science and Medicine*, 41 (8): 1111–8.

Francis, Corinna-Barbara (1996) "Reproduction of Danwei Institutional Features in the Context of China's Market Economy: The Case of Haidian District's High-tech Sector," *China Quarterly*, 147: 839–59.

Gao Qiang (2004) "Yi 'sange daibiao' zhongyao sixiang wei zhidao jianchi kexue fazhan guan jiakuai weisheng shiye gaige yu fazhan – zai 2004 nian quan guo weisheng gongzuo huiyi de jiang hua" (Using important thought of "the three representatives" as a guide, maintain a scientific outlook and speed up health sector reform and development), speech to the 2004 National Health Work Conference: Ministry of Health.

Grogan, Colleen M. (1995) "Urban Economic Reform and Access to Health Care Coverage in the People's Republic of China," *Social Science and Medicine*, 41 (8): 1073–84.

Gu Xingyuan and Tang Shenglan (1995) "Reform of the Chinese Health Care Financing System," *Health Policy*, 32: 181–91.

Hesketh, Therese and Zhu Wei Xing (1997) "Health in China: The Health Care Market," *British Medical Journal*, 314: 1616–8.

Hillier, Sheila and Jie Shen (1996) "Health Care Systems in Transition: People's Republic of China. Part 1: An Overview of China's Health Care System," *Journal of Public Health Medicine*, 18 (3): 258–65.

Hillier, Sheila and Zheng Xiang (1991) "Township Hospitals, Village Clinics and Health Workers in Jiangxi Province: A Survey," *China Information*, 6 (2): 51–61.
Hindle, D. (2000) "China in Transition: The New Health Insurance Scheme for the Urban Employed," *Australian Health Review*, 23 (3): 122–31.
Ho, L. S. (1995) "Market Reforms and China's Health Care System," *Social Science and Medicine*, 41 (8): 1065–72.
Hossain, Shaikh I. (1997) "Tackling Health Transition in China," Washington, DC: World Bank.
Hsiao, William C. L. (1995) "The Chinese Health Care System: Lessons for Other Nations," *Social Science & Medicine*, 41 (8): 1047–55.
Hsiao, William C. L. and Liu Yuanli (1996) "Economic Reform and Health: Lessons From China," *New England Journal of Medicine*, 335 (6): 430–1.
Huang, S. M. (1988) "Transforming China's Collective Health Care System: A Village Study," *Social Science and Medicine*, 27 (9): 879–88.
Hussain, Athar (2000) "Social Welfare in the Context of the Three Transitions," unpublished manuscript.
Kan Xuegai (1990) "Village Health Workers in China: Reappraising the Current Situation," *Health Policy and Planning*, 5 (1): 40–8.
Liu Yuanli (2002) "Reforming China's Urban Health Insurance System," *Health Policy*, 60 (2): 133–50.
Liu Yuanli, Hsiao, William C. and Eggleston, Karen (1999) "Equity in Health and Health Care: The Chinese Experience," *Social Science and Medicine*, 49: 1349–56.
Liu Yuanli, Hsiao, William C., Li Qing, Liu Xingzhu and Ren Minghui (1995) "Transformation of China's Rural Health Care Financing," *Social Science & Medicine*, 41 (8): 1085–93.
Liu Yuanli, Rao Keqin and Hu Shanlian (2002) *People's Republic of China: Toward Establishing A Rural Health Protection System*, Manila: Asian Development Bank.
Lü Xiabo and Perry, Elizabeth J. (1997) "The Changing Chinese Workplace in Historical and Comparative Perspective," in Lü Xiabo and E. J. Perry (eds.) *Danwei: The Changing Chinese Workplace in Historical and Comparative Perspective*, Armonk, New York: M.E. Sharpe.
Mackintosh, M. (2001) "Do Health Care Systems Contribute to Inequalities?" in D. A. Leon and G. Walt (eds.) *Poverty, Inequality and Health*, Oxford: Oxford University Press.
Ministry of Civil Affairs, Ministry of Health and Ministry of Finance (2003) "Guanyu shishi nongcun yiliao jiuzhu de yijian" (Opinions concerning implementation of rural medical financial assistance), *Minfa*, 158, Beijing.
Ministry of Health (2000) *Zhongguo weisheng nianjian 2000 (Health Yearbook of China 2000)*, Beijing: Renmin wiesheng chubanshe.
Ministry of Health (2002) *Zhongguo weisheng nianjian 2002 (Health Yearbook of China 2002)*, Beijing: Renmin weisheng chubanshe.
Ministry of Health (2004) *2004 nian zhongguo weisheng tongji tiyao (China Health Statistics Extract, 2004)*, Beijing.
Ministry of Health, Ministry of Finance and Ministry of Agriculture (2003) "Guanyu jianli xinxing nongcun hezuo yiliao zhidu de yijian" (Opinions on establishing new-type rural) CMS, *Guobanfa*, 3, Beijing.
Ministry of Health Office (2003) "Guanyu zuo hao xinxing hezuo yiliao shidian gongzuo de tongzhi" (Notice concerning doing well new-type CMS trial work), *Weiban jifu fa* (2003), 47, Beijing.
Ministry of Labor and Social Security (2003) *Zhongguo laodong tongji nianjian 2003*

*(Yearbook of China's Labor Statistics, 2003)*, Beijing: Ministry of Labor and Social Security.

Naughton, Barry (1996) *Growing out of the Plan: Chinese Economic Reform, 1978–1993*, Cambridge: Cambridge University Press.

Östlin, Piroska, George, Asha and Sen, Gita (2001) "Gender, Health and Equity: The Intersections," in T. Evans, M. Whitehead, F. Diderichsen, A. Bhuiya and M. Wirth (eds.) *Challenging Inequities in Health: From Ethics to Action*, New York: Oxford University Press.

Park, Albert, Rozelle, Scott, Wong, Christine and Ren Changqing (1996) "Distributional Consequences of Reforming Local Public Finance In China," *China Quarterly* 147: 751–78.

Peter, Fabienne and Evans, Timothy (2001) "Ethical Dimensions of Health Equity," in T. Evans, M. Whitehead, F. Diderichsen, A. Bhuiya and M. Wirth (eds.) *Challenging Inequities in Health: From Ethics to Action*, New York: Oxford University Press.

Shi Yuxiao (2004) *Cooperative Medical [System]: World Developments and Chinese Experience (Huezuo yiliao: shijie fazhan yu zhongguo jingyan)*, CASS Social Policy Center; available online at <www.social-policy.info/930.htm> (accessed 13 September 2004).

Sidel, Ruth and Sidel, Victor W. (1982) *The Health of China*, Boston, MA: Beacon Press.

Solinger, Dorothy J. (1999) *Contesting Citizenship in Urban China: Peasant Migrants, the State and the Logic of the Market*, Berkeley and Los Angeles, CA: University of California Press.

State Council (1999) "Guowuyuan guanyu jianli chengzhen zhigong jiben yiliao baoxian zhidu de jueding" ("State Council decision concerning the creation of an urban employee basic health insurance system"), issued on 12 December 1998, in *Shehui baozhang: changyong zhengce fagui (Social Security: frequently used policies and regulations)*, edited by State Council & Ministry of Labor and Social Security, Beijing: Falü chubanshe.

State Council (2003) "State Council New-type Rural CMS Inter-ministerial Conference System" ("Guowuyuan xinxing nongcun hezuo yiliao buji lianxi huiyi zhidu"), Beijing.

State Council (2004) *China's Social Security Situation and Policies* [White paper] (*Zhongguo de shehui baozhang zhuangkuang he zhengce, bai pi shu*), Beijing.

State Council System Reform Office, State Planning Commission, Ministry of Finance, Ministry of Agriculture and Ministry of Health (2001) *Guanyu nongcun weisheng gaige yu fazhan de zhidao yijian* (Guiding Opinions on Rural Health Reform and Development), Beijing: State Council.

State Statistical Bureau of China (1992) *Zhongguo tongji nianjian 1992 (Statistical Yearbook of China 1992)*, Beijing: Zhongguo tongji chubanshe.

State Statistical Bureau of China (1996) *Zhongguo tongji nianjian 1996 (Statistical Yearbook of China 1996)*; available online at <http://www.stats.gov.cn/> (accessed 24 September 2004).

State Statistical Bureau of China (2001) *Zhongguo tongji nianjian* (*State Statistical Yearbook of China 2001*); available online at <http://www.stats.gov.cn/> (accessed 24 September 2004).

State Statistical Bureau of China (2004) *Statistical Communique on the National Economic and Social Development of the People's Republic of China in 2003*, Beijing: PRC State Statistical Bureau.

*Taiyuan Daily*; available online at <http://www.tynews.com.cn> 13 September 2004 (accessed 25 September 2004).

Tang Jun (2002) "Dangqian Zhongguo chengshi pinkun de xingcheng yu xianzhuang" (The formation and current situation of urban poverty in contemporary China), *Shehuixue (Sociology),* 6: 16–19.

Tang Wenfang and Parish, William L. (2000) *Chinese Urban Life Under Reform: The Changing Social Contract*, Cambridge: Cambridge University Press.

Whyte, Martin K. and Parish, William L. (1984) *Urban Life in Contemporary China*, Chicago, IL: University of Chicago Press.

World Bank (1983) *China: Socialist Economic Development (Volume III: The Social Sectors)*, Washington, DC: World Bank.

World Bank (1992) *China: Long-Term Issues and Options in the Health Transition*, Washington, DC: World Bank.

World Bank (1997) *Financing Health Care: Issues and Options for China*, World Bank (ed.) *China 2020*, Washington, DC: World Bank.

World Bank (2002) *China National Development and Sub-National Finance: A Review of Provincial Expenditures*, Poverty Reduction and Economic Management Unit, East Asia and Pacific Region.

World Health Organization (2000) *World Health Report 2000*, Geneva: World Health Organization.

Wu Yi (2004) Speech at the National Health Work Meeting ("Zai quanguo weisheng gongzuo huiyi de jianghua").

Xinhua (Anhui) (2002) *Wo guo nongcun hezuo yiliao zhidu de jianli* (*The construction of our country's rural cooperative medical system*) Xinhua news agency; available online at <http://www.ah.xinhua.org/jiandu/2002–11/12/content_44308.htm> 12 November 2002 (accessed 25 August 2004).

Yin Jidong (1997) *Zhongguo shehui baozhang yanjiu (Research on China's social security)*, Nanchang: Jiangxi gaoxiao chubanshe.

# 4 Paying for education in rural China[1]

*Rachel Murphy*

Chinese policy advisors, as well as the general public, see surmounting the "rural problem" as the key to overcoming China's delayed modernization, and they identify education as central for "solving all lingering rural problems and lifting millions of farmers out of poverty."[2] They also see education as a private benefit that enables individuals to improve their own lives. While it is agreed that education is both a public and private good, the question of who should pay and how much is more contentious. Education is therefore a pivotal domain in which the public discourse about entitlements (claimed and held by the people) and responsibilities (assumed with difficulty by the governing authorities) is negotiated. How the balance of entitlements and responsibilities is constituted in relation to rural education is of crucial importance for inequalities and social justice in China. This is because throughout the 1990s and 2000s the taxes and levies to cover education expenses comprised the largest part of the onerous "farmers' burden" (Guo 2002; Wang and Wang 2003), and because educational disadvantage has a negative impact on the life chances of rural children, thereby tending to sustain rural–urban inequality.

Throughout the 1990s and early 2000s the Chinese Party-state neglected to invest adequately in either general education or rural education. The proportion of GDP invested in education throughout the 1990s in all countries, in developing countries and in China was 5.1 percent, 3.9 percent and 2.1 percent respectively (Rong and Shi 2001). Aware of the lag, in 2003, the central state increased the proportion of GDP allocated to education to 3.41 percent, 0.8 percent more than the previous year but still 0.6 percent below the average for developing countries (Chen 2004).

Within China, per student investment in education was much lower in rural than urban areas (see Table 4.1). In rural areas parents paid for school buildings and teachers' wages – the latter of these expenses having increased several times because of teachers' wage rises (Shih and Zhang, Chapter 7)[3] – while in the cities the municipal governments paid. The difference in the financial burden was such that in 2002 rural parents contributed 60 percent of the costs of compulsory education whereas urbanites contributed only 13 percent despite enjoying incomes that were five times higher (Wang and Wang 2003). The economic advantage of urban parents enabled them to invest more than rural parents in their children's

*Table 4.1* Per capita investment in rural and urban students, 2002 (yuan)

| | *Rural* | *Urban* | *National average* |
|---|---|---|---|
| **Total investment per primary student** | 519.16 | 841.11 | 625.45 |
| **Total investment per junior high student** | 861.64 | 1423.85 | 1102.5 |

Source: adapted from Lu 2003

education. Parents in county seats and cities commonly paid for their child to participate in vacation and Sunday tuition classes. They also bought special equipment for them such as musical instruments, English audio-dictionaries, computers and books. Although urban parents felt burdened by trying to keep apace of rising expectations about what constituted necessary support (Milwertz 1997; Fong 2004), their burden differed from that of many rural parents who struggled just to afford the fees for basic education.

This chapter charts the course of crucial debates and policy experimentation carried out during the late 1990s and the first half of the 2000s over the best way to fund rural education. It draws on ethnographic material collected in September to December 2000 and August 2004 from Rivercounty, an agricultural settlement in southeast China, as well as Chinese documentary sources. An examination of this period focuses on how the struggle over who should pay for education was shaped by incentives in the wider political structures in which rural schools were embedded, and articulated through an emerging partly old, partly new language which combined a neoliberal emphasis on individual responsibility with existing socialist and Chinese humanist ideas about the state's responsibility to promote the public good. The following substantive sections consider, in turn, how the public understanding of entitlements and responsibilities were continually negotiated and remade; how various factors affected the political will to fund education at different levels of the state apparatus; how educational funding pressures were shaped by incentives in the wider system of governance; how schools took action to raise revenue for themselves; and how the state responded to the general funding crisis. The conclusion considers the trajectory of these policy debates and practices beyond the mid-2000s and associated shifts in the substance of neoliberalism and approaches to human development in rural China.

## Changing public discourse of entitlements and responsibilities

The changing public discourse on the entitlements and responsibilities of state and society in China during the 1990s and early 2000s shared much with trends in other countries in that national leaders maintained that in an environment of global competition and flexible labor markets, investment in human capital was to replace direct state security-provisioning as the principal tenet of its welfare regime (Giddens 2000; Ferrara et al. 2001). With the ascendancy of neoliberal policies, Chinese leaders increasingly emphasised personal transformation as the key to citizenship rights, thus seeming to blame what was actually the state's own failure to guarantee social rights such as decent education and living standards on the low physical, intellectual and moral "quality" (*suzhi*) of Chinese villagers. But at the same time, the Party-state continued to claim its socialist and developmental credentials by representing itself as central to facilitating the qualitative improvement of the population.

Nowhere was the focus on individual quality failings more pronounced than in discourses about the countryside. Television documentaries and newspaper articles commonly lamented inherent rural backwardness, a lack of parental commitment to their children's education and the inadequacies of rural teachers, demonstrated, for instance by their desultory professional commitment and imperfect Mandarin. At the same time emotive documentaries portrayed rural parents scrimping and saving to send their children to school, and depicted the triumphs of determined students who preserved the canvas on their shoes by walking barefoot over mountainous terrain to attend classes, eventually even passing university entrance exams. Many teachers I met in Rivercounty used the truism common in such media reports – "the child of paupers matures early" (*qiongren de haizi zao dangjia*) – to insist that poverty need not disadvantage a child's education, and that many university students have arisen out of adversity. Implicit in such claims was the belief that although material deprivation is one kind of poverty, true poverty lies in attitudinal and "quality" deficiencies. This popular discursive motif assumed that there were opportunities for upward social mobility for those who strived, and thus obscured the entrenched structural inequalities that hindered educational achievement for the poor, for example, the requirement that students from interior provinces and rural areas obtain higher national exam scores for university entrance.

Alongside the ethos of individual responsibility there was nevertheless a very real and also popular perception that the state should provide quality education for all citizens of the nation. This could be seen in television programs which used the idiom of national unity and belonging to appeal to government bodies and urbanites to support farmers' demands for affordable education and safe school buildings. One program that I watched in Rivercounty told the story of Teacher Yang who often paid the school fees for her students and who dreamed of taking them from their poor mountain hamlet to see national treasures such as Tiananmen Square and the Great Wall, which they had only ever seen in textbooks (Jian Television Station, 9 September 2000, 20.00hrs). Another program exposed an instance of exorbitant school fees and dangerous crumbling buildings,[4] with the investigative journalists invoking sympathy for individual children while expressing concern about the implications of their deprivation for national modernization (*Jiaodian fangtan*, 20 November 2000).

A further source of ideas informing popular perceptions about the state's responsibility to provide affordable education was historical memory. Farmers

I talked with in Rivercounty recalled that during the Mao era no one was forced out of school because of an inability to pay tuition and that Mao "really cared" about the farmers. This belief reflected the success of educational provisioning during the Mao era in meeting the needs of individuals who lived in the poor and relatively undiversified rural economy of the time. While some scholars argue that the low quality of rural education under Mao and the paucity of job opportunities caused students to give up on studying (Peterson 1994; Unger 1982), the recollections of Rivercounty farmers suggested a more positive evaluation: even though opportunities for spatial mobility were closed off in the Mao era, education still enabled socio-economic mobility through access to better jobs within the commune, and practical literacy and numeracy lessons improved livelihoods.

In the reform era too, the Chinese government still boasted considerable achievement in expanding educational coverage, but the successes claimed were far from unmitigated. Some scholars use enrolment and progression figures as indicators of China's educational achievements (Knight and Li 1996 cited in Hannum and Park 2002). In the case of Rivercounty, the figures recorded in the 1999 *Jiangxi Statistical Yearbook* are 100 percent for enrolment and 96.1 percent for progression from primary to junior high, with provincial averages reported as 99.6 percent and 94.2 percent respectively. By this measure, Rivercounty exceeded the year 2000 targets of 99 percent and 94 percent, which were set by the State Council in 1995 (*Zhongguo wushi nian de Jiangxi*, 2000: 515–6).[5] But in China as in other countries, enrolment and progression figures tell only part of the story (Hall and Midgley 2004: 148). The "enrolment" figure is the proportion of children whose names are registered with a school at the start of an academic year, while the "progression" figure measures the proportion of final year primary school students entering the first year of junior high, and so omits those students who have left primary school before graduation. According to year-by-year and grade-by-grade enrolment figures for 1979 to 1999 provided by the Rivercounty Bureau of Education, only 68 percent of students in the 1995 primary school intake graduated (in 1999) and only 64 percent started junior high (in 2000) (Murphy 2004a).[6] As shown in Figure 4.1, although the overall trend in Rivercounty was towards longer periods of schooling, large numbers of children continued to drop out.

The figures for Rivercounty as well as for other rural areas across China suggested that the government rhetoric about commitment to compulsory education was not fully realized at the local level (Brown and Park 2002; Wang 2004).[7] As Brown and Park pointed out, despite the 1986 Compulsory Education Law mandating that all children stay in school for nine years, children whose families failed to pay fees were not allowed to attend class. Some parents in poorer families avoided school fees by delaying their child's attendance by one or two years so their children were usually in their early teens by the final year of primary school, an age when they may have felt ready to work (Brown and Park 2002). Children in hardship households were also less likely to receive financial support from their parents for their studies when it was believed there was little hope of them entering university or being allocated a secure job. In these cases both parents

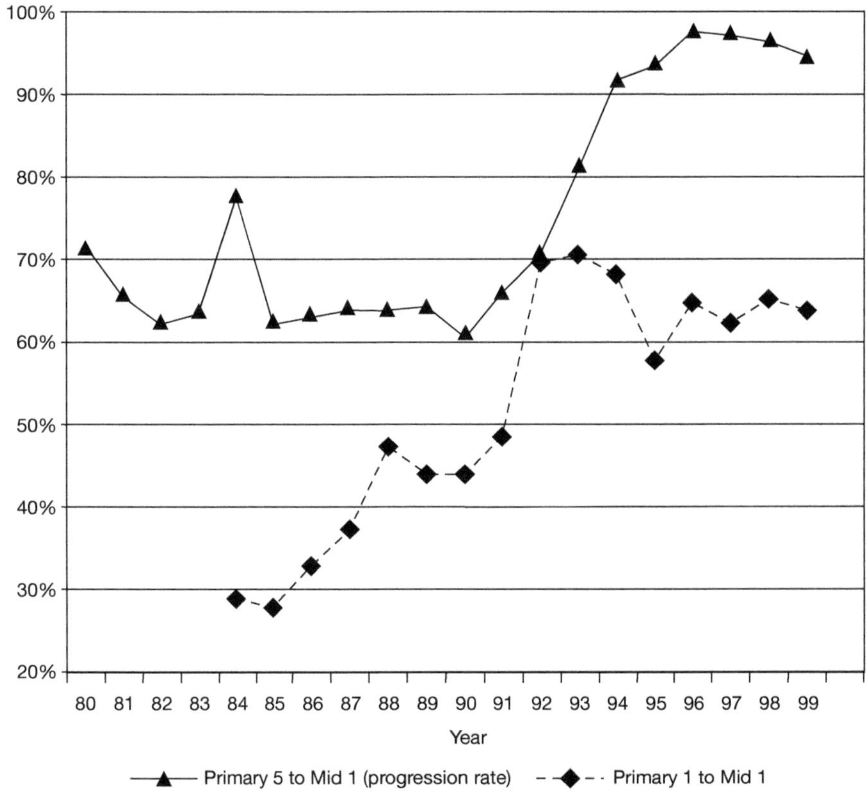


*Figure 4.1* Percentage of students progressing in Rivercounty (Murphy 2004a: 9)

and students often thought that it was better to count losses early, and for the child to leave school and earn money. This situation was well described in the official newspaper for the prefecture in which Rivercounty is located:

> The problem of primary and junior high students dropping out of school and going to work is common, especially in poor households. Even though these youths (aged ten-plus years) may earn as much as 500–600 *yuan* a month which they can contribute to the family, the villagers are still being short-sighted [in sending them to work] and are hindering rural society's progress to *xiaokang* (a comfortable standard of living). . . . Now in poor rural households there is often not enough money to pay for the school fees of two or more children. If a disaster should befall the household, then it must certainly go into debt and there would often be no other choice but for the child to go to work. And of course there are many other farmers who simply hold onto a backward perspective and believing that because there is no guaranteed allocation of jobs after university that the student may as well go and earn some money sooner rather than later. . . . Now that we are moving

> into a knowledge economy, village and township governments must pay attention to the problem of children dropping out of primary and junior high school. They should increase investment in rural education and decrease the miscellaneous school fees. . . . They should also raise farmers' enthusiasm for investing in education.
>
> (*Jinggangshan bao*, 10 July 2004)

## State commitment to education

When examining the performance of the state in ensuring that its citizens receive access to public goods, some scholars use the concept of "political commitment" (Tomasevski 2003) or "political will" (Chambers 1997: 12–14; Fraser and Restrepo-Estrada 1998; Hall and Midgley 2004: 159–61). "Political will" refers to the willingness of those who have institutional authority and control over resources to give priority to a particular project or course of action. In China, as in any country, the task of discerning whether or not the state has the will to mobilize individuals and resources to ensure the adequate provisioning of a public good is complicated by the fact that the state is not a coherent homogenous actor. Instead the state is characterized by tensions among different levels of its hierarchy, with its functioning dependent on a diverse range of actors and institutions, each responsive to different incentives and constraints and engaging in society in different ways (Migdal 2001; Shue 1988).

In the case of rural China, the relevant state actors include village cadres, township cadres and educators. The factors shaping the political will of these state actors include the political and economic rewards for completing top-down work targets, the competing demands of different kinds of work targets, the resource and institutional limitations of their localities and opportunities for personal gain (Shue 1988). In poor agricultural counties during the 1990s and early 2000s, state actors faced tremendous hardship in raising the funds needed to support the large numbers of functionaries who carried out multifarious top-down work tasks. Moreover, the costs of supporting the revenue-collectors often exceeded the total taxes collected. This meant that township governments incurred debt and failed to make public investment or provide services for farmers. Despite repeated calls by central state leaders to slim down the ranks of local level bureaucracy, the former recognized that the political cost of removing or seriously eroding the presence of the latter could be the complete loss of Party-state control in rural areas (Cao 2004). Hence central and local state officials remained locked in a structural stalemate with the genuine retrenchment of local cadres stalled.

In Rivercounty, as elsewhere in rural China, farmers' perceptions of the Party-state's commitment to promoting the public good was expressed in the common phrase "above there is a policy, below there is a counter-policy." In this popular construction the central state was conceived as genuinely committed to enacting policies which improve the lot of farmers. But local officials, who were seen as self-serving, distorted these policies in the process of implementation, leading to ills such as a heavy peasant burden, shoddy school buildings, and the waste of community or public funds. This view – promoted in the media and reinforced by initiatives aimed at intensifying villagers' supervision of cadres (Yep 2004) – deflected attention away from structural deficiencies within the Party-state apparatus which distorted incentives and constrained policy implementation at the local level.

Examining the ways in which schools were embedded within rural political and social institutions helps to elucidate the incentives and constraints that worked for and against investment in rural education. This is because schools are inseparable from the state (Reed-Danahay 1996; Rival 1996; Unterhalter 1999). They are visible emissaries of the state's nation-building agenda. They are regulated by national and provincial laws and regulations, subject to the supervision and certification of state administrative institutions, and funded at least in part by the state. At the same time, they are embedded in the local community, share horizontal and vertical relationships with a range of state institutions at the village, township and county levels, and engage with social actors such as cadres, parents and students.

## The political embeddedness of education provisioning

During my fieldwork it was clear that education in Rivercounty was embedded in a wider top-down system of governance. At the township level, the education office (*jiaoban*) followed plans devised and directed by the County Bureau of Education. The township government was also subordinate to relevant county departments for its work in other policy areas such as family planning, land use, economic development, tax collection and public security. Villages were designated as self-governing, with villagers' committees entrusted to help organize villagers in promoting the construction of socialism. In practice, this meant they had to manage village affairs, help the township oversee agricultural production, economic development, tax collection and the coordination of public works projects such as maintaining irrigation channels, and building and repairing schools.

When facing their subordinates, cadres at each level enjoyed substantial power. But when facing their superiors, they were constrained by tightly defined responsibilities and all manner of quotas. Cadres attached much importance to top-down work tasks because attaining or surpassing quotas directly affected their personal advancement. County and township cadres who performed well stood a better chance of being assigned to a good location and institution, and to a higher level appointment on their next posting. For many leading cadres in local areas, reappointments to new locations and institutions occurred every two to seven years, creating pressures on them to generate visible evidence of "progress" within a relatively short time period. Village cadres similarly gave high priority to quota completion because they regularly hosted township inspection teams and were rewarded with salary bonuses if they could demonstrate that local targets had been met and kept up good relations with higher-level officials. Cadres at all levels who failed to reach targets risked public criticism (Cao 2004: 132; Edin 2000; Wu 2003: 49).

Within the top-down system of governance, rural education provisioning encountered two kinds of pressure. First, since the early 1980s, fiscal decentralization made local governments responsible for raising a substantial portion of the revenue needed for meeting development goals, including stipulated education targets such as building schools and implementing restructuring programs and curriculum reforms. Second, cadres and school principals were evaluated on their capacity to meet these targets, which led to their penchant for expensive "showcasing projects" that demonstrated progress to superiors.

### *Fiscal pressures*

To take up the first theme, previously all fiscal revenue was surrendered to the center, with a portion then redistributed downward through the state apparatus to the local levels as a budgetary allocation. Following fiscal decentralization only a portion of fiscal revenue was directed upwards, in the form of a negotiated "tax-assignment" or *jishu*. Although township and village governments were permitted to retain a greater share of their revenue, they also became responsible for raising the extra-budgetary revenue needed to meet local expenditure for overheads, administrators' salaries, welfare provisioning and public works (Oi 1992; Wong 1992). Starting in 1996, a further decentralization requiring county and township governments to "eat in separate kitchens" meant that lower levels of government were unable to turn to the county for emergency help in covering these expenditures (Zuo 1997).[8]

Under this decentralized tax system, education funding depended heavily on local fiscal resources. The 2001 breakdown of the sources of funding for education in rural Jiangxi was as follows: township finance – 78 percent, county finance – 9 percent, provincial funding – 11 percent and central government funding – 2 percent (Xie and Guo 2003). Clearly, paying for education in rural China placed a huge strain on local level finances: in the year 2000 in Rivercounty numerous township heads told me that over two thirds of their fiscal resources would commonly go to support education.

Under the decentralized fiscal system, agricultural regions in Jiangxi raised most of their revenue for social expenditure and for tax assignments by levying special taxes on cash crops and animal-raising (Peng 1996; Wu 2003: 49). In 2000, Rivercounty farmers living in poor townships were strongly urged to plant tobacco and to pay the taxes due on it even if they had not grown the crop. Tobacco cultivation was popular among county governments precisely because they were authorized to levy heavy taxes on the crop. The monopoly Rivercounty Tobacco Company was paying the county government around 30 percent of the gross purchasing price it paid to farmers: for reference, special taxes on pigs, watermelons and tea were 8 percent, 5 percent and 15 percent respectively. When the tobacco company resold its goods to factories, it also paid a value added tax of 13 percent, and surcharges for education and for town construction at a rate of 8 percent of its VAT. Year 2000 estimates from the Rivercounty Statistical Bureau and from various township accounts indicated that tobacco taxes made up well over one third of all fiscal revenue collected in the county.[9]

By 2000 the funding crisis resulting from fiscal decentralization meant that in many agricultural counties, schools became a new site through which the local state flexed its extractive muscle in collecting general taxes. Much to the chagrin of Rivercounty parents, in some townships cadres went so far as to attend village schools on enrolment day to collect outstanding local taxes and special tobacco taxes: the threat was made that if this money was not paid, the children might be prevented from attending school. So in the eyes of farmers, both schools and government institutions formed part of a united, top-down instrument of predation.

Within the overall tax burden that was placed on farmers, there were special local levies specifically to fund education. Up until the implementation of new tax reforms in 2004 which are discussed later in the chapter, township and village governments charged a tax which was technically not to exceed 5 percent of the average per capita income of a village for the previous year, and one component of this tax, the educational surcharge – 1.5 percent of per capita income – went to the township education fund to pay teachers' wages. This surcharge was augmented with additional unauthorized education fees levied on a per *mu* basis. School repairs and equipment, the responsibility of the village committee, were also financed through fees and levies exacted on a per *mu* basis. Between 1996 and 2000 fiscal shortages became so acute that teachers' wages in most Rivercounty townships remained unpaid for several months, resulting in some teachers providing lessons in a half-hearted manner. In Rivercounty, only the top two tobacco producing townships, as well as two townships located near towns that had many commercial activities, were able to cover teachers' wages.

Given the fact that education funding was largely a local level responsibility, it is not surprising that repeated studies of schooling in rural China found that local wealth emerged as a key determinant of schooling quality, progression rates and fee levels (Brown and Park 2002; Connelly and Zheng 2003; Hannum 1999; Hannum and Park 2002). In light of this, Chinese social scientists argued that the redistribution of fiscal resources was necessary for remedying the cash shortage in rural education, pointing out that when aggregated to the national level, there was an adequate total sum of fiscal resources to fund education (He et al. 2003). This lends weight to a wider argument that in China the failure of the state to fund public goods adequately lay not in an incapacity to extract sufficient fiscal resources, but in an overall systemic failure to redistribute revenue in ways that ensured effective public goods provisioning across regions and communities (Saich 2001). But in China, as has been documented in numerous other developing countries, the positioning of the countryside away from urban centers of power and a preoccupation with economic growth meant that basic rural education was for a long time a "soft" political target, with government authorities on the whole being more committed to GDP targets than to making the necessary budgetary adjustments and spending allocations (Hall and Midgley 2004: 152, 159, 161).

### *Top-down evaluations*

Educational provisioning was affected not only by the local-level fiscal crunch but also by the pressure to reach the targets that formed part of top-down performance evaluations. One such target was the requirement that townships build modern schools with dormitories so that restructuring could take place. This restructuring occurred throughout many interior provinces (Huang and Zhang 2003) and arose in part because lower fertility and decreasing class sizes generated a demographic impetus for closing some village schools, making others infant-only, and concentrating resources on key "complete" schools: children reside at a complete school (away from their villages) for the final year of primary school. A further impetus for the restructuring was ideological. The "enclosed method" of these "complete" schools was seen as easier logistically and superior pedagogically: the students were said to be better able to concentrate on their studies and to share the advantages enjoyed by boarders in prestigious private urban schools. So students at junior high schools boarded, regardless of the distance from their homes. Owing to capital shortages, however, in some schools these rural students lived in partially constructed and unsafe dormitories and in some schools there were times when there was not enough food in the canteen for everyone (for an account of the situation in Anhui province see Huang and Zhang 2003). Some rural parents expressed concern to me that their children were living in poor conditions and boarding away from home at too young an age. Teachers also had their reservations, with a deputy head in a junior high school telling me that: "the economic conditions here are not yet ripe for the enclosed system of schooling" (Field Notes, 20 November 2000).

The physical restructuring of schools overlapped with a wider drive to construct modern schools, so-called "brand-name schools" (*pinpai xuexiao*), which boasted facilities associated with advanced teaching methods and subjects. Local-level officials and principals faced immense pressure to build schools with libraries, computers, sporting facilities and musical instruments which could be "showcased" when higher-level inspection teams visited (see also Zhang 2000).[10] The showcase imperative was such that township education management offices demanded that even very poor schools transformed themselves into "garden style schools" (*huayuanshi xuexiao*) if they were to be recognized as delivering quality education. This is not to deny that students should have good quality buildings and attractive grounds, and that there were many well-built and equipped schools in Rivercounty. But there is a fine balance between providing quality public goods and showcasing. Showcasing distorts resource allocation. For instance, in some Rivercounty townships, officials went so far as to divert money from poorer schools to favoured display schools, a practice which was explicitly condemned by teachers in a 2000 public criticism campaign designed to rectify problems in rural governance (Field Notes, 13 November 2000).[11]

The top-down extractive and evaluative political system was manifest not only by showcasing but also through more subtle aspects of schools' everyday operations. The position of school principal had a semi-official flavour, and primary and junior high schools regularly entertained township and county officials who visited to inspect school performance, with some junior high schools spending nearly ten thousand yuan on food and drink each year (see also Zhang 2000). Schools were obliged to subscribe to periodicals marketed through different county offices such as law books from the county procurate and Party ideological materials from the county branch of the Party School. Teachers were also required to attend ideological education classes at the Party School, with fees paid by the school.

## School revenue-raising

As local government did not finance schools adequately, schools were also forced into raising some of their own funds. The main way of raising funds was by charging student fees. In 2000, Rivercounty farmers commonly paid 600 yuan per year for a primary school student and at least 1,000 yuan for a junior high student: in a household with two primary school children this was equivalent to nearly 10 percent of average household income. Children were also required to pay fees in-kind with contributions of vegetables, oil and grain: in one village the in-kind contribution was five kilograms of rice, several catties of vegetables and one litre of oil. Even heavier school fees were reported for other rural areas: in some Hunan villages visited by the Chinese sociologist, Cao Jinqing (2004), school fees claimed as much as 40 percent of household income. The full weight of the burden becomes apparent if we consider that roughly one third of the reported per capita income of a rural household was in-kind. In 2004 the central state ruled that miscellaneous school fees were to be replaced by a fixed-sum fee, the "one fee system" (*yi fei zhi*), an initiative that proved difficult to implement in the face of capital shortages.

In addition to regular matriculation fees, schools also raised money by charging for the allocation of different kinds of "favor" places. Primary schools charged 80 yuan for students to attend school a year early and audit the first grade.[12] The impetus to raise money was such that some key-point junior high schools even accepted money from a parent to place a weaker student in a top stream class which had the advantages of more motivated students and the best teachers. This practice was criticized in provincial newspapers as immoral because privileging one student necessitated removing another student, who was typically from a poor rural family that lacked social connections (*Jiangxi ribao*, 8 September 2000). Finally, senior high schools sold places to students who failed to make the cut-off entry grade: farmers referred to this as selling or "buying a senior high" (*mai ge gaozhong*) (Tape 23, 9 November 2000).

Schools also tried to make up the funding shortfall through entrepreneurial activities, which often placed a further burden on students. The Rivercounty Number Two Middle School set up a printing factory in 1991 which produced the exercise books that the students had to buy. This was one of many school enterprises established throughout the prefecture between 1990 and 1993 in response to an upper-level exhortation. By 2000, however, few of them were still operating, and after nine years, the Number Two Middle School Printing Factory was also forced to close, apparently because the removal of tax breaks for such businesses made continuing unprofitable.[13] In other parts of Jiangxi province, there were reports of children doing piece-rate work in handicraft industries as part of an activity class or during lunch breaks: the fireworks tragedy in Wanzai county was a much publicized example which led the National People's Congress to call for a campus protection law, which the delegates argued was especially necessary for protecting students in poor rural localities (Li 2001). Schools also arranged various activities for which payment was required. For instance, as part of the labor skills class in Rivercounty Junior High School, a hairdresser visited and the students each had to pay for a haircut.

### *State solutions to the funding crisis*

The state, at its various levels, initiated a range of measures which aimed to increase the real and perceived involvement of the government in meeting its responsibilities and delivering entitlements by reining in the farmers' burden, offering some band-aid monetary relief to poorer county governments and urging rural parents to accept greater responsibility for their children's human capital investment. The measures fell under the three broad categories of fiscal initiatives, revenue-raising from and for education, and charity.

### *Fiscal initiatives*

Fiscal initiatives to alleviate the under-funding of schools included giving priority to the payment of teachers' wages, rural taxation reform, and central government monetary transfers to support rural education.

In April 2000, acting on provincial level instructions, the Rivercounty government issued a document ordering township officials to pay the wages of teachers before allocating funds for their own wages, mobile phones or official car expenses. The document warned that failure to ensure the payment of teachers would result in negative career evaluations for officials on the basis of "one strike and you are out" (*yipiao foujue*). Township governments responded by arranging for individual cadres to take out personal loans. In one township, the head of the education office, the township Party Secretary, the deputy and the township head each borrowed over 10,000 yuan. By indirectly incurring debt, the township was able to both circumvent the regulation forbidding government departments from borrowing against future tax earnings and avoid censure for failing to pay teachers' wages.

In the latter half of 2000, following national directives, the Jiangxi provincial government ruled that the county rather than the township had to assume responsibility for issuing the wages of primary and middle school teachers. Then, in 2002 as part of a nationwide attempt at a rural tax reform, counties in Jiangxi province began preparing to "convert fees to tax," a reform that only started to be truly implemented in 2004. This reform involved abolishing the village and township tax levied at 5 percent of per capita income, and abolishing miscellaneous informal levies and fees, replacing them with a fixed-rate tax. The aim was to relieve the burden on farmers by preventing local governments and village committees from imposing arbitrary charges and increasing supervision over the deployment of the collected revenue.

In the closing months of 2000, education officials and school principals expressed mixed views about the likely impact of these two reforms. One optimistic official explained:

> These changes will be beneficial. At the moment all we get from the township education supplement is 20 yuan per person, which is less than 1.5 percent. In reality the most we are actually able to obtain from the education supplement is 15 or even only 10 yuan. This means relying on the village committee for the rest, and the village committee tends not to have the ability to invest so much. If the fee is changed to a tax we will be able to levy 30 yuan per capita for education. Moreover, the usage of this money will be controlled by the county, which will ensure that more investment reaches education instead of going to other places.
>
> (Interview, education official, 1 December 2000)

Another official was more sanguine, saying:

> Which ever way, the money has to come from farmers and the farmers here do not have so much money. It is hard to implement such reforms when the conditions are not ripe. Like here, we have said it will be at least three years before the county will be able to take responsibility for teachers' wages.
>
> (Interview, education official, 12 November 2000)

Reports from the Jiangxi countryside and from other agricultural provinces as well as my own interviews with Rivercounty education officials in August 2004 suggested that the "fees-for-tax" reform had severely exacerbated the capital shortage of rural schools. County governments which subsequently bore the main responsibility for the administration of compulsory education commonly defaulted on spending due to their own fiscal shortages (Bao and Deng 2002; Chang 2002; Huang and Zhang 2003; Lai 2003; Wang and Wang 2003; Wu and Wang 2003; Yan 2002; Yu and Cheng 2002). Although the payment of the basic subsistence component of teachers' wages was on the whole more stable, the loss of the township education surcharge, the village education levy and other fees meant that there was no money to pay teachers' benefits and subsidies which were issued by the township as crucial contributions to their wages. Local governments and schools also lacked the funds to pay for building new schools and dormitories, repairing and maintaining existing schools, expanding from eight to nine years of compulsory education, or meeting the general operating costs of schools. The crisis in rural education reflected a wider fiscal crunch that followed in the wake of the reform, with government institutions in many predominantly agricultural localities being forced to reintroduce informal fees in order to meet top-down development targets, including educational ones.

The central government used transfers to local governments to compensate for the funding shortfall: in 2002, 24.35 billion yuan was transferred and a compulsory education fund of 9.58 billion yuan was established. In 2004 the levels of the province and prefecture were also instructed to contribute to these transfers, this money in turn being levied from the lower levels. In Rivercounty in 2004 the transfers took the form of a government contribution to each junior high school of 30 yuan per student per semester and to each senior high school of 12 yuan per student per semester. While these transfers offered some help, they were far from adequate and many county and township governments and schools in agricultural localities were forced into debt, with the burden being ultimately transferred to the farmers.

### *Raising revenue from education*

During the first half of the 2000s, the Party-state trod a fine line over how to obtain money from parents for their children's non-compulsory education without explicitly commercializing it. Accordingly the Party-state was cautious in the choice of language used to describe payment schemes, and there was considerable ambiguity in the policy pronouncements from different levels and institutions within the state. On the one hand, education was a public good and a right which could not be traded as a commodity in a socialist society. On the other hand, fees could be charged according to the differing demand for places at different kinds of schools: on 1 September 2003 the Private Education Law even came into effect permitting market entities to run schools and charge fees. Moreover, the increasing importance of fees was accompanied by a line in public discourse which urged rural parents to abandon their "little peasant mentality" and foster the progressive mentality that would make them willing to save for and invest in education (Long 2003). Against this background of ambiguity in official policy discourse, Rivercounty introduced a range of experiments aimed at raising revenue from and for the provisioning of education. These measures included turning non-compulsory education into an industry (*jiaoyu chanyehua*), introducing fees for non-compulsory education such as "top-up fees" for better quality schools, and permitting different non-state actors to establish and run schools.

To take the first measure, towards the end of 1999, in Rivercounty as in numerous rural counties, local officials began to turn non-compulsory education into an industry. This involved turning senior high and vocational schools into businesses and charging fees for non-compulsory education at market rates. Such measures were seen by Rivercounty officials as a way to make non-compulsory education support compulsory education. According to one local report:

> As the government has too much fiscal responsibility for non-compulsory education, making education into an industry will free up resources for improving the quality of compulsory education, which includes expanding

> from eight to nine years compulsory education, a target to be reached throughout Jiangxi province by 2005.
>
> (JX Township Peoples' Government 2000)

In Rivercounty the initiatives to make education into an industry were not just confined to non-compulsory education. As mentioned earlier, primary and junior high schools implemented a compulsory boarding system and under the "education as an industry" initiative, logistical services for the dormitories and canteens were also commercialized. The Rivercounty government even went so far as to urge schools to "attract commercial investment and encourage investors to construct and manage dormitories and canteens, then after several years, return the premises to the schools" (Rivercounty Government 2000). Whereas previously rural parents provided food for their children from their grain reserves and accommodation with the family house, under the commercial system they had to pay cash, which exacerbated their financial burden.

But four years later (on 6 January 2004) and following a series of experiments throughout poorer counties and a proliferation of supportive media articles, the Minister for Education, Zhou Ji, convened a press conference at which he criticized the *chanyehua* of non-compulsory education. He stated that the *chanyehua* of education had never been an approved government policy and he reprimanded local governments for turning education into a "cash cow" and using it to alleviate local fiscal shortages. He also stated that using non-compulsory education to raise revenue is different from inviting different social and market actors to participate in the funding and provisioning of education (He 2004; Yi 2004).[14]

While senior high schools in Rivercounty no longer pursued the *chanyehua* of education, they charged fees. In particular, since the latter half of 2004 key-point senior high schools and other schools with good reputations obtained the legal right to levy a "fee for choosing the school" (*ze xiao fei*) which was paid in addition to the regular school fee (Interview, Jiangxi Provincial Government Secretary, August 2004). Although in theory this fee was paid in circumstances where parents wanted to send their children to preferred schools outside their catchment areas, in practice the fee was also paid in other circumstances, for instance, when students wanted to secure entry to a good school despite their inadequate grades. At Rivercounty Senior High the regular fee was 6,000 yuan including board while the top-up fee could reach 1,500 yuan, with higher top-up fees being paid the lower the entrance exam score of the student. There were, however, reports of top-up fee schemes in other localities, for example Chongqing city, that exceeded 10,000 yuan and that extended even to junior high schools. Critics of the new fee scheme argued that it exacerbated regional inequalities in educational investment because schools that already had the benefits of better equipment and more qualified teachers gained even more investment. Also fee-paying students potentially deprived other students of places (*Renmin ribao*, 14 August 2004: 5; *Jinghua shibao*, 4 August 2004: AO2).

Charging fees and using the language of markets and commercialization when discussing vocational education seemed to be far less controversial than for senior high education. This was possibly because a person's chances for university education were not affected by whether or not they could afford to attend vocational school, a problem highlighted by several high profile cases wherein rural students or parents committed suicide because of an inability to pay senior high fees (*xuefei zisha* – literally "school fee suicide"). It could also have been because vocational education was more directly associated with training individuals to earn money for themselves in the market place.

The pressure to obtain fees made vocational schools in Rivercounty ever more proactive in their publicity and recruitment drives. In 2000 the main vocational school in Rivercounty instituted a requirement that all of its 65 teachers recruited two students each, while the school leaders had to recruit three. The teachers visited rural households with photos of school computers and equipment. They also obtained the county education bureau's list of students who had failed the entrance exams for senior high, and issued them all with an information letter. A further recruitment measure involved vocational school leaders visiting first and second grade junior high classes to find out which students had poor grades and to persuade them to leave early and transfer to the vocational school. In 2000 the Rivercounty Vocational School set itself the target of increasing its student body from 560 to over 600 students and upgrading its equipment in order to compete for the status of "provincial model school," an honor that would bring 100,000 yuan in funding (Tape 33, Interview, 28 September 2000). On my return visit in 2004 the vocational school had not yet earned the honour of "provincial model school."

County vocational schools such as that in Rivercounty faced ever increasing competition in their recruitment drives from some large city-based *minban* vocational schools which advertised on county television stations and promised job placements for all graduates. For instance, in 2002, the Blue Sky Vocational School based in Nanchang city had 8,000 students but by 2004 it had 30,000 students and moved to a newly built larger campus. Founded by a Jiangxi native who is also a member of the National People's Congress, the school was one of two large-scale *minban* vocational schools in the province. Of its total student body 60 percent were from the countryside and 40 percent were from other provinces (Interview, Jiangxi Provincial Government Secretary for Education and visit to the school, August 2004).

While the Party-state was careful to avoid referring to education as an "industry" (*chanye*) or as an item of consumption, fees and market forces were clearly important for sustaining and expanding both senior high education and vocational education that was responsive to the needs of the students. Accordingly, official and media texts increasingly referred to education as an enlightened investment and a worthy goal for personal savings. Tang and Parish (2000) argued that in the cities, the changing discourse of entitlements and responsibilities (discussed earlier) caused individuals to accept that expanding economic opportunities reward individualistic effort and human capital investment through competition, and that this, in turn, made them willing to invest their increased incomes in education. Chinese commentators increasingly debated whether or not farmers were likely to become similarly progressive so that they too would begin to save for and invest in their children's education. One view was that meagre incomes, low returns to education, and a general lack of competition meant that rural parents were reluctant to invest in their children's education (Li 2002). A second view was that rural people were able to afford to contribute towards the costs of education and that "thought work" could help them develop the appropriate progressive mindset to recognize the benefits (Liu and Yan 2000; Xu 1999). A third view, and the one that rang true for Rivercounty, was that despite their limited income, rural parents were willing to invest in their children's education so long as they could perceive benefits (Yan and Zhang 2003; Bai 2003). Scholars espousing this view pointed out that although returns to education were low in the rural economy, the vast majority of parents wanted their children to become anything but farmers (Bai 2003). This was also the case in Rivercounty, as suggested by the breakdown of 112 parents' answers to the question "What occupation do you want your child to do in the future?"[15]

| | |
|---|---|
| Don't know | 5 |
| Farmer | 5 |
| There is no point in thinking of this/Why hope? | 19 |
| It is up to the child, not me | 11 |
| If the child studies well, s/he will have some choice | 13 |
| States a non-farm job | 37 |
| Anything but farming | 12 |

There were essentially two ways of leaving farming – by attending university or by working off the farm and in the cities (Chong and Feng 2003).

The first of these options, attending university, required attending senior high school. As already noted, Rivercounty parents were willing to pay the fees if their child was perceived to stand a good chance of university entrance. Even following the 1998 disbanding of the job allocation system for university graduates, and the phasing out of the financial sponsorship of diploma and degree education by government departments, many parents I met in Rivercounty in 2000 insisted to me that having a university graduate in the family would ultimately benefit everyone. But, as also mentioned previously, the downside to this focus on senior high schools as a path to university was that if students were seen as unlikely to pass the entrance exams, then even good grades would not be enough to prevent them from being withdrawn before graduating from junior high. This was particularly true for daughters whose parents were generally less inclined to insist that they stayed in school because they would eventually marry into another family. Rising school fees were therefore likely to exacerbate the disparity in male and female progression, with adverse knock-on effects because lower maternal education reduces educational investment in the next generation (Brown and Park 2002).

Vocational schools, especially county level ones, were not as popular as senior high schools among the parents and students of Rivercounty. People complained that university entrance was impossible from these schools and that job prospects for graduates were poor. The view that the county vocational school would not lead to good job opportunities was clear in the words of a mother who told me the following:

> Now the money from the early rice is only enough to pay for the schooling of my son. This year my son is 16. He is studying the second year of middle school in Jinping Party School.[16] When he was first allocated a place at that school he really didn't want to go and blamed us for not going to entreat someone to help him get into the Number Two Middle School. He cried at home for several days and I also cried. He did not want to study at the vocational college but his grades were not good and what else could I do? There are two people in our village who study at the vocational school. Aye! . . . The fate of this generation has been bitter, starting from my parents right up to me, and now this bitterness is on the bodies of my children. My only son does not know how to study, and in the end has had to go and study at the vocational school. Fate is really bitter.
>
> (Tape 9, 20 October 2000)

Even so, increasing economic diversification and rural–urban migration caused some Rivercounty farmers to start to perceive that there could be more routes in life than a narrow road to university and a wide road back to the village. Their own observations led them to concur with state publicity that individuals were responsible for learning a skill to forge a good life. One father in Rivercounty expressed the following view:

> I wanted my son to repeat and take the exam but he was unwilling. He said: "With the present reforms of the educational system, even if you graduate from a key university, the state does not allocate a job to you and you must rely on yourself to find a job. Seeing as that is how it is, I may as well learn some computing skills and go out into society to earn money a little earlier." . . . My daughter, well her grades are not so good. . . . When the time comes I'll send her to learn a technical skill. Nowadays everyone needs a skill. If you don't have a skill it is not feasible to migrate to find work.
>
> (Tape 16, 16 October 2000)

During the early 2000s, vocational schools in agricultural counties were accordingly phasing out agricultural skills classes in favour of courses in electronics, computing and sewing.

In response to the fact that growing numbers of people wanted vocational education, and that the Chinese government saw education as a way to alleviate surplus labor in rural areas by facilitating off-farm employment, in 2003 the central authorities took the dramatic step of launching a plan to provide free or subsidized training for rural people who were either preparing to migrate or who had already migrated to the cities. This plan was financed by funds allocated at the central and local government levels; in 2004 the central government allocated 300 million yuan (US$36.1 million) to this project (*China Daily*, 9 March 2004). Under the plan, over seven years, an estimated 70 million migrant workers were to receive training or additional professional training. Yet while this training initiative was laudable, its implementation in rural areas was thwarted by the fiscal system and by the top-down cadre evaluation system. One problem was that in many agricultural localities the funds allocated for training were diverted to alleviate county governments' fiscal shortages: particularly in the wake of the "tax-for-fee" reforms, funds were used to finance cadres' wages. Another problem was that many training courses operated in a formalistic manner with the organizers paying more attention to qualifying for centrally transferred funds than to meeting the needs of the participants, so often the participants stopped attending (Conversations with Chinese labor bureau officials and migrant NGO representatives, Lanzhou City, China, 2005). At the time of my fieldwork in 2004 there were no free vocational training courses available in Rivercounty, and access to quality vocational education continued to depend on the willingness and ability of parents to pay.

So far, it can be seen that during the 2000s fees became increasingly important for funding non-compulsory as well as compulsory education. This development was accompanied by an official and media discourse that strenuously avoided the language of *chanyehua* and commercialization because the Party-state needed to act in ways that appeared consistent with the public perception that education was a basic right and public good for which the state was responsible. The public discourse therefore focused on whether or not rural parents had the progressive outlook and sense of responsibility necessary for them to save for and invest in education. The public discourse also increasingly placed emphasis on the willingness of the state to help people in their pursuit of education and "*suzhi*" improvement. But despite these good intentions, in cash-strapped agricultural localities state efforts to expand rural people's access to vocational education were undermined by the fiscal system and absence of independent supervision over the final usage of earmarked funds. So access to quality vocational education continued to require the payment of fees.

### *Charity*

State institutions co-ordinated charitable activities which supported schools in poor communities and students in poor households. These well-publicized activities served several functions. During the 1990s and early 2000s they enabled the Party-state to demonstrate to rural people that, despite withdrawing from public goods provisioning, it nevertheless fulfilled its caring responsibilities, helping to create the conditions under which citizens could claim basic social entitlements. Involvement in such activities also helped cadres to maintain a positive self-image so that they felt that their work entailed more than exacting levies and pushing farmers to plant specified crops such as tobacco. Finally, charitable activities assisted different levels of the government in meeting upper-level targets for school enrolment and progression, and for school building and maintenance. Three examples of charitable activity in rural Jiangxi included the fundraising and support activities of quasi-NGOs, local government activities to send "warmth" to poor households and grants for senior high students.

A key quasi-NGO education charity is Project Hope (*Xiwang Gongcheng*), which was founded in 1991 under the auspices of the China Youth Development Foundation. It has branches at all administrative levels, down to the township, which actively raise funds and allocate money to cases of need. In Rivercounty, cadres were periodically required to donate to their local branch of Project Hope. For many cadres, finding external benefactors became an important part of their officially assessed contribution to local development. A female township deputy explained her involvement in Project Hope as follows:

> I felt that Project Hope was a realistic and down to earth project so we [the Party Youth Corps] . . . made it the focus of our work. I used all kinds of methods to obtain donations from various places and within four years, that is by 1999, we had built six Hope schools and taken in 1,800,000 yuan. I was once awarded the provincial honour of "Outstanding Youth Corps Cadre". Our County Corps was also commended at the provincial and prefectural levels as an advanced work unit. Raising funds and building schools is difficult. Apart from luck, I relied on running all over the place. For example the Shelou Hope School was the result of unremitting endeavour. It was only after much pleading that we moved the heart of the general manager of the Shanghai Shelou Photocopy Company and obtained support. . . . Right until last year when I transferred out of the Corps people from the Shelou Company would visit us here in Rivercounty.
>
> (Tape 20, 22 October 2000)

Project Hope contributed significantly to education provisioning in Rivercounty. Seven primary schools were built with money from the charity, with benefactors including a local airport, the Jiangxi Province Tobacco Company, the Fumin Tobacco Company, the Guangdong Coca-Cola Company and a Taiwanese entrepreneur, and donations ranging from 80,000 to 200,000 yuan per school. In 2000 10 percent of school children in the county received some subsidy from the foundation, even if this amounted only to a few donated books. Three percent of children received more substantial sponsorship, though administrators noted that in cases of full sponsorship, donors commonly specified that their money be used to support students with good grades.

Another quasi-NGO that supported education was the Jiangxi Charity Foundation. Founded in September 2002 under the auspices of the Jiangxi provincial government, it exists alongside the Jiangxi Poverty Relief Foundation and solicits donations from relatively wealthy members of society that are then distributed to the needy. Within its sights are over one million Jiangxi farmers who face problems with basic subsistence, over three million farmers who need disaster relief in the course of any one year, over two million handicapped persons in rural and urban areas, and the urban poor. The education needs of primary and junior high students in these households are a key area of attention for the foundation and in 2004 it teamed up with the Jiangxi public television broadcaster, Jiangxi Station Five, to launch an education donation appeal. The commercials showed black and white images of poor rural children set against the theme tune of the Sound of Silence. On-screen text listed the names and the particular hardships of individual students. And a channel five celebrity urged city people to deposit donations in the charity bank account that had its details displayed on the screen.

A second example of charitable support involved local cadres co-ordinating activities to "send warmth" (*song wennuan*) to hardship households: giving money for school fees to households designated as poverty-stricken and food to households with sick members.[17] In a neoliberal economic environment, these benevolent actions demonstrated the caring credentials of the cadres. Often though, the farmers still perceived the gap between the performance of caring by cadres and their own experiences of cadre exactions. When watching televised programs about such caring activities the farmers quipped that when they wanted permission to build houses or needed special help, they themselves had to send warmth to cadres!

A final instance of charitable support was the issuing of grants and loans to rural senior high school students. In 2004, the Jiangxi provincial government established a fund of 6 billion yuan which included a 4.3 billion contribution from the State Development Bank, one of the country's policy banks, as well as locally raised sources. In allocating these grants, priority was given to students who were an only-child (*China Daily*, 22 April 2004). The grants were designed to offset the increasing costs of senior high education and to promote human capital formation (*suzhi* development) among rural youth.

## Conclusion

Understanding how education was funded into the mid 2000s is central to understanding the rural disadvantage that has prevailed in incomes, livelihoods, human development indicators and life chances. This is because education expenses in the form of levies and school fees accounted for the lion's share of the crippling farmers' burden. It is also because the ability of the village, township and county to fund education and the willingness and ability of parents to pay for education has had a strong bearing on the life chances of children.

State planners increasingly have identified rural education as the solution to both rural and national underdevelopment, but they have been unsure about how to fund it. During the 1990s and early 2000s, the answer seemed to involve reshaping the public understanding about entitlements and responsibilities. This reshaping process entailed promoting a public discourse that encompassed two main elements. First there was a neoliberal emphasis on individual responsibility for human capital investment and wealth creation. By urging farmers to adopt a progressive mentality whereby they invested in education, an emphasis on individual and societal responsibility excused the state from much of the burden of educational investment. Second there was a socialist and Chinese humanist emphasis on state responsibility for promoting the public good. Activities used by the state to demonstrate the fulfillment of this responsibility included increasing the proportion of GDP invested in education, issuing loans and grants, coordinating vocational education programs and transferring funds to local-level education. The state also coordinated charitable activities, retaining for itself a form of moral authority that in more liberal governing systems is ceded to society and individuals.[18]

While these measures led to some improvements in rural educational provisioning and education costs, they fell far short of fully redressing the inadequacies in the provisioning of affordable quality education that so disillusioned rural people. Rural families continued to be burdened by school fees. Urban dweller became increasingly alarmed at the plights of rural people, especially children, depicted on television and in reportage accounts. At the same time, policymakers grew ever more perturbed at the destabilizing effects of widening disparities in wealth and living standards, and recognized that the immense hardship in rural areas undermined state claims to be socialist and to stand for social justice.

Subsequent to the fieldwork for researching this essay, key shifts in policy discourse and practice about rural development and "building a harmonious society" promoted under the new Hu-Wen leadership (2002/2003) gained momentum, and basic education became ever more clearly defined as an entitlement and a public good. Conversations with farmers during return visits to rural Jiangxi in July and December 2006 indicated that school fees had fallen and that on account of this and other initiatives, such as tax reductions and grain subsidies, they felt their situation had improved somewhat over the past one to two years (*hao yidian*). With regard to education, a series of documents released in 2006 ruled that an increased educational budget was to be used mainly for rural education. Moreover, the policy requiring the eradication of tuition and miscellaneous schools fees for compulsory education in rural areas is to be fully implemented by 2007 and included within top-down local cadre evaluations (Feng 2006; Zhang 2006). The neoliberal dimension of human development in China has thus been undergoing gradual substantive modification. Indeed, over the course of an ongoing period of uncertainty, debate and experimentation, the state has increasingly accepted responsibility for providing the resources and creating the environmental conditions necessary for rural people to assume their responsibilities of improving their own *suzhi* and contributing to "harmonious" national development. Even so, the extent to which local governments facing severe fiscal shortages will ensure that rural children receive their entitlement to free compulsory education remains to be seen.

## Notes

1 I am grateful to Vivienne Shue for extensive written feedback, to Kun-Chin Lin for reading an early draft and to Tao Ran for helpful discussions. I am grateful also to the British Academy and Simon Population Trust for funding the fieldwork in 2000 and to the Oxford University Contemporary China Studies Program for funding the fieldwork in 2004.

2 Lin Yifu, a member of the National Committee of the Chinese People's Political

Consultative Conference, in "Members Urge Funding for Rural Schools," *China Daily*, 12 March 2004.

3 Item 16 of The Jiangxi Province Promulgation on Methods for Implementing China's Education Law states that teachers should receive higher wages than civil servants while item 17 states that teachers with an education level of vocational diploma (*zhongzhuan*) or above who teach in the village or township primary schools and junior high schools should be paid at one grade higher (*Jiangxi Daily*, 25 October 1996). So teachers in rural schools are supposed to receive higher wages than their counterparts in urban schools.

4 In 1999, out of 30 provinces, the ones with the largest areas of dangerous school buildings were Guangxi – 545,000 sq metres, Guizhou – 517,000 sq metres, and Guangdong – 418,000 sq metres, followed by Jiangxi – 415,000 sq metres (see Liu 2002).

5 The 1995 target for 2000 was to have 99 percent of children enrolled in primary school and 85 percent enrolled in junior high school.

6 These levels of primary school completion fall below the official provincial average of 88.2 percent.

7 A survey of lower middle schools in 14 counties in Liaoning, Heilongjiang, Shandong, Henan and Jilin found that over 40 percent of students dropped out in the first one or two years and over half of the dropouts said that they did so because they disliked school. The researchers also found that children were rounded up into classrooms when upper level inspection teams came to visit. The survey was conducted by the Rural Education Research Office of Northeast Normal University. For students dropping out from compulsory education in other Jiangxi counties see Murphy 2004b.

8 This further decentralization began nationwide in 1994, but implementation in Jiangxi province lagged by two years, starting only in 1996.

9 This is based on the estimate given to me by the head of the county statistical bureau in October 2000. Interviews with township accountants also suggest that in 2000 in key tobacco growing townships well over half and even up to 70 percent of fiscal revenue came from tobacco (Tape 15, TL Township, 15 November 2000; Tape 18, GP Township, 21 November 2000). One official report written in 2000 says that in 1993, two thirds of revenue in Rivercounty came from tobacco and the proportion has increased since then, and that there is further potential for development as suggested by the fact that in a neighbouring county in Guangdong province, 70 percent of fiscal revenue comes from tobacco (Yuan 2000). Although plans are currently underway to phase out special agricultural taxes nationwide, tobacco is likely to remain important as a source of revenue for local governments because it is the only crop that will be exempt from the tax cancellation.

10 School visits. Item on *suzhi* education and equipment, Jian Prefecture News, 11 November 2000, 22.30hrs.

11 The public criticism campaign was called the "three stresses" (*sanjiang*), these being "study," "politics" and "a healthy atmosphere." *Sanjiang* lasted from the end of 1999 to early 2001. One of the education devices used in *sanjiang* was the circulation of "opinion boxes" so that people could anonymously lodge petitions against their superiors and make appeals for particular kinds of change. One of the grievances that some officials and teachers noted had been lodged concerned the diversion of funds from poorer schools to showcase key schools. Another problem raised in the *sanjiang* campaign concerned unpaid teachers' wages.

12 Some parents pay willingly for such places because they see it as a way to give their children a head start in life; to avoid the child having to repeat a year further down the track; and a source of childcare that frees other family members to work in the fields.

13 According to rumour, strict new pollution regulations meant the factory had to close.

14 Details of this press conference were first reported in the influential publication *Zhongguo Qingnian bao* (China Youth News) in an edition published 7 January 2004. This article was then citied in articles in a series of other magazines and newspapers such as those by He (2004) and Yi (2004).
15 These were parents whose children were still in school or who were yet to start school.
16 Jinping Party School is a vocational school.
17 There are also special relief schemes for particular categories of household: students in daughter-only households are theoretically entitled to reductions in school fees, as are children in households that have lost one or both parents.
18 Thanks to Vivienne Shue for making this point.

## References

Alpermann, Björn (2001) "The Post-Election Administration of Chinese Villages," *China Journal*, 46: 45–67.

Bai Junhong (2003) "Nongcun jiaoyu touzi siren baochoulü cesuan" (Calculations of private returns to rural educational investment) *Zhejiang daxue xuebao* (Journal of Zhejiang University), 33 (4) (July): 144–50.

Bao Chuanyou and Deng Tao (2002) "Shuifei gaige dui nongcun jichu jiaoyu de yingxiang" (The influence of fee for tax reforms on rural basic education), *Liaoning Shifan daxue xuebao* (Journal of Liaoning Normal School), 25 (5) (September): 31–3.

Brown, Phil and Park, Albert (2002) "Education and Poverty in Rural China," *Economics of Education Review*, 21 (6) (December): 523–41.

Cao Jinqing (2004) *China Along the Yellow River*, trans. Nicky Harman, London: Routledge.

Chambers, Robert (1997) *Whose Reality Counts? Putting the First Last*, London: ITDG Publishing.

Chang Wanxin (2002) "Nongcun shuifei gaige dui yiwu jiaoyu de yingxiang ji duice" (The effects of rural fee for tax reform on compulsory education and countermeasures), Simao shifan gaodeng zhuanke xuexiao xiaobao (Journal of Simao Teachers' College) 18 (2) June: 74–6.

Chen Xiaodong (2004) "Levelling School Playing Field," *China Daily*, 31 August.

Chong Haijun and Feng Xiaotian (2003) "Ye tan cheng xiang jiating renli ziben touzi chayi de yuanyin" (Discussing again the reasons for the rural and urban difference in family investment in human capital), *Jingji yu jiaoyu* (Economy and Education), 4: 27–30.

Connelly, Rachel and Zheng Zhenzhen (2003) "Determinants of Primary and Middle School Enrollment of 10–18 Year Olds in China," *Economics of Education Review*, 22 (4): 379–90.

Edin, Maria (2000) *Market Forces and Communist Power: Local Political Institutions and Economic Development in China*, Uppsala: Uppsala University Press.

Feng, Jianhua (2006) "Equal Education", *Beijing Review*, 49 (49) (7 December):28–9.

Ferrera, M., Hemerijck, A. and Rhodes, M. (2001) "Recasting European Welfare States for the Twenty-First Century," in S. Liebfried (ed.) *Welfare State Futures*, Cambridge: Cambridge University Press.

Fong, Vanessa (2004) *Only Hope: Coming of Age Under China's One-Child Policy*, Stanford, CA: Stanford University Press.

Fraser, Colin and Restrepo-Estrada, Sonia (1998) *Communicating for Development: Human Change for Survival*, London: I.B. Tauris.

Giddens, Anthony (2000) *The Third Way and Its Critics*, Cambridge: Polity Press.

Guo Yongzhong (2002) "Dangqian zhongguo nonmin fudan wenti yanjiu" (Research into the present problem of Chinese farmers' burden), *Beijing daxue xuebao* (Journal of Peking University) 39 (10) (January): 47–54.

Hall, Anthony and Midgley, James (2004) *Social Policy for Development*, London: Sage Publications.

Hannum, Emily (1999) "Poverty and Basic-Level Schooling in the People's Republic of China: Equity Issues in the 1990s," *Prospects: the Quarterly Journal of Comparative Education*, 29 (4): 561–77.

Hannum, Emily and Park, Albert (2002) "Educating China's Children in the 21st Century," *Harvard China Review*, 3 (2): 8–14.

He Guangwen, Ma Xingyuan and Li Lili (2003) "Nongcun jiaoyu rongzi wenti yanjiu" (Research into the problem of funding rural education), *Guojia xingzheng xueyuan xuebao* (Journal of the National Administration Institute), 5: 75–9.

He Yonghai (2004) "Shei chui da jiaoyu chanyehua de qipao?" (Who blew the big bubble of making education into a product?), *Beijing Shibao*, 13 January: AO2.

Huang Feng and Zhang Puan (2003) "Shiying nongcun shuifei gaige xin xingshi, jiagou nongcun jiaoyu chanye da juge" (Adapting to the new situation of rural fees-for-tax reforms, structuring the rural education enterprise), *Jiaoyu zhengce yu guanli* (Education Policy and Management): 15–18.

JX Township Peoples' Government (2000) "Greatly Develop Education as a Product, Accelerate the Regional Development of the County," *Rivercounty Government Affairs*, 19, 1 September (Rivercounty County Peoples' Government Office).

Knight, John and Li Shi (1996) "Education Attainment and the Rural–Urban Divide in China", *Oxford Bulletin of Economics and Statistics* 58 (1) (February): 81–115.

Lai Jinsheng (2003) "Ying dui nongcun shui fei gaige chuangxin jiaoyu touru jizhi" (Creating a new funding mechanism for education in response to fee for tax reforms in the countryside), *Nongcun caizheng yu caiwu* (Rural Public Finance), 76: 26–7.

Li, Clara (2001) "Delegates Urge Law to Protect Children," *South China Morning Post*, Friday, 9 March; available online at <http://special.scmp.com/npc2001/main/ZZZGRA165KC.html> (first accessed 29 January 2004; last viewed 7 September 2006).

Li Wen (2002) "Jiating renli touzi de chengxiang chayi fenxi" (Analysis of the rural–urban difference in family human capital investment), *Shehui* (Society) 7.

Li Xiande (2004) "Rethinking the Peasant Burden: Evidence from Village China," in Peter Ho, Jacob Eyferth and Eduard B. Vermeer (eds.) *Rural Development in Transitional China*, London: Frank Cass, pp. 45–76.

Liu Xiaohua (2002) "Overview of Educational Needs and Philanthropic Opportunities in China," San Diego, CA: International Community Foundation, September.

Liu Yunfeng and Yan Hesheng (2000) "Jiaoyu chanyehua' de zhanlüe sikao" (Strategic thoughts on the industrializing of education), *Jiaoyu yu jingji* (Education and Economy), 1: 5–11.

Long Shouxing (2003) "Nongmin de tezhi: nongcun jiaoyu de zhuolidian" (Special characteristics of farmers: points of effort in rural education) *Jiangxi jiaoyu keyan* (Jiangxi Educational Research), 7: 3–5.

Lu Yarong (2003) "Guanzhu nongcun gaige zhong de jig e bu gongping wenti" (Concern about a few inequities in rural reform), *Nongcun jiangji wenti* (Issues in Agricultural Economy), 11: 19–23.

Migdal, Joel (2001) *State in Society*, New York: Cambridge University Press.

Milwertz, Cecelia Nathansen (1997) *Accepting Population Control: Urban Chinese Women and the One-Child Family Policy*, Richmond: Curzon.

Murphy, Rachel (2004a) "Turning Peasants into Modern Chinese Citizens: 'Population Quality' Discourse, Demographic Transition and Primary Education," *China Quarterly*, 177 (March): 1–20.

Murphy, Rachel (2004b) "The Impact of Labor Migration on the Well-Being and Agency of Rural Chinese Women: Cultural and Economic Contexts and the Life Course," in Arianne M. Gaetano and Tamara Jacka (eds.) *On the Move: Women in Rural-to-Urban Migration in Contemporary China*, New York: Columbia University Press, pp. 243–78.

Oi, Jean (1992) "Fiscal Reform and the Economic Foundations of Local State Corporatism in China," *World Politics*, 45: 99–126.

Peng Yali (1996) "The Politics of Tobacco: Relations Between Farmers and Local Governments in China's Southwest," *China Journal*, 36: 67–82.

Peterson, Glen (1994) "State Literacy Ideologies and the Transformation of Rural China," *Australian Journal of Chinese Affairs*, 32 (July): 95–120.

Reed-Danahay, Deborah (1996) *Education and Identity in Rural France: The Politics of Schooling*, Cambridge: Cambridge University Press.

Rival, Laura (1996) "Formal Schooling and the Production of Modern Citizens in the Ecuadorian Amazon," in Bradley A. Levinson and Douglas E. Foley (eds.) *The Cultural Production of the Educated Person*, New York: State University of New York Press, pp. 153–68.

Rivercounty Education Office (2000) "Urgent Notice on the Delayed Payment of Teachers' Wages."

Rivercounty Government (2000) "Document on the *Chanyehua* of Education."

Rong Xue Lan and Shi Tianjian (2001) "Inequality in Chinese Education," *Journal of Contemporary China*, 10 (26): 107–24.

Saich, Tony (2001) *Governance and Politics of China*, London: Palgrave.

Shue, Vivienne (1988) *The Reach of the State*, Stanford, CA: Stanford University Press.

Tang Wenfang and Parish, William L. (2000) *Chinese Urban Life Under Reform: The Changing Social Contract*, New York: Cambridge University Press.

Tomasevski, Katarina (2003) *Education Denied*, London: Zed Books.

Unger, Jonathan (1982) *Education Under Mao*, New York: Columbia University Press.

Unterhalter, Elaine (1999) "Citizenship, Difference and Education: Reflections on the South African Transition," in Nira Yuval-Davis and Pnina Werbner (eds.) *Women, Citizenship and Difference*, London: Zed Books, pp. 100–17.

Wang Huangqing and Wang Shuhua (2003) "Jiejue sannong wenti libukai nongcun jiaoyu de fazhan" (Resolving the three rural problems cannot be separated from the development of rural education), *Shijian yu tansuo* (Economic Tribune), 24: 68.

Wang Junrong (2004) "Fazhan tese jiaoyu, zhengjiu nongcun xuesheng zhuixue" (Develop special education, save rural students from dropping out), *Kejiao Zhoukan* (Education Weekly) 15 July 2004: 13.

Wong, Christine P. W. (1992) "Fiscal Reform and Local Industrialisation: The Problems of Sequencing Reform in Post-Mao China," *Modern China*, 18: 197–227.

Wu Qingze and Wang Qiang (2003) "Nongcun shuifei gaige hou nongshui zhengguan de xin wenti ji duice" (New problems and counter-measures for collecting taxes after the rural fees for tax reform), *Nongcun caizheng yu caiwu* (Rural Finance): 39–40.

Wu Bin (2003) *Sustainable Development in Rural China: Farmer Innovation and Self-Organization in Marginal Areas*, London: RoutledgeCurzon.

Xie Lijun and Guo Xiangtian (2003) "Jiangxi nongcun jiaoyu tansuo" (Exploration of education in rural Jiangxi), *Fuzhou shizhuan xuebao* (Journal of Fuzhou Teachers College), 22 (4) (December): 35–7.

Xu Guangyu (1999) "Survey on the Public Mind-Set Regarding the Development of Private Schools and the Public's Ability to Pay for Them," *Chinese Education and Society*: 70–9.

Yan Jianzhang (2002) "Qiantan shuifei gaige dui nongcun yiwu jiaoyu de chongji" (Discussing the blow of the fees-for-tax reform on rural compulsory education), *Zunyi shifan xueyuan xuebao* (Journal of Zunyi Normal College), 4 (2) (June): 52–6.

Yan Shumin and Zhang Shengtai (2003) "Zhongguo nongcun jiating renli ziben touzi dongtai fenxi ji zhengce jianyi" (Dynamic analysis on human capital investment of the rural family in China and policy suggestions), *Yuce* (Forecasting), 22 (1): 7–10.

Yep, Ray (2004) "Can Tax-for-Fee Reforms Reduce Rural Tension in China? The Process, Progress and Limitations," *China Quarterly*, 177 (March): 42–70.

Yi Hong (2004) "Cong jiaoyu bu neng chanyehua shuoqi" (You can't start from making education into a product), *Huanan yaowen* (South China Digest), 13 January.

Yu Liqing and Cheng Ping (2002) "Dangqian nongcun jiaoyu cunzai de wenti ji duice" (Existing problems and countermeasures in rural education), *Anhui jiaoyu* (Anhui Education): 14–15.

Yuan Yansheng (2000) "Tong xia juexin, hen zhua zhiliang, ba yanye chanye zuo you zuo qiang, shi qi zhenzheng chengwei wo xian de zhizhu canye" (Firmly resolve, grasp quality, make tobacco production excellent and strong, make it truly become the pillar industry of our county), Transcript of 17 page speech by the head of the Rivercounty Tobacco Company, 12 November.

Zhang Huaqiao (2000) "Nongcun jiaoyu zai weiji zhong jiaohan" (The shout of rural education in crisis), *Zhongguo nongcun* (Rural China), 3: 30–2.

Zhang Xianguo (2006) "Quanguo nongcun xiaoxue chuzhong mingnian jiang quanbu mian shou xue za fei" (Next year miscellaneous school fees will be eradicated in rural primary and junior high schools across the country), *Guangming ribao* (Guangming Daily), 12 December: 1.

Zuo Xuejin (1997) "China's Fiscal Decentralization and the Financing of Local Services in Poor Townships," *IDS Bulletin*, 28 (1): 80–91.

*Zhongguo wushi nian de Jiangxi 1949–1999* (*Fifty Years of Jiangxi 1949–1999*) (2000) Beijing: Zhongguo tongji chubanshe.

# 5 Social security in transition

*Athar Hussain*

## Introduction

Viewed from the perspective of well-being and social security, four developments over the reform period[1] stand out. The first is the dramatic fall in rural poverty in the train of the transformation of the rural collective economy. The second is the emergence of a large population of migrants, who suffer from a host of disadvantages. The third is the combination of the steady erosion of the inherited social security regime, a massive retrenchment of labor from the state sector and the appearance of urban poverty as a major social issue. The fourth is the setting-up of a new social security regime, a process that is still under way.

The downward trend in rural poverty was set off by the distribution of collectively owned land to rural households on long-term leases, which as well as generating economic incentives for output growth also ensured that income from farming was distributed far and wide across the rural population, though not equally. The downward trend was given a further momentum by the expansion of employment in town and village enterprises (TVEs), which grew almost five-fold from 28 million in 1978 to 135 million in 1995 (NBS 2005b). The number of rural poor fell particularly sharply immediately following the beginning of rural reforms in 1979. Reckoned in official figures,[2] the headcount of the rural poor fell from 250 million in 1978 (31 percent of the population at that time) to 85 million in 1985. The downward trend continued but slowed down in the 1990s. The urban–rural income gap, which narrowed substantially in the early 1980s, began to widen and is now wider than it was in 1978.[3] There still remain pockets of severe poverty, not only in the poorer western but also in the central and the coastal regions. The notable feature of the dramatic fall in rural poverty in the first ten or so years of the reform period is that it was due entirely to output growth. Not only did anti-poverty schemes play a negligible role or none in the fall, but also it went in parallel with the collapse of most of the local cooperative health insurance schemes, which had been perhaps the most notable achievement of the period of the Cultural Revolution (1966–76). This left a large gap in health care in the countryside, which the government would belatedly recognize and try to fill by reviving cooperative health insurance schemes. With the disappearance of abject and endemic poverty from large parts of the countryside, new issues concerning rural social security have come to the fore. These include social assistance to poor households in localities not regarded as poor, and widening access to basic health care which has assumed a particular urgency following the outbreak of Severe Acute Respiratory Syndrome (SARS) in 2003 and the looming threat of an avian flu pandemic.

A stringent control on rural-to-urban migration had been an abiding feature of Chinese economy following the famine of 1959–61. The control rested on the complementary combination of restriction on travel, the rationing of necessities on the basis of the place of residence and the "household registration system" (*hukou*), which recorded personal details. The registration system which still survives, though modified, resembles the national identity card schemes in many European countries except in one crucial respect: the permanent place of residence in the "household register" can only be altered by administrative discretion and does not change with migration.[4] Thus *hukou* partakes of a central feature of citizenship and is similarly used to control migration or to sort individuals into categories with differing entitlements. Following a lowering of impediments to travel and labor mobility and the displacement of rationing with an open market in necessities, migration grew and became substantial in the 1990s. As a result, the *hukou* mutated into a mechanism for dividing the population into "permanent residents" and "outsiders" (migrants) with differential access to social goods, such as basic education, and opportunities in the labor market. The migrant population[5] or the "floating population" is huge – just over 134 million according to the 2000 population census, around 11 percent of the then national population (NBS 2002). In the Chinese context, the category "migrants" is an anomaly created by treating individuals as residents of a locality other than where they have actually been living and working for a long time. With a large percentage excluded from participation in Social Insurance and means-tested social assistance, the migrant population represents a huge blind spot in the social security cover.

The inherited urban social security regime, which gradually collapsed with the transition to a market economy, rested on three pillars. The first was the imperative on the able-bodied to work and the obligation on the government to provide them with a job, albeit with a delay and at a very low rate of pay. This was the planned economy version of "welfare through work" or workfare. The strict control on rural-to-urban migration helped to keep the numbers of those to be provided with jobs manageable. Social assistance in cash and kind was confined to those unable to work. The second pillar was the extended social welfare role of work units (*danwei*) – including enterprises, social service units (*shiye danwei*) and government departments. These organizations, in particular enterprises, administered and financed Labor Insurance, the precursor of what in the second half of the 1990s would begin to be called "Social Insurance." They also provided free or at subsidized prices a wide assortment of social services and also public utilities to their current and retired employees and often to their families as well. These benefits went together with the prevalent practice of employees remaining in the same work unit for a long time, if not for life. Thus the third pillar was no lay-offs or redundancies. Once employed, a worker could confidently expect to stay in the same unit for life, if not the same job.

By the mid-1990s, changes in the urban economy had eroded the ground from beneath all three components. The delegation of economic decision-making to enterprises severely curtailed the ability of the government to provide jobs. The traditional arrangement of "employment for life" ended as a result of two developments. One was the introduction of employment on terminable contract for new recruits in 1986. The other was the relaxation of restraints on state enterprises to lay off surplus labor, which was forced upon the government by the rapid worsening of the financial situation of the state sector in the 1990s. The extended social welfare responsibilities of enterprises came under strain from the beginning of the reform process. With their budgets separated from the government budget, many enterprises could no longer maintain those responsibilities. To maintain the social welfare regime the government had to subsidize insolvent enterprises, which went against the grain of enterprise reforms. By the second half of the 1990s the government was forced to take on the extended social welfare responsibilities of work units, a process that is still not finished. A by-product of the disappearance of the inherited urban social welfare regime has been the appearance of urban unemployment which, unlike in the past, is both open and substantial. This has gone together with the emergence of poverty as a salient feature of the urban landscape, which previously was regarded as an almost exclusively rural phenomenon. The combination of urban unemployment and poverty emphasized the issue of the income maintenance of the urban population in the late 1990s and led to the extension of unemployment insurance, which until then remained a small scheme, and the introduction of the Minimum Living Standard Assistance (MLSA), which provided a means-tested cash allowance to urban households falling below the poverty line and marked a formal end of "income maintenance through work."

Reform of the social security regime, particularly of the schemes covering the urban population, has been a strand running through the transition period since 1978. Until the middle of the 1990s, these reforms consisted mostly of piecemeal measures to prop up the schemes carried over from the pre-1978 period, particularly the old-age pension scheme. The principal innovation in the 1980s was the introduction in 1986 of unemployment insurance so as to mollify resistance to the replacement of permanent with fixed term employment in state enterprises. The reforms since 1995 have been aimed at instituting a new system in urban areas to replace the one carried over from the pre-1978 period. But over the last few years an overhaul of the system for the rural population, previously regarded as a task for the distant future, has risen higher on the reform agenda. There have been three principal motive forces behind the reform of the urban social security regime: first, the widening incompatibility between the inherited system and the exigencies of a market economy; second, the emergence of new problems during the course of the transition such as the massive labor retrenchment in the state sector and rise in urban poverty from the mid-1990s; third, extraneous developments such as the aging of the population and the risk of epidemics.

The purpose of this chapter is to outline and assess the developing social security system. This is done in the wider context of the socio-economic changes

China has been undergoing since 1979, which are grouped under the heading of "three transitions" and discussed in the next section. The third section presents an overview of the schemes that make up the current social security system focusing on its salient features rather than on the details of particular schemes. The final section concludes with an analysis of the salient trends of change in the social security system.

## Three transitions

The transition to a market economy dominates the socio-economic setting for the emergence of a new social security system but does not exhaust it. Also relevant are two other transitions that China has been undergoing. One is the demographic transition set by the downward fertility rate and its salient feature is the changing age structure of the population. The other is economic development, broadly, the transformation of an agrarian into an urban economy dominated by industry and services. For the present purpose, its salient aspect is the shift of labor out of farming into industry and services. Closely correlated with this shift is rural-to-urban migration and urbanization.

### *Demographic transition*

The demographic transition that has been under way in China was set in motion by the downward trend in the fertility rate that dates back to 1970, preceding the "one child policy" by a decade or so. In recent years it has been sustained by a below-replacement fertility rate of 1.9 children per woman over life according to the 2003 figures (NBS 2005c). A notable feature is the exceptionally rapid pace of the fertility decline, with associated changes in the age structure of the population crowded in a much shorter period than in other countries such as Japan, South Korea, Taiwan and Hong Kong (Feeney 1996; Leete and Alam 1993). Aside from a slow-down in the growth rate of population, down from 2.6 percent in 1970 to 0.6 percent in 2004 (NBS 1999; NBS 2005c), and a lower population total than would otherwise be the case, it is accompanied by the progressive aging of the population; one indicator of which is the rising median age of the population. This trend is expected to persist for several decades and has three consequences that are relevant for social security. The first is the rising ratio of the elderly (above 65) in the population. The second is a falling ratio of children, (under age 15) and the third is a rising percentage of older relative to younger members in the labor force.

Amongst the three, the first has attracted most attention in China and has stimulated a widespread discussion of the financial support and the personal care of the rising numbers of the elderly. The ratio of the elderly in the total population will keep on rising for some decades, reaching a high 25 percent by 2050, according to various forecasts. A similar upward trend holds for the closely related "dependency ratio" (the ratio of the elderly to the working population). This is brought out by a comparison of the population profiles provided by the population censuses of 1982[6] and 2000 and the projection for 2020 (Table 5.1).

*Table 5.1* Population profile, 2000 and 2020

| | *1982* | *2000* | *2020* |
|---|---|---|---|
| Total (1,000) | 1,016,540 | 1,265,830 | 1,441,980 |
| Population ratio of children[a] (dependency ratio)[b] | 33.6% (54.2%) | 22.9% (32.7%) | 19.3% (28.0%) |
| Population ratio of the elderly[c] (dependency ratio) | 4.9% (7.9%) | 7.0% (10.0%) | 11.4% (16.5%) |
| Total dependency ratio | 62.1% | 42.7% | 44.5% |

Notes: The age division here follows the convention in demographic literature:

a aged (0–14)
b following the convention in demography the denominator of the dependency ratios is the population aged 15–64
c aged 65+

Sources: NBS 1982; NBS 2004c and NBS 1998d

As shown by Table 5.1, the rise in dependency ratio of the elderly goes together with a fall in the dependency ratio of children, with the latter wholly or partially offsetting the former. Thus the total dependency ratio, including both children and the elderly, may fall while the dependency ratio of the elderly rises, as it did between 1982 and 2000 when the total ratio fell by almost 20 percentage points. The total dependency ratio in 2020 will be higher than that in 2000, but still substantially less than the level in 1982. The argument is that the exploration of the economic implications of the demographic transition requires an analysis of the change in the whole of the age structure, covering not only the elderly and working-age adults but also the children (see Easterlin 1998).

Further, in drawing conclusions from a rise in the elderly dependency ratio, one has to take into account that China is, and will for some time remain, a labor surplus economy, which means that there is substantial unemployment, both open and disguised. The implication is that even a sizeable reduction in the population of working-age adults relative to that of the elderly, which is what the rise in the dependency ratio of the elderly means, may have little or no effect on the burden of supporting the dependent population. Here it is important to note that the rise in the observed ratio of the elderly has been and will continue for some decades to be due entirely to a lower number of working-age adults and children than what would have existed in the absence of the fertility transition. Assuming it began in 1970, the fertility decline will only affect the number of elderly after 2035; until then the number of the elderly will be what it would have been in the absence of the downward trend. However, eventually the burden of supporting the elderly will rise in tandem with the rising ratio of the elderly to working-age adults. China has had a pension problem since the beginning of the reform period. But that problem is largely caused by the absence of any long-term financial planning concerning pensions.

What are the implications of the rising ratio of the elderly to the working-age population for social security? Assuming that the living standard of the elderly does not fall, a rising elderly dependency ratio implies the elderly consuming an increasing share of GDP. How this increased cost is distributed across the economy depends on the sources of support for the elderly. Currently, the three main sources in the order of importance are, first and foremost, the family, then the social security schemes (including old-age pension and social assistance to the indigent elderly) and personal savings. Most of the cost arising out of the rising ratio of the elderly has fallen and will continue to fall on the families, which also bear much of the cost of children. The implication is that any offset that the falling ratio of children provides against the rising of cost of supporting the elderly accrues to families. As increasingly realized in China, the current heavy reliance on the family for old-age support fits ill with the demographic trends and socio-economic changes. The general trend is towards nuclear households and a majority of the elderly live separately from their offspring. With rising life expectancy, especially at old age, each succeeding cohort of the elderly would need support for a longer period than did the preceding. Added to this, because of the birth control policy, which in many localities means one child per couple, the future cohorts of the elderly will have fewer offspring to depend on than does the present cohort. The conjunction of birth control policy and the rising ratio of the elderly in the population has brought to the fore the issue of replacement of family financial support with old-age pensions. Currently 43 percent of the urban labor force is covered by the pension scheme under Social Insurance, which excludes the rural labor force. There are small-scale rural pension schemes but these cover only 54 million people (just 11 percent of the rural labor force) and promise to provide only a percentage of the minimum subsistence. Although almost all of the discussion of pensions in China is focused on urban areas, the problem of the support of the elderly is more serious in rural than in urban areas. Not only do the rural elderly not receive a pension but also, given the trend of emigration of working-age adults from the countryside, the ratio of the elderly to working-age adults in the near future will be higher in rural than in urban areas.

As dramatic as the falling ratio of children and the rising ratio of the elderly, but less discussed, is the aging of working-age adults. This matters because age, either on its own or as a correlate of features such as educational attainment and experience, is a central consideration in labor recruitment and is also a determinant of labor productivity. The change in the age structure of working-age adults over the 22 years to 2004 has been substantial. This is shown by Table 5.2 that compares the age structure of working-age adults in 1982 and 2004, before and after the effect of the fertility decline from the late 1960s and early 1970s fed through to the population of working-age adults. The working-age population in 2004 includes those born between 1970 and 1989 (aged 15–34 in 2004), the birth cohorts affected by the fertility decline and who received all of their post-primary education in the reform period and thus benefited from the revival of the educational system after the Cultural Revolution.

*Table 5.2* Age structure of working-age adults, 1982 and 2004

| *Age group* | *1982* | *2004* |
|---|---|---|
| Aged 15–34<br>(Number in millions) | 59.2%<br>(365) | 43.7%<br>(410) |
| Aged 35–64<br>(Number in millions) | 40.8%<br>(252) | 56.3<br>(528) |

Sources: NBS 1982 and NBS 2005c

Over the 22 years from 1982 to 2004, the number of working-age adults has risen by 52 percent. The notable feature is that most of the increase (86 percent), 276 out of 321 million, is in the older age-group of 35–64. As a result, the percentage of younger working-age adults (aged 15–34) has dropped by 15.5 percentage points. As in other economies, the average educational attainment of younger cohorts is higher than that of older cohorts of workers, but the gap in China is particularly wide because of the damaging impact of the Cultural Revolution (1966–76) on the educational system. Many in the age group 40–55 in 2003 missed out partially or completely on higher secondary, technical and vocational and tertiary education. Currently, a common refrain in China, especially in the north-east, is that once laid off, men aged 50 and above and women 40 and above have little hope of finding a job comparable to what they previously had. This is precisely the age group most affected by the deleterious impact of the Cultural Revolution on secondary and tertiary education.

Unemployment is a major concern in present-day China and included in this is a specific problem of long-term unemployment due to a conjunction of three factors. One is the sharp increase in the number of older workers relative to younger ones. The second is the long shadow of the Cultural Revolution on human capital amongst older age cohorts. The third is the labor retrenchment in the state and urban collective sector. Furthermore, the problem of long-term unemployment among older workers may persist over the next 15 to 20 years because of a combination of increasing labor force and a rising median age of the labor force driven by the falling size of cohorts entering the labor force.

### *Process of development*

As in other countries, economic development in China involves two interrelated processes with extensive socio-economic ramifications:

- population migration, mostly rural-to-urban, and associated urbanization;
- shift of labor from farming to industry and services often coupled with a change from self- to wage-employment.

These processes largely concern the rural population and take on special forms in China because of two particular features. The first is the household registration system, referred to earlier. The second is the land tenure pattern shaped by two decades of collectivization up to 1978 and the subsequent distribution of collectively owned land to rural households on a long-term lease.

Here it is relevant to point to a particular feature of the Chinese economy: whereas the share of farming in its GDP is a low 15 percent, similar to that in middle-income economies, the labor share of farming is a high 47 percent, which is similar to that in low-income economies[7] (NBS 2005a; NBS 2005b). A GDP share of farming that is a small fraction (say less than half) of its labor force share is a common feature of developing economies (Stern 1996). But with a GDP share of farming less than one third of its labor force share, the gap between the two ratios in China is wide even for a developing economy. The wide gap between the two ratios explains why the average personal income in rural areas is a fraction of that in urban areas. A significant narrowing of the rural–urban gap in personal income, which is a major policy aim, will require reducing the difference between the GDP and the employment share of farming. This can be done by either raising the GDP share or reducing the employment share. The first, which requires the farm sector growing much faster than industry and services, is impossible because of natural factors, such as cultivable land area and water availability, and limitations on the demand side. The second is the only feasible alternative and requires policies to promote a shift of labor out of farming, which is premised on urbanization often combined with migration.

The wide difference between the two ratios points to a stark asymmetry in the adverse impact of natural hazards. This is of some importance because China is one of the most natural hazard-prone countries in the world. Its varied climate and complex geology result in a wide range of natural hazards. Floods and droughts are recurrent threats to much of the rural population. Areas particularly vulnerable and prone to floods include the southern and eastern coastal provinces. The north central part of China, running from Gansu to Henan, suffers from a high risk of drought while the provinces of Hubei, Hunan and Anhui can experience both flood and drought in the same year. Given the low GDP share of farming, even a major natural disaster would have a limited impact on GDP. By the same logic, even a minor hazard may have a damaging impact on a large number of people, given that almost half of the labor force is employed in farming. Much of the social protection in rural areas has been and continues to be concerned with the alleviation of suffering caused by floods and droughts.

Notwithstanding the impediments implicit in the *hukou* system and the land tenure condition, migration has risen substantially over the reform period. Coinciding with the beginning of economic reforms, the control on rural-to-urban migration was loosened, and then later in 1992, as part of the strategy to deflect rural-to-urban migration away from large cities, immigrants with stable jobs were allowed to acquire permanent residency or *hukou* for small cities and towns. The provision was generalized in 1997. However, the details and implementation were left to towns and cities; as a result, how the system operates varies widely across localities. The system underwent a fundamental change in 2002 when the quota of the conversion of "agricultural" into "non-agricultural" registration, first introduced in 1995, was finally abolished and the conditions for acquiring permanent residency in towns and cities, except the large ones, were further relaxed.[8] The Chinese statistics on migrants have to be treated with some care because of their particular meaning. The category "migrants" includes all those resident for more than six months in a place other than the one named on his/her *hukou*. A migrant remains a migrant until a change in the place of residence is officially registered. In contrast, in most countries internal migrants automatically acquire the status of permanent residents after a period. The Chinese statistic for migrants has two salient characteristics. First, it covers a very wide range in terms of time since arrival. Second, the reported number of "migrants" for a particular period is determined not only by the movement of people in the preceding period but also by the evolution of the policies concerning the change of *hukou*.

Though the changes since 2000 have widened the local differences in details and operation of the *hukou* system, the goal is to institute a unified national system without any distinction between rural and urban residents. But the central government has yet to decide on the details of such a system. In the meantime, 11 provinces (mostly coastal) are pressing ahead with the introduction of a unified system for their urban and rural populations. The pattern is reminiscent of numerous reforms since 1979, that is, to begin with an experiment in selected localities followed by extension and finally universalization across the country and formalization through laws and regulation. The size of the migrant population matters for social security because migrants do not enjoy the same access to employment, housing and public services as bona fide residents do. But the pattern of discrimination between the migrants and local residents differs across cities and recent years have seen the attenuation, if not abolition, of particularly objectionable forms of discrimination against migrants. For example, many cities no longer refuse to admit children from migrant families in local schools or charge them a higher than usual tuition fee. Similarly, many cities now allow, and often encourage, migrant workers, especially those in regular employment, to join the Social Insurance schemes. But this affects only a small percentage of migrant workers because many of them are self- or informally-employed or are on a short-term contract.

The obverse of the transfer of labor out of farming and associated population migration is urbanization, which both widens economic opportunities open to the labor force and creates problems such as increased pressure on the environment and public services. In China, as elsewhere, the process has taken two forms: first, the expansion of existing urban settlements combined with rural-to-urban migration and, second, the urbanization of rural localities involving a switch of labor from farming to industry or services without migration, which has been encouraged by the government with the slogan "leave the land but not the village." Compared with international experiences, the second has been far more prevalent in China and the driving force behind it has been the growth of rural ("town and village") enterprises (TVEs), which accelerated sharply following the decollectivization of the rural economy from 1979 to 1984. The TVE labor force grew rapidly until 1996, but has since grown only slightly (NBS 2005b). As a result, "urbanization without migration" is no longer as relevant as it was in the past.

The shift of labor from farming into industry and services in many cases involves a changeover from self- to wage-employment. The shift of the rural labor force to non-agricultural activities, although it contributes to rising personal incomes, goes together with two changes that have implications for social security. One is the rapid expansion of wage-employees in rural areas, bringing with it the risk of unemployment and retirement at a particular age. This is relevant here because two of the principal social security schemes, old-age pensions and unemployment benefits, have traditionally been linked closely to wage-employment (Atkinson 1991), and so too in China. Compared to income from self-employment, especially when in kind, wages provide an easily verifiable standard for defining benefits and a convenient tax handle for financing contributory social security schemes. Thus a shift from self- to wage-employment widens the scope for the application of social insurance schemes with a benefit entitlement tied to the contribution record. Changes in the modes of employment since 1978 in rural China have gone through two phases: first, the redeployment of labor engaged in farming from collectively owned land to the plots assigned to households. The second has been the outflow of labor from farming to industry and services. Though a majority of the rural labor force is still engaged in the cultivation of its own land plots, a substantial and rising percentage is employed in non-farming activities. Town and village enterprises (TVEs), including household units, employ 138.7 million, which constitutes 28.5 percent of the rural labor force (NBS, 2005b). Among these many are wage-employees. However, because of the long-standing definition of the term "rural economy," TVE employees, even those in sizeable establishments, are not recognized as wage-employees. Neither Social Insurance nor many of the labor laws apply to them. Both the growth in wage-employment in rural areas and rural out-migration, though massive, remain yet to be fully incorporated into the framework for the Chinese social security system.

### *Transition to a market economy*

Compared with that in Eastern Europe and the former Soviet Union, China's transition to a market economy has been benign. It has gone together with a rapid and sustained growth rate, and an unprecedented rise in living standards, and a dramatic fall in rural poverty. But, as with other transitional economies, China has also witnessed a sharp rise in income inequality, in particular between persons and between regions. Amongst the multifarious changes associated with the transition, the following have been of particular importance in the present context:

- a shift in the respective roles of the government and enterprises;
- a shift of urban employment away from the public sector (state and collective units);

- lay-offs and severance on a large scale and the appearance of urban unemployment and poverty as major issues.

At the outset of the transition, while economic decision-making such as that concerning output and prices was centralized in government departments, the provision of social services and collective goods and the operation of social security schemes were dispersed across a large number of work units. Broadly, the transition has reversed this pattern by decentralizing economic decision-making to enterprises and centralizing the financing and administration of social security schemes in government departments. Thus stated the process seems like a straightforward change of roles. But it was complicated by the fact that the government lacked the ready capacity to take on the welfare role of enterprises. In turn, enterprises, not having been created on the basis of financial viability or "naturally selected" for survival in a market economy, could not operate as independent financial units. Many of them could not survive without government assistance.

The interchange of roles was far from smooth or coordinated. Whereas the decentralization of economic decision-making began early with the start of the transition in 1979, the centralization of social security schemes followed, with a long lag of almost two decades, only in the second half of the 1990s. This extended hiatus was accompanied by a steady erosion of Labor Insurance that assumed crisis proportions in the mid-1990s, when default on the payment of pensions and the reimbursement of medical expenses became a common occurrence. The assumption by the government of its extended role in the running of Labor Insurance (renamed Social Insurance) and in the provision of education and health care was impeded by two factors: first, a sharp decline in the ratio of government revenue to GDP up to 1995 followed by an upturn to a level still well short of the share in 1978. The second was the precipitous fall in the profitability of the state sector, which not only reduced the tax base but also raised outlay on subsidies to enterprises (see Hussain and Zhuang 1998). The government has over time assumed an enlarged role in the provision of social services and in the running of social security schemes but it has also, in the process, shifted much of the cost to households. The percentage of the cost of publicly provided education and health care borne by households has gone up sharply over the reform period. Added to this, since the latter half of the 1990s, employees have had to contribute towards the cost of Social Insurance, which in the past they were not required to do.

Historically, the state and urban collective sector (hereafter "state-collective sector") has been the principal source of employment for the urban labor force. But beginning from the 1990s, not only was the sector unable to provide jobs to fresh entrants to the labor force, it also began shedding existing employees. As shown in Table 5.3, in the 10 years from 1994 to 2004, the state-collective sector saw its share of urban employment plunge from 78.7 percent to 28.7 percent. The sector also lost jobs on a massive scale. Job losses from urban collective enterprises began from 1992 and from state units in 1996. In just 10 years from 1994 to 2003, the combined sector lost 68.9 million jobs (37.4 percent of the 1994 total),

*Table 5.3* Distribution of urban employment by ownership units, 1994–2000

| | *1994* | *1995* | *1996* | *1997* | *1998* | *1999* | *2000* | *2001* | *2002* | *2003* | *2004* |
|---|---|---|---|---|---|---|---|---|---|---|---|
| Urban labor force, million | 184.1 | 190.9 | 198.2 | 202.1 | 206.8 | 210.1 | 212.7 | 239.4 | 247.8 | 256.4 | 264.8 |
| In the state sector | 112.1 | 112.6 | 112.4 | 110.4 | 90.6 | 85.7 | 81.0 | 76.4 | 71.6 | 68.8 | 67.1 |
| (Percentage of urban labor force) | 60.9% | 59.0% | 56.7% | 54.7% | 43.8% | 40.8% | 38.1% | 31.9% | 28.9% | 26.8% | 25.3% |
| In collective units | 32.9 | 31.5 | 30.2 | 28.8 | 19.6 | 17.1 | 15.0 | 12.9 | 11.2 | 10.0 | 9.0 |
| (Percentage of urban labor force) | 17.8% | 16.5% | 15.2% | 14.3% | 9.5% | 8.1% | 7.0% | 5.4% | 4.5% | 3.9% | 3.4% |
| Other | 39.1 | 46.9 | 55.6 | 62.8 | 96.6 | 107.3 | 116.7 | 150.1 | 165.0 | 177.6 | 188.7% |
| (Percentage of urban labor force) | 21.3% | 24.5% | 28.1% | 31.1% | 46.7% | 51.1% | 54.9% | 62.7% | 66.6% | 69.3% | 71.3% |

Source: NBS, *China Labor Statistical Yearbook*, various years

of which 45 million were from the state sector (enterprises, public institutions and the government).

The trend is expected to continue for some years. Offsetting the downward trend of employment in the public sector, the non-public sector (comprising foreign-invested, private and household enterprises) saw its employment share jump from 21 percent in 1994 to 71 percent in 2003 and its total labor force rise almost five-fold from 39 to 189 million. Such a shift of employment fits in with the transition from a planned to a market economy. But it raises important issues of unemployment and of income maintenance for the unemployed because of the differences that exist in the terms and conditions of employment and in social security coverage between the public and the non-public sectors.

In 2003, the state and urban collective sector, although employing 26.8 percent of the urban labor force (Table 5.3), accounted for 72.1 percent of employees categorized as "staff and workers" (*zhigongren*). Here it is interesting to note that the number of such employees has been steadily falling since 1995, in parallel with the downward trend for public sector employees. In the eight years from 1995 to 2003 their total number fell by 30 percent from 149 million to 105 million (NBS *Labor Statistical Yearbook*, various years). The category of "staff and workers" is relevant in the present context because such employees have formal labor contracts and are covered by Social Insurance. In contrast, other employees do not have formal labor contracts, have less secure jobs and a large percentage of them are outside the umbrella of Social Insurance. Thus the shift in the pattern of employment away from the state and urban collective sector represents a significant shift in the terms and conditions of employment, which goes together with more frequent job terminations and, more consequential for poverty alleviation, a reduction in the percentage of the unemployed who are entitled to unemployment benefits. The implication is that the shift in the pattern of employment away from the public sector, which is a central feature of the transition to a market economy, involves a substantial shift of risk to employees.

A by-product of labor retrenchment in the state and urban collective sector in the second half of the 1990s was the emergence of open unemployment and of urban poverty as a major problem. Previously, the urban poor were small in number and characterized by the so-called "three nos": no ability to work, no savings or other income source and no relatives to depend on. The "new urban poor" in the period since the 1990s have not only been more numerous but also, for the most part, able and willing to work but unable to find jobs. Unlike in the past, the government can now, for the most part, respond only by providing a subsistence allowance instead of a job. In addition to the emergence of open unemployment and labor lay-offs, the second half of the 1990s also saw the establishment of the Minimum Living Standard Assistance (MLSA), which provides a cash allowance to all bona fide urban residents with an income below the local poverty line.

## Overview of China's social security system

A social security system with its own administration, regular sources of finance and separated from the organization of economic activity is largely a development from the second half of the 1990s, one that is still under way. In the pre-1978 period income maintenance was woven into the fabric of economic organization. Those able to work were sooner or later provided with a job or assigned a task. This regime of "welfare through work" was complemented by a policy of keeping the prices of necessities low. The payment of an allowance in cash and kind was confined to a very small group unable to work. Notably absent from the social security system was an unemployment insurance scheme which has only been introduced more recently, as part of the economic reforms. In principle, employees of the state sector and larger collective enterprises, constituting most of the urban labor force, were covered by the comprehensive Labor Insurance, the precursor of the present-day Social Insurance. But the system, which was set up in the 1950s, was transformed into "work-unit" or occupational welfare during the period of the Cultural Revolution. Over the period, retirement was suspended; employees kept on working as long as physically capable. Thus the reform period started with a social security system that was partly out-of-operation and comprised a disparate collection of arrangements to cater for various contingencies.

The current system[9] consists of an assortment of schemes aimed at the following:

- poverty alleviation;
- income maintenance in the events of unemployment, occupational injury, sickness and retirement;
- subsidized, including free, medical care as and when needed.

These schemes divide into the familiar categories of "social insurance" and "social assistance (social safety net)."[10] Both categories include a variety of schemes and the distinction between them is based on two salient aspects: first, the conditions attached to the provision of benefit (entitlement qualification) and, second, the method of financing.

As is usual, social assistance is conditional on a means test, which in China can be stringent and intrusive and may discourage a substantial number of genuine cases from claiming assistance. Being non-contributory the social assistance schemes have to be financed from general government revenue, which, in the Chinese context, leads on to the vexed issue of the apportionment of expenditure responsibilities among various government tiers. The issue has risen in importance in recent years with the establishment of a number of new social assistance schemes and a huge growth in the number of their beneficiaries. Prominent examples include two schemes. One is the Minimum Living Standard Allowance (MLSA), which was set up at the end of 1997. The number of its beneficiaries rose from 1.8 million in 1998 to 22.1 million in 2004 (MOCA 2005). The other example is the new Rural Cooperative Medical Insurance Schemes (RCMIS), which began to be set up in 2003, are heavily subsidized and cover a rural population of over 100 million. The dramatic increase in the number of beneficiaries of these two schemes is due largely to the central government covering most of the cost of the schemes and thus circumventing the issue of the division of costs among government tiers.

The contributory schemes fall into two categories, first, Social Insurance and, second, the two rural schemes: the local pension schemes, which cover a rural population of 54 million (only 7 percent of the total) and provide no more than part-subsistence, and, with qualification, RCMIS. These two are still in the pilot stage and it is the first that constitutes the core of the contributory schemes. In design, China's Social Insurance system is very similar to those in welfare states and includes five separate schemes covering old-age pensions, injury compensation, health care, maternity benefits, and unemployment compensation. Participants are mostly urban residents in formal employment, so called *zhigongren*, though many localities now enrol migrant workers. The principal impediment to the enrolment of migrant workers is not rules and regulations which exclude them but the reluctance of migrant workers themselves to participate. An unusual feature of China's Social Insurance system is a wide variation in the number of participants in particular schemes. For example, the figures on participants in 2004 were 165 million in the old-age pension scheme, 106 million in the unemployment insurance scheme with 106 million and 90 million in the medical insurance scheme. The work injury compensation scheme had only 68 million participants (NBSb 2005). Even in the case of the old-age pension the number of participants came to 62 percent of the urban labor force. The participation rate of the urban labor force also varies across localities; it is high in Shanghai and other coastal provinces and low in the interior provinces. In law, participation in Social Insurance is mandatory for the whole urban labor force. In practice, the participation rate is high in the state sector and in large non-state units; and the rate is low in small units, mostly in the service sector. As outlined earlier, a particular impediment to the extension of Social Insurance is the steady shift of employment away from the state sector into small enterprises in the services.

Social Insurance provides a limited social security cover in that it not only excludes by design the non-participants in the labor market but also fails to extend to the whole urban labor force. The implication is that a social security system has to include both social insurance and social assistance schemes, if it is to cover a substantial section of the population, which is what the Chinese and other social security systems do. The transition towards a market economy has drastically curtailed the scope of "welfare through work" and the void that created has been largely filled by social assistance schemes. The trend looks likely to continue. Taken together the contributory and non-contributory schemes are characterized by two salient features, the ramifications of which run wide and deep through the system:

- segmentation and striking differences in provision across groups;
- highly decentralized financing and management.

### *Segmentation*

All social security schemes in China are earmarked either for the urban or the rural population; as yet, there is none that covers the whole population. Furthermore, "rural" and "urban" are defined with reference to the entry in the *hukou*, not the actual place of residence. As a result persons living and working in cities on a long-term basis may still be classified as "rural" and excluded from the schemes for the urban population. From the point of view of social security, the population is divided along two lines: first, rural and urban and, second, permanent residents and immigrants, a distinction which is mainly relevant in an urban setting. In the past, there also existed a deep division between the state sector employees and other employees, which has almost disappeared. The first two divisions are fading, but will still take some time to disappear completely.

The difference in the social security provision for the urban and for the rural population is glaring. In principle, though not always in practice, those with *bona fide* urban registrations benefit from a complementary combination of a comprehensive Social Insurance and the MLSA, which bridges any shortfall of household per capita income up to the local poverty line. As a result, the urban population enjoys a comparatively high level of social security by the standards of developing economies. In contrast, social security provision in rural areas is sparse. Apart from two limited contributory schemes, all rural schemes fall under the category of "social assistance," aimed at relieving severe poverty only. Social Insurance does not apply to the rural labor force, not even to wage-employees of TVEs, who number 139 million compared to 67 million employees in the state sector (NBS 2005b). Notwithstanding the rising ratio of the elderly in the population, there is as yet no clear policy towards the development and extension of rudimentary rural pension schemes.

An urban bias in social security provision is common in developing economies and not by any means unique to China. The bias is to a degree unavoidable, given serious problems in designing contributory social security (Social Insurance) schemes for the self- or the informally-employed. There are two professed rationales for the limited social protection cover in China's rural areas. One is that each rural household is assigned a plot of agricultural land that serves as a floor to household income, a feature that is particular to China and a few other economies. The other is the high cost of introducing a social security regime comparable to the one in urban areas relative to the limited capacity to collect taxes and social security contributions in rural areas. Both are valid justifications, but under strong qualifications. The protection provided by land plots is highly variable and has diminished over time because of the combination of the increase in the rural population and the diversion of land to non-farm uses. The latter has given rise to a substantial rural population without any land. As for the second, the rural–urban distinction is maintained even where it is possible to extend some schemes to the rural population. For example, 139 million employees of TVEs are by design excluded from Social Insurance, even when employed in large enterprises on terms similar to those in urban enterprises. The differential treatment of the urban and rural population is also based on the anachronistic assumption that the rural labor force is self-employed and engaged in farming.

### *Decentralization*

Both rural and urban social security systems are highly decentralized, the former more than the latter. In the case of the urban schemes, although Social Insurance and MLSA are based on regulations issued by the central government, many of the details of the schemes are left to the discretion of the provincial or municipal governments. More consequential, for both Social Insurance and MLSA, the budgetary units are 269 cities (excluding county-level cities and towns),[11] and generally cities are expected to cover from their own budgets any deficit on Social Insurance and the cost of MLSA in their respective jurisdictions. As is to be expected, the balance between contributions and expenditure varies across cities, depending on the number of pensioners relative to contributors and the unemployment rate, and so do their general finances. As a result, the operation and benefit levels can vary widely across cities even within the same province. Apart from a few very large ones, cities are too small a budgetary unit to provide sufficient risk pooling to ensure the sustainability of Social Insurance. The financial decentralization also has an adverse effect on the operation of MLSA, which has to be financed from the general revenue of the cities. In many cases, cities with a comparatively heavier burden of MLSA have more strained budgets because the factors that cause households to slip into poverty also act as a drag on city finances.

Decentralization in rural areas runs deeper than in urban areas. Apart from a few schemes run by the national or by provincial governments, most of the rural social security schemes are organized at the grass roots level of villages. Such schemes include assistance to poor households and the rural pensions and cooperative medical insurance schemes. The initiation, operation and financing of rural schemes largely rests with lower government tiers; the higher government tiers (provinces and the center) confine themselves to the supervision and setting-up of pilot schemes. Associated with this, variations in social security provision are much wider in rural than in urban areas.

There are *ad hoc* transfers from the central and provincial governments to lower tier governments so they can meet their social security obligations under Social Insurance and MLSA. But there is as yet no regular framework for fiscal transfers from higher to lower government tiers to cover expenditure responsibilities of the latter. An overhaul of the system of intergovernmental finances has been high on the reform agenda for a number of years but, as emphasized in several of the other chapters in this volume, it still remains to be realized. A pooling of Social Insurance contributions and expenditures at the provincial level is the policy aim. In most cases, this would be sufficient to put the urban social security system on a sound financial footing because many of China's provinces are as populous as sizeable countries. The upgrading of the level of budgeting from cities to provinces for Social Insurance can take a number of forms ranging from a full integration to compensatory transfers within a decentralized system. Each of these has implications for the administrative structure. The national pooling of social security contributions and expenditures does not seem to be feasible. It would also be inequitable in that, under the present financing arrangements, poorer provinces would be making transfers to richer provinces because the latter tend to have a higher ratio of pensioners to contributors than do the former.

## Trends of evolution

The most notable trend at present is the progressive erosion of the distinction between urban and rural, which has cast a long shadow on the Chinese social security system and on a wide range of other institutions and social phenomena. The driving forces behind the trend are three developments since the mid-1990s. One is the emergence of a large population of immigrants,[12] who find themselves in "no man's land," excluded from social security at their destination and also at their place of origin by virtue of their absence. Migrants already constitute a substantial percentage of the total population and are likely to grow in numbers. For example, the migrant population of 134 million reported by the census in 2000 came to almost 11 percent of the total population in that year. Migrants have existed in substantial number since the early 1990s. But recent years have seen a major change in government's attitude towards migrants and rural-to-urban migration. It has come to be widely accepted that rural-to-urban migration is irreversible and the absorption of migrants is the appropriate policy response. The indicators of change include the ongoing transformation of the *hukou* system and the phasing out of negative discrimination against school children from migrant families, such as denying them admission in the local schools or charging them a higher fee. Underlying the change of stance is also the recognition that a narrowing of the gap between rural and urban incomes, which is wider than ever before, requires the removal of impediments to migration and that in some cases migration is the most cost-effective way of lifting the rural population out of poverty.

The second driver is the flux in the *hukou* system. The predominant orientation of the change is towards the abolition of the division "agricultural/non-agricultural" or "urban/rural." A major landmark in the transformation of the *hukou* system was the document on the urbanization strategy issued by the Central Committee of the Party in September 2000. The document entitled migrants with a regular job and a fixed residence to obtain a change in *hukou.* The prescription is universally implemented, though details vary locally. Another radical change is the decision by 11 provinces to set up a unified *hukou* system that does away with the division between rural and urban altogether. As these are to be provincial systems, they will highlight the division of the population by provinces. These ongoing transformations of the *hukou* system on a piecemeal basis raise questions concerning, first, the likely final outcome and, second, the impact on the social security system. The likely outcome is the consolidation of disparate changes in a national framework that permits provinces and municipalities to decide on particular details. But as the new system will be operated by a sub-national government tier, the new *hukou* will throw into relief the particular province or the municipality that issues the registration document.

On its own, the elimination of the distinction between urban and rural is merely a matter of relabelling. There are now reports of numerous cases where it has been just that and has therefore made no difference to social security entitlments.[13] Actual steps to extend the coverage of existing urban schemes to the rural population have so far taken three forms. The first is to bring immigrants in cities within the ambit of the urban social security system. Following the example set by Guangdong and Shanghai, many cities extend Social Insurance to immigrant workers. The impediment here is in solving the question of how the participating workers, who are meant to be temporary residents, would actually receive the future benefits due to them, such as pension or unemployment compensation. The removal of the tag "agricultural" should help in lifting the impediment. The second is to extend Social Insurance to wage-employees in TVEs, especially large ones, which a number of cities have begun to do. The third, which is the most radical, is to extend the urban social security schemes to the rural population in the jurisdiction of the city or the province. Shanghai is already implementing a staged transition to an integrated system covering both the rural and urban inhabitants of the city. In the first stage, which is already introduced, the rural inhabitants of the city are offered a social insurance package that covers the same contingencies as does the scheme for urban inhabitants but with a reduced contribution rate in return for reduced benefits.

The third development eroding the distinction between rural and urban inhabitants is the appearance of a sizeable population of landless rural households, which is an anomaly in the context of the Chinese social security system. Classified as "agricultural," they are excluded from the social security cover for the "urban" households on the grounds of having a plot of land, which they no longer have. Until the late 1990s such households were small in numbers and most of them had given up land voluntarily. In recent years they have grown rapidly in numbers due mostly to the requisition of land for "development zones," in return for a derisory compensation. The households are paid a fraction of the value of their plots as agricultural land, which is usually a small percentage of their value in non-farming use. In 2003 the total area of the development zones exceeded the total area used for new municipal construction. A rough estimate is that there are 40 million such households, which comes to 16 percent of the total number of rural households in 2004. Regarding them as a potential source of social instability, the government has extended the MLSA for the "non-agricultural" households to rural households with no or insufficient land. This constitutes a major breach of the separation of social security schemes for the rural and urban populations. Extrapolated over time such extensions of the urban schemes will not mean an end of the distinction between "rural and urban" per se, but rather a progressive shrinkage of the category "rural."

## Notes

1 This refers to the period since the end of 1978.
2 The official figures are calibrated with reference to the official poverty line, which is regarded as too low by external observers. Using a higher poverty line changes the headcount of the poor but does not affect the downward trend.
3 The rural as a percentage of the urban per capita income rose from 39 percent in 1978 to 54 percent in 1985 and thereafter began to fall, reaching an all-time low of 31 percent in 2004 (NBS 2005a: Table 10.2)
4 For an account of the *hukou* system see *Beijing Review* (2004) 47 (1) and *Beijing Review* (2005) 48 (49).
5 In Chinese statistics a migrant is defined as a person living for six months or more in a locality different from the registered place of residence.
6 The first population census, undertaken in conformity with best international practice, was carried out in 1982.
7 The categories "low-income" and "middle-income" refer to the World Bank classification of countries in terms of GDP per person.
8 See *Beijing Review* (2004) 47 (1) 1 Jan: 32–3 and *Beijing Review* (2005) 48 (19) 8 Dec: 22–5.
9 For an outline of the current system see the white paper issued by the State Council "China's Social Security and Its Policy," Sept 2004, available online at <http://peopledaily.com.cn>
10 For an account see the "White Paper on Social Security," Ministry of Labor and Social Security, Sept 1994.
11 Chinese cities divide into a five-level hierarchy: provincial, sub-provincial, prefecture- and county-level. All included there are 662 cities and towns. The above figure of 269 excludes 393 county-level cities.
12 Classified with reference to origin and destination (whether rural or urban), migrants divide into four categories, but a vast majority fall in the category rural-to-urban.
13 See *Beijing Review* (2005) 48 (19) 8 Dec: 22–5.

## References

Atkinson, Anthony B. (1991) "Social Insurance," *Welfare State Programme Discussion Papers*, 65, London School of Economics.

*Beijing Review* available online at <http://www.bjreview.com.cn>

Easterlin Richard A. (1998) *Growth Triumphant*, Ann Arbor: Michigan University Press

Feeney, G. (1996) "Fertility in China: Past, Present, Prospects," in W. Lutz (ed.) *The Future Population of the World – What Can We Assume Today?*, London: Earthscan Publications for International Institute for Applied Systems Analysis.

Hussain, A. and Zhuang, J. (1998) "Enterprise Taxation and Transition to a Market Economy", in D. S. Brean (ed.) *Taxation in Modern China*, New York and London: Routledge.

Kingson, E. R. and Schulz, J. H. (1997) *Social Security in the 21st Century*, Oxford: Oxford University Press.

Leete, R. and Alam, I. (eds.) (1993) *The Revolution in Asian Fertility – Dimensions, Cause and Implications*, Oxford: Oxford University Press.

Ministry of Civil Affairs (2005) *China Civil Affairs Yearbook 2005*, Beijing: China Statistics Press.

NBS (State Statistical Bureau) (1982) *The 1982 Population Census of China (Results of Computer Tabulation*, Beijing.

NBS (State Statistical Bureau) (1999) *Comprehensive Statistical Data and Materials on 50 Years of New China*, Beijing.
NBS (State Statistical Bureau) (2002) *China Population Yearbook 2002*, Beijing.
NBS (State Statistical Bureau) (2005a) *Statistical Yearbook of China 2005*, Beijing.
NBS (State Statistical Bureau) (2005b) *China Labor Statistical Yearbook 2005*, Beijing.
NBS (State Statistical Bureau) (2005c) *China Population Yearbook 2005*, Beijing.
Stern, N. (1996) *Growth Theories, Old and New and the Role of Agriculture in Economic Development*, FAO Economic and Social Development Paper 136, Rome: FAO, 10.

# 6 Investing in rural China

## Tracking China's commitment to modernization[1]

*Zhang Linxiu, Luo Renfu, Liu Chengfang and Scott Rozelle*

Two decades of economic reform have changed the economic landscape of China. During the 1980s and 1990s, per capita grain output reached a level similar to that in developed countries (FAO 2002). Agricultural productivity has risen steadily for two decades (Jin et al. 2002). Many farmers have shifted into higher valued agricultural enterprises, making decisions increasingly on market-oriented principles (Huang et al. 2006). Off the farm, more than 40 percent of rural residents have employment; about 100 million of them – most of them young and eager to make new lives in the city – have left home and moved to urban areas for employment (de Brauw et al. 2002). Rural incomes have risen significantly and hundreds of millions of people have escaped poverty during this time (World Bank 2001). Indeed, economists looking at China from a comparative perspective praise China's reforms as the "biggest antipoverty program the world has ever seen" (McMillan 1997: 210) and have claimed that the reform policies have led to "the greatest increase in economic well-being within a 15-year period in all of history" (Newsweek 2005).

While the recent success of China's poverty alleviation efforts is indisputable, there are still great challenges ahead. More than 100 million farmers and their families still live below the poverty line (World Bank 2005).[2]

Inequality within the rural economy rose during the early reforms and has remained high since the mid-1990s (see Chapter 2 by Riskin in this volume). Despite nearly continuous growth, the gap between urban and rural incomes has not narrowed (Fleisher and Yang 2003). Visitors to most parts of rural China find that, while life has improved immeasurably in recent years, the landscape is still one of a poor, developing country. Understanding the importance of keeping the rural economy strong and reducing the glaring differences between the rural and urban economies, national leaders during the recent sixteenth National Congress of the Communist Party of China (CPC) reiterated several times that one of the main goals of the coming decade was to integrate the rural and urban economies, ensure a more balanced pattern of growth between city and countryside, shift massive amounts of labor out of agriculture and generally to seek a modern, urban-based society.

To achieve such lofty goals, not only do leaders need to continue to push reform policies, but the experience of other nations demonstrates that massive investments

– from both fiscal and financial sources – are needed to facilitate the modernization of China's rural sector. In countries that have gone through this development transition in the past, Timmer (1998) has described a process by which modern nations at a certain point in their development path make a fundamental shift in priorities and begin to increase investment into the rural sector. While recent work has quantified the nature of the capital flows between the agricultural and non-agricultural sectors and between the rural and non-rural sectors, there is almost no understanding of the channels through which these investments flow, how the decisions are made at the micro-level to invest or not, how much support is provided by upper-level government and how much by the village itself, or of how to explain the great heterogeneity that we observe in rural China.

In this chapter we will seek to better understand how investments – both those from above and those made by villagers themselves – have contributed to the process of rural development and poverty alleviation in China. In particular, we will use a new, nationally representative data set from nearly 2,500 villages to describe the contours of investment in rural China. We will also present profiles of investments in rich and poor areas, and examine the nature of the heterogeneity in investment. Finally, we will attempt to explain why some villages have received and made heavy investments while others have not.

In this analysis, we will focus on the village and its role as the entity to which public goods are being provided. While it is possible to have centered our attention on other levels of administration – for example, towns or counties – we chose the village because of its immediacy to the livelihoods of China's rural population. By far the great majority of China's rural residents live and work within the confines of the village community. Traditionally village leadership councils, while they are not formally part of the government hierarchy, have acted as quasi-government entities and have taken on responsibility for the provision of public goods. We understand that by focusing on villages we miss a certain amount of public investment that provides services to rural residents that are not within the boundaries of village communities (e.g. schools in townships; interprovinical roads, etc.). Our field work however has taught us that, for many public goods, farmers are most aware and take most frequent advantage of those that are provided within their villages.

## Data

At the heart of our analysis is our data set. We use a unique set of data on the institutions and public goods investments in rural villages in China. The data were collected in 2003 from six provinces and 36 counties in a nearly nationally representative sample. The sample provinces were each randomly selected from each of China's major agro-ecological zones and the counties were randomly selected from within the provinces.[3] After counties were selected, a sample of six townships was chosen from each of the 36 counties. A total of 216 townships were chosen. Within each of the 216 townships (six provinces × six counties × six townships) visited by our enumerator teams, officials asked each village to send two representatives (typically the village head and accountant) to a meeting in the township. On average, enumerators surveyed around 11 villages in each township. The number of villages per township ranged from two to 29.[4] In short, we surveyed the village leaders from each of the villages in a sample of 216 randomly drawn towns and 36 randomly drawn counties in six representative provinces. To our knowledge, this is the only nationally representative data set on investments in public goods at the village level that exists in rural China.

A unique feature of the data set is that it is based on information provided by representatives of the villages. Most other studies have used data from more aggregated sources, such as data at the county or provincial level (e.g. Huang et al. 2006; Fan et al. 2002). Relying on village leader input, however, is important for two reasons. First, historically villages in China have taken responsibility for raising money and in-kind labor from their villagers and other assets (e.g. village-run enterprises and/or land sales) in order to invest in the village. Second, even when funds for investments in villages are provided from above level governments, they almost always are run through projects that are implemented, managed or monitored by village leaders. Hence, to an extent not possible with information from either upper-level government officials (who only know at most part of the flow) or farmers (who often do not have access to information on investment activities (either from above or by the village itself), village leaders are in a unique position to provide a comprehensive portrait of investment at the village level.

After answering questions about the economic, political and demographic conditions of their villages in 1997 and 2003, the respondents answered a set of questions about the investment activities in and around their villages between the years 1998 and 2003. The questionnaire was designed to elicit information about the size of each investment, its primary objective, sources of funding and the level of participation in terms of investment and labor contribution of the village. The survey instrument collected information on both the *number of investment projects* in the village between 1998 and 2003 and the total *level of investment*. The information was collected for 17 different types of *public goods projects* and 10 different types of *development projects*. A public goods project is an investment activity in which the benefit of the investment is enjoyed by all or most of the residents in the village and where it is difficult to exclude individuals from access to the services of the project (see Table 6.1 for a list of public goods projects). A road or an irrigation project is an example of a public good investment. Development projects were defined as projects with the major objective of promoting an economic enterprise that is normally run by a household as a primary income generating activity. Unlike public goods, individuals in the village can be excluded from enjoying the benefits of development projects. For example, development projects include investments in orchards, cash crop enterprises and livestock raising activities. In this chapter we focus on public goods projects.

*Table 6.1* Number and size of public goods projects (regional population weighted), 1998–2003

| *Project* | *Number of projects* | *Average size (1000 yuan)* | *Accumulated distribution of projects* |
|---|---|---|---|
| Roads and bridges | 1266 | 112 | 21.2 |
| Grain for Green | 892 | 67 | 36.1 |
| School construction | 850 | 99 | 50.3 |
| Irrigation and drainage | 819 | 65 | 64.1 |
| Drinking water | 636 | 75 | 74.7 |
| Loudspeaker for village committee | 379 | 60 | 81.0 |
| Recreation center | 262 | 50 | 85.4 |
| Build clinic | 163 | 25 | 88.2 |
| Beautify environment | 157 | 24 | 90.8 |
| Watershed management | 151 | 298 | 93.3 |
| Forest closure | 140 | 34 | 95.6 |
| Land leveling | 124 | 136 | 97.7 |
| Eco-forest | 55 | 34 | 98.6 |
| Land improvement | 52 | 110 | 99.5 |
| Build pasture | 19 | 134 | 99.8 |
| Other public project | 10 | 244 | 100.0 |
| N/mean | 5,975 | 108 | – |

Source: Authors' survey

## Tracking investment in rural China

Despite the suggestion by some that China's rural areas are being neglected, our survey shows a surprising level of investment activity in rural China. During the five years of our study, enumerators recorded that there were 9,138 investment projects in the 2,459 sample villages. On average this means that during the five-year sample period, each village had 3.75 projects, nearly one per year. More than 85 percent of villages in the sample had more than one investment project between 1998 and 2003. While it is hard to say if this level of investment is high enough to facilitate China's modernization, compared to some other developing countries, it appears that China in recent years is generating a relatively high degree of investment. For example, in a study by Khwaja (2002) that canvassed several hundred villages in Northern Pakistan enumerators found only 99 villages that had at least one public goods or development project during the previous decade. Only 33 villages had more than one project. A recent national representative sample of villages in Mexico found, on average, that there was only approximately one public good or development investment project that had been implemented in a typical village during the past 10 years. At least compared to other developing nations, China's villages appear to be receiving substantial investments.

In addition, China's investment targets are increasingly focusing on investment in public goods. In the 1980s local leaders put a lot of effort into managing village-run development projects (Rozelle 1990). For example, during the 1980s and

1990s leaders themselves often took an active role in starting and running local enterprises instead of maintaining a more traditional regulatory role. In some parts of China the vast tracts of fast-growing forests, citrus and apple orchards and large-scale livestock projects testify to the efforts of entrepreneurial village and township leaders who were trying to diversify the economic bases of their communities (Rozelle 1990). After 1998, however, our data show that leaders focused most of their effort on public goods-oriented investment projects (87 percent).[5] In value terms, 77 percent of rural investment was spent on public goods.

Although most new investment projects since 1997 were public goods in nature, leaders invested in a wide variety of different types of infrastructure projects. Specifically, of the 5,975 public goods projects, there were at least 20 sample villages that invested in 15 different types of public goods investment projects (Table 6.1, Column 1).[6] The average size of each type of project was fairly small – 108,000 yuan (Table 6.1, Column 2) – although these vary from project to project (from a high for watershed management projects – 298,000 yuan – to projects such as clinics and village beautification that were only around 25,000 yuan).

Some types of investment projects, however, were much more popular than others; a large majority of all types of public goods investment were made in one of five categories of projects (Table 6.1, Columns 1 and 3). For example, over half of the villages (1,266) invested in roads or bridges. Roads and bridges accounted for 21.2 percent of all of public goods projects. Between 800 and 900 villages invested in Grain for Green, school construction or irrigation and drainage projects.[7] More than 600 villages invested in drinking water projects.[8] In total, three quarters of all projects (74.7 percent) were accounted for by investment into these five investment activities.

The top five projects – roads and bridges, Grain for Green, irrigation, school construction and drinking water – also commanded a large share of total investment. Of all investment in value terms, leaders invested 81 percent of their funds in the top five projects. In fact, of all the investments made in China's villages, according to our data, 22 percent of investments are in roads and bridges.

## Sources of funding

While investment activity in China's villages has been fairly robust and varied, the extent of decentralization and the sources of investment need to be tracked before one can assess the commitment of the central leadership to the rural economy. Many government functions in China are decentralized (Wong 1997). In many cases, the degree of decentralization is more than in any other country of the world. For example, while in most countries the national government takes responsibility for most agricultural research and development and rural educational programs, in China provincial and sub-provincial governments bear most responsibility for investment into agricultural technology and agricultural extension.

Despite the decentralized nature of China's economy, the national and provincial governments have funded significant amounts of investment into rural areas

(Table 6.2, Column 4). For example, in 2003 the central government spent about 12 billion yuan on roads and bridges in rural areas. This is part of a national effort that was announced in 2000 which set a goal of improving China's rural road network (Ministry of Communications 2000). In the same year, 26 billion yuan was spent on irrigation and drainage projects and more was spent on drinking water (although the precise figure is difficult to know, given the absence of statistics). While a large fraction was devoted to salaries, in 2003 the central government spent more than 82 billion yuan on rural education. Although statistics also are difficult to find, it is estimated that upper-level officials and local leaders invested 7.2 billion yuan annually into the construction of schools. Although expenditure on Grain for Green was low in 2000, the first year of the program, by 2003 the government had spent 5.3 billion yuan. Clearly, at least according to national statistical sources, there are large volumes of funding being directed to rural public goods.

However, because of China's decentralized fiscal system, local governments and communities are expected to take responsibilities for the provision of local public goods, including investment in the infrastructure that is needed to provide access to or improve access to the public good. This is confirmed in our data, which show that China's villages also contribute a large share of the funding for public goods investment to their villages (Table 6.3, Columns 1 to 4). For example, after dividing projects into three types – those fully invested from above (henceforth, *subsidized investments*); those fully invested by the village (*own investments*) and those that are jointly funded (*joint investments*) – our data show

*Table 6.2* Total annual investment in rural China's infrastructure at village level, 2003 (billion yuan)

| *Project type* | *Our sample survey data*[a] | | | | | |
|---|---|---|---|---|---|---|
| | *Total investment at village level* | *Subsidized investment* | *Own investments* | *Budgeted investment*[b] | *Percent of budgeted investment spent at village level*[c] | *Total investment (Columns 3 plus 4)* |
| Column | 1 | 2 | 3 | 4 | 5 | 6 |
| Roads and bridges | 11.01 | 5.19 | 5.83 | 12 | 43 | 17.83 |
| Irrigation | 4.67 | 1.77 | 2.90 | 26 | 7 | 28.90 |
| Grain for Green | 4.66 | 3.85 | 0.81 | 5.3 | 72 | 6.11 |
| Schools | 7.19 | 3.51 | 3.68 | 82 | 4 | 85.68 |
| Drinking water | 3.70 | 1.90 | 1.80 | na | na | na |
| Others | 7.60 | 4.25 | 3.35 | na | na | na |

Notes:

a Data from columns 1, 2 and 3 are from authors' survey and using its representative nature are scaled up to the national level;

b Data from column 4 are from secondary sources and are tabulating budgeted investment from above (Huang et al. 2005; Fan et al. 2002; Xu and Cao 2002);

c Column 5 is calculated as the ratio of Columns 2 and 4.

*Table 6.3* Funding source of public goods projects by province, 1998–2003

| *Province* | *Total number of projects* | *Wholly subsidized-funded projects* | *Wholly own-funded projects* | *Jointly funded projects* | *Subsidized investment* | *Own investment* |
|---|---|---|---|---|---|---|
| | (*Number of projects*) | | | | (*Percentage*) | |
| Jiangsu | 1,646 | 436 | 392 | 818 | 26.0 | 74.0 |
| Gansu | 1,085 | 481 | 67 | 537 | 76.9 | 23.1 |
| Sichuan | 1,037 | 567 | 92 | 378 | 64.3 | 35.7 |
| Shaanxi | 1,352 | 525 | 142 | 685 | 72.2 | 27.8 |
| Jilin | 1,130 | 420 | 135 | 575 | 44.7 | 55.3 |
| Hebei | 1,473 | 318 | 557 | 598 | 50.4 | 49.6 |
| Whole sample | | | | | | |
| Number of projects | 7,723 | 2,747 | 1,385 | 3591 | — | — |
| | (*Percentage*) | | | | | |
| Percentage of total | 100 | 36 | 18 | 46 | 53 | 47 |

Note: Subsidized investment is the amount of investment from higher-level governments; own investment refers to funds invested by the village itself

Source: Authors' survey

that villages fund 18 percent of all public goods projects as own investments (Table 6.3, Row 8). And, while 36 percent of projects are from subsidized investments, nearly half (46 percent) are joint investment projects. In rural areas in other countries, such as Indonesia and Malaysia, local governments contribute little if any to public goods investment.

Examining the total contribution from villagers in value terms, in fact, the role of the village is even higher (Table 6.3, Columns 5 and 6). While 53 percent of the monetary value of total investment is from subsidized investment, villagers in China are funding 47 percent of their public goods investment with their own investments (Table 6.3, Row 8). In addition, China's villages also help by investing in-kind labor. In 56 percent of projects, villagers contributed labor. On average, for each project towards which villagers invested their labor, villagers contributed 1,121 days of labor (on average about five days per household). Hence, if the time that villagers work is monetized and is counted towards the overall contribution, the local share of public goods investment is far greater than 50 percent.

Counting investment in public goods from both sources – both from above and from villagers – the nature of our sample allows us to estimate the total volume of investment funds that are channelled into China's villages each year for public goods investments and to demonstrate that a substantial amount of investment is now going into China's villages. For example, according to our data, during the five-year study period, China invested 11 billion yuan per year into the construction of roads (Table 6.2, Column 1). The simultaneous appearance of investment at the local levels and nation-wide infrastructure improvement programs demonstrate that at least to some extent the central government's investments do make their way down to rural communities and help supplement the village's own efforts. While such large levels of investments are impressive, especially when compared to other developing countries, it is important to note that because of the nature of our data, we still only count the part of total investment that is spent at the village level. Our figures do not count the part of the total of investment funds budgeted by upper level officials (henceforth, budgeted investment funds) that is spent on projects or project components outside of China's villages. Likewise, budgeted investment data from yearbooks and other information sources do not typically include spending by villages on public goods. Village spending is counted as self-raised and therefore is almost never counted.[9] Hence, in the same way that our data do not include all of budgeted investment figures, budgeted investment figures do not capture all of the investment going into China's villages. Hence, when we add budgeted investment to the investments from villagers, overall investments rose further (Table 6.2, Columns 3, 4 and 6).

Our data also let us examine in part how rural public goods investment funds are managed and what fraction of budgeted investments is spent in China's village. When we compare the part of village level investment coming from above with budgeted investments, we find that only a relatively small share of total budgeted investment is ultimately spent in China's villages. For example, according to national data sources, about 12 billion yuan per year has been expended by upper level governments on roads (Table 6.2, Column 4). According to our data, however, only 5.2 billion yuan of the 12 billion, or 43 percent of total budgeted investment funds, that are spent in the village is from above (Table 6.2, Row 1, Columns 2, 4 and 5). In fact, the proportion of budgeted investment that is spent at the village level varies greatly. In the case of Grain for Green, 72 percent of the funds allocated from above make it to the village level. In the case of irrigation projects, only 7 percent is spent at the village level. While it is beyond the scope of our chapter to analyze the reasons for these differences, certainly, it is a combination of technology (e.g. a large fraction of irrigation money goes to maintain the large irrigation infrastructure that is needed to deliver water from its source to the village), the nature of the data (in the case of roads, we are comparing funds spent at the village to the total budgeted for rural roads; funds invested in inter-provincial roads and urban roads are not included), and any diversion of investment funds that occurs for administration and/or other less transparent reasons.

## Changing investment strategy and pace of investment

Our data also suggest that China's commitment to investment in rural public goods is not static. During our survey, in response to our inquiries about the objective of investments in the past (that is, before the study period in the 1980s and early 1990s), village leaders told us that most projects would only be implemented if they had a close connection to village incomes or would increase employment opportunities for villagers. For the study period, we asked a series of more formal questions about the motivation for investments. Specifically, enumerators asked village leader respondents about the *primary* goal of each investment that their village made. They were asked to choose among several pre-coded answers: increase income of villagers; improve the standard of living (apart from any direct rise in rural incomes); raise village fiscal revenue; employment generation; improve the environment; or some other unspecified reasons. While a large share of respondents (34 percent) still said that the primary reason for a project was to increase farmer income, many did not. In fact, the most frequent response about the motivation of public goods investment (41 percent) was to improve the quality of the standard of living in the village. Moreover, a significant proportion (16 percent) stated that projects were primarily being implemented in order to improve the environment. Only an insignificant share stated the projects were to generate employment or increase village revenues. If our data are accurate, these responses indicate that there has truly been a shift in the quality of the projects being implemented.

In addition to the change in the *quality* of China's investment projects, our data also show a modest increase in the *quantity* of investment funds flowing into China's villages. According to our data, during the first part of our study period (before 2001), on average, China implemented 0.46 projects per year (survey weighted). In other words, during this time, there was less than one project implemented in each two villages during each year. There was no province in which upper-level officials and village leaders reached an investment rate that exceeded one project per year. In fact, most of the provinces in our sample did not achieve a project implementation rate greater than 0.5 project per year.

The rate of project implementation rose, however, during the latter period of our study. After 2001, according to our data, on average each village in China was implementing 0.57 project per year (survey weighted). Officials and leaders in Shaanxi and Jilin implemented almost one project per year. Although not shown, if we include improvements to the electrical web and telephone network, the number of investment projects per village almost reaches an average of one for each year. Investments calculated in value terms give us similar results.

Hence, when examining descriptive statistics, we see a profile of a rural economy that is in the midst of an emergence of investment activity. As required for the fundamental transformation of its villages, according to our data, it does appear as if China's rural areas are getting greater amounts of investment than before. The amount of investment appears to be larger than that in many other developing nations. Moreover, most of the investment appears to be going into public goods.

Despite the progress, however, it is important to note that comparisons (that are at best rough) with other East Asian nations during their take-off periods show that China is still far short of the level of investments in rural areas that supported the transformation of their economies (CCICED 2004). While China currently is only investing between 40 to 50 US dollars per capita into rural areas, Japan during the

1950s and 1960s was spending about 400 US dollars per capita. South Korea was spending more than 200 US dollars per capita during the 1970s and 1980s, its take off period. Hence, the bottom line is that while it appears as if China is moving in the right direction, it also seems clear that the current level of public goods investment is still not sufficient to push the nation decisively toward rural modernization.

One unique characteristic of China's investment pattern is the important role being played by villages in financing public goods investment. This feature is almost absent in other developing countries today where the central government is the driving force behind most public goods investment. Perhaps it is because of the active role played by villages that China is outperforming other developing nations in recent years. However, it is possible that over-reliance on local sources of investment may lead to inequitable levels of public goods provision across China's communities, since it is presumed that the poor will be less able to afford to invest. A local government-dominated system of public goods investment may also not yield the best mix of investments since many public goods investments (e.g. schools) tend to provide great benefits outside the community (e.g. when children are educated they frequently leave for urban centers, taking their skills with them). It is possible that when much of the benefit of public goods investments can be seen to accrue to the economy outside the locality, local officials and village leaders may have significantly less incentive to invest. Pointedly, although Japan and South Korea both had considerable participation by local governments during their take-off periods, most funding came from the national government.

## Explaining inter-village differences in public goods investments

While the profile of investment for rural China in general is positive, there are still a number of unanswered questions, many of which include questions about the distribution of investments. Are the poor benefiting? How have ethnic minority groups fared? In such a decentralized system, who is paying for the investments and are the investments being put into the areas that demand investments? Who is receiving subsidized investments and what are the factors that determine the allocations of public goods investment funding?

In this section the primary purpose is to answer some of these questions and to help identify the determinants of investments in public goods. To do so, we proceed in two steps. First, we need to examine the degree of heterogeneity of public goods investments. Second, we need to identify the factors that lead to high investments in some villages and low ones in others. We do so with both descriptive statistics and multivariate analysis.

The importance of determinants analysis is underscored when examining the distribution of China's investments. While our data show that the number of investment projects in China is fairly substantial and rising over time, it also can be demonstrated that the number of investments varies significantly among our sample villages (Figure 6.1). For example, although the mean of the distribution

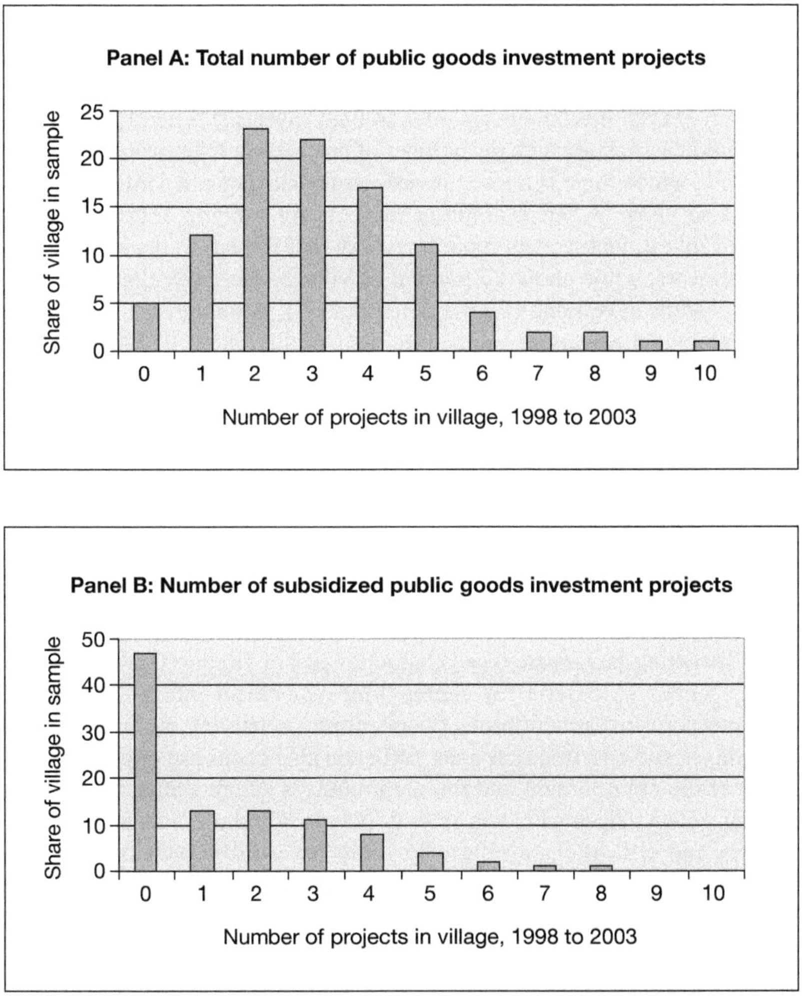


*Figure 6.1* Distribution of public goods projects, total number of investment projects and number of subsidized investment projects in rural China, 1998 to 2003 (authors' survey)

is 3.7 (that is, on average, each village implemented nearly four projects during the sample period, 1998 to 2003), there are some villages that have implemented many more projects than others. Nearly 20 percent of villages have run five or more projects during the five-year study period; several have had up to 10 (Figure 6.1, Panel A). At the same time, however, a significant share of villages had only one project (12 percent of villages) or none at all (5 percent of villages) during the entire period.

In addition, there is also substantial heterogeneity in the size of projects and the amount of investment in each village. On average, each public goods project required about 50,000 yuan. However, some projects are very large (up to 500,000 yuan or more). In contrast, a substantial share of projects came in under 20,000 yuan. When we examined the correlation between the number of projects and the size of projects, it was found to be insignificant from zero. This means that the distribution of total investment (in total amount invested) is nearly as skewed as the distribution associated with the number of projects. In other words, there are some villages in which there is a lot of investment occurring and some with little.

Our data also show, when examining projects by funding source, that the distribution of investment is even more unevenly distributed. In the case of subsidized investments, while about 20 percent of villages have three or more such projects, 48 percent have none (Figure 6.1, Panel B). Although not shown, the distribution of own investment projects is also highly skewed. For example, around 25 percent of villages have implemented at least two projects without any assistance from above. However, nearly two thirds of our sample villages have never done so.

### *Determinants of public goods investment*

In a system in which there are two main sources of funding (those from subsidized investments and own investments), there are two major types of factors – targeting factors and demand-side factors – that could affect the intensity of public goods investment. Targeting factors are those characteristics of villages that are used by upper-level officials as criteria for channelling investment into a village. For example, a pro-poor investment project concentrates relatively more investment into poor villages and less into rich ones. Officials also could use criteria such as the fragility of the environment and the community's ethnic status. It could be, however, that poor villages have less growth potential and officials are trying to target growth and will allocate relatively more investment towards non-poor villages. Demand-side factors can be thought of as characteristics of the village that would make villagers more or less inclined to invest in their village's public goods or to take the time and put out the effort to lobby upper-level officials for public goods investment. In this part of the chapter, we are interested in understanding which targeting and which demand-side factors are guiding the allocation of investment funding.

One of the most surprising targeting factors that is correlated with the intensity of public goods investment in our descriptive statistics is the community's income level, although the relationship differs when using different definitions of income and examining different dimensions of the relationship.[10] In fact, when examining the relationship between per capita income and the number of public goods projects during the entire sample period, there is little pattern to the data (Figure 6.2, Panel A). As villages move from the lowest quintile when ranked in terms of

*Figure 6.2* (opposite) Relationship between number of public goods projects and per capita income, richer (Jiangsu province) and poorer (Shaanxi province) areas, 1998–2003.

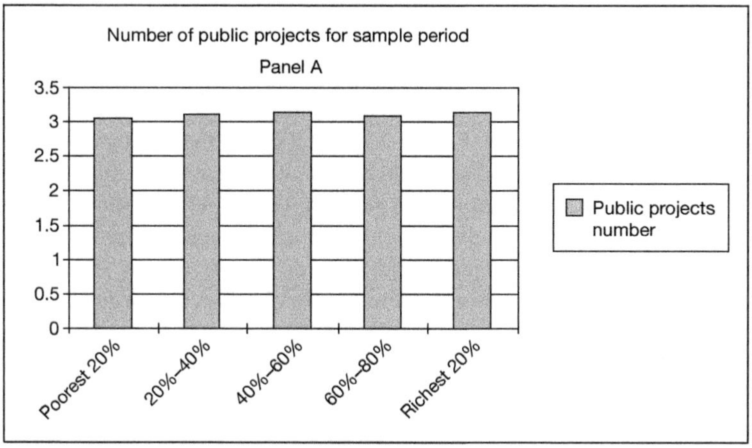

Number of public projects for sample period
Panel A
3.5
3
2.5
2
1.5
1
0.5
0
Poorest 20%
20%–40%
40%–60%
60%–80%
Richest 20%
Public projects number


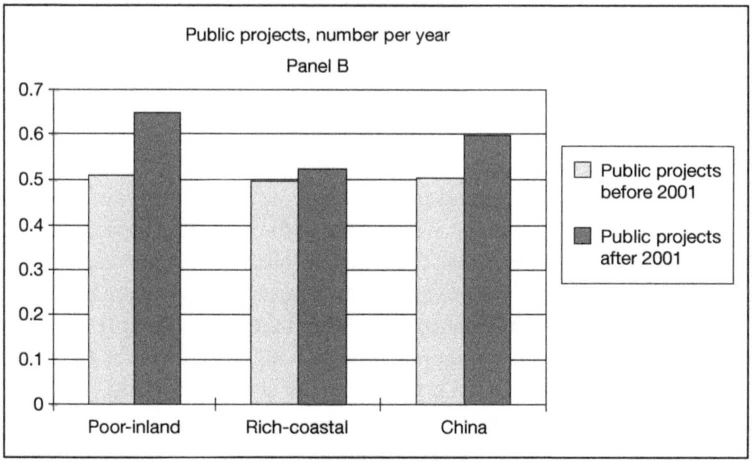

Public projects, number per year
Panel B
0.7
0.6
0.5
0.4
0.3
0.2
0.1
0
Poor-inland
Rich-coastal
China
Public projects before 2001
Public projects after 2001


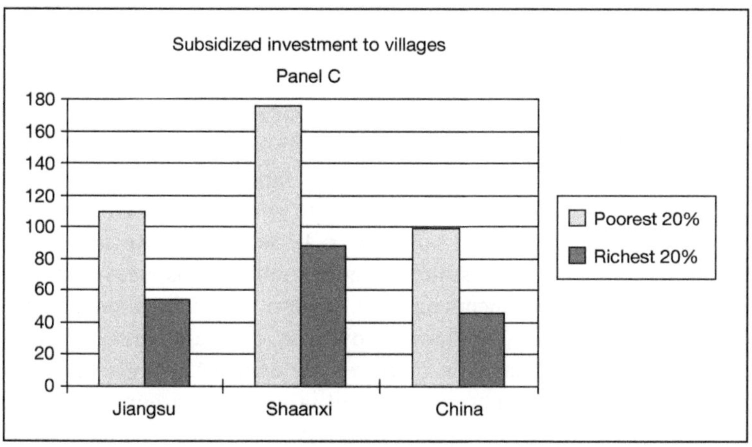

Subsidized investment to villages
Panel C
180
160
140
120
100
80
60
40
20
0
Jiangsu
Shaanxi
China
Poorest 20%
Richest 20%

per capita income to the highest quintile, the number of projects ranges between 3.0 and 3.2; there is little apparent relationship.

In contrast, when comparing the number of public goods investments over time between rich and poor villages, we see a positive shift in the government's commitment towards poor areas (Figure 6.2, Panel B). In the first part of our study period, not only, as noted in the discussion above, was the average investment low, but there was slightly more investment in richer areas (about 0.46 project per year) than in poor areas (0.43 project per year). In the second part of our study period, however, China's investment patterns became more progressive. In that period, officials and leaders in poor areas were implementing 0.6 project per year. Although public goods investment also rose in richer areas, the rate of rise was low enough that the annual rate of investment was lower (only 0.55).

Our data also identify the emergence of China's progressive investment strategy when looking at the level of subsidized investment for different groups of villages when we rank them on a per capita income basis (Figure 6.2, Panel C). On average, subsidized investment into China's poorest villages is almost twice as great as the richest villages. The same pattern appears in Jiangsu, the richest province in our sample, and Shaanxi, a poor western province. Indeed, our descriptive data show that on a number of dimensions China's investment behavior is favoring the poor, especially when considering subsidized investment.

A number of other correlations using our descriptive statistics to compare public goods investment and targeting and demand-side determinants can be identified in an array of cross tabulations that we created with our data (Appendix 6.1). For example our descriptive data show that, unlike the case of per capita income, there is little overt effort by the government to target minority areas (Appendix 6.1, Section 1). There are no evident trends, either in the number or level of investments, as the data range from villages with no or negligible shares of minorities to those with substantial shares. While this result is disappointing for those that were hoping that more investment would be channelled to minority communities, it should be remembered that the cross tabulations are using all investments, both subsidized and own investments. It could be that upper-level officials are allocating more to minorities, but this is being obscured in the descriptive statistics by the fact that minority villages are poorer and have fewer of their own resources to invest.

The descriptive data do show, however, that officials appear to be targeting investments according to several criteria, some of which appear to be progressive in nature and others that could be interpreted as being regressive. For example, somewhat more projects and significantly more investment are being put into areas that are more mountainous (Appendix 6.1, Section 2). Most likely driven by recent efforts to increase investment in poor mountainous areas with projects such as Grain for Green, it appears as if the government is beginning to be concerned about environmental problems. However, our data show that officials are not targeting smaller villages in more remote areas (Appendix 6.1, Sections 3 and 4). Instead, relatively more investment is going to larger villages and to villages that are nearer roads. Investing in villages near roads may be done for the convenience of project implementing teams or by officials wishing to showcase their results. If officials are targeting growth, there may be greater growth potential in villages near roads. By doing so, officials may be sacrificing deeper needs in more remote villages for the benefits that come from being able to show off their investment efforts.

In addition to a number of targeting factors, our descriptive data show clearly that several demand-side factors also could be associated with the demand by villagers for higher or lower rates of investments. In particular, villages with more collective enterprises and those with more self-employed private entrepreneurs have more projects and higher levels of public goods investments than those without (Appendix 6.1, Sections 5 and 6). In contrast, villages with a large share of the population in the migrant labor force have less investment (Appendix 6.1, Section 7). While there are a number of reasons why such patterns may emerge, they are also consistent with a story in which those with economic interests in the village (e.g. those running or working in collective enterprises and those running self-employed business) welcome and/or are willing to contribute to public goods investments. When a large share of the village lives and works outside the village in the city, however, those outside and those left in the village may be less inclined to support public goods projects. Somewhat surprisingly, given the government's commitment to national food security, those villages with more land, or those that may be more reliant on agriculture, have relatively less investment (Appendix 6.1, Section 8).

Finally, when looking at other factors, we find in some cases there are other factors that might affect the number or level of investment projects. Above all, we find a strong correlation with the number of villagers who hold positions as officials in the village's township or county (Appendix 6.1, Section 9). According to our data, having connections – or *guanxi* – in the places where investment decisions are made matters. Such a finding of course is not surprising in a society that has thrived over the years on informal networks. In contrast, there is little support for a hypothesis that would predict an association between village governance and investment. In the descriptive data, few, if any, of our village governance variables are associated – either positively or negatively – with investment (Appendix 6.1, Section 10).

### *Multivariate analysis*

To further examine the determinants of investment intensity, we use a series of regressions to examine the factors that induce high investment in some villages and low investment in others. In order to implement the multivariate analysis, we examine the effect of a number of factors on the number and level of public goods investment. Because we want to both run a regression that is population weighted in order to produce results that are nationally representative and because of the limited nature of the dependent variable, we use two separate estimating strategies: one, a weighted Ordinary Least Squares (OLS) estimator; and two, a tobit estimator (which is used by econometricians when the dependent variable is a limited number – that is, it is limited to between zero and one, as would be the case if we explain the number of investment projects). The explanatory variables include three types: a) targeting factors (including per capita income levels – both a linear and squared term; the share of the population that is minority; the share of the village's land that has a slope greater than 25 percent; two location variables – the distance of the village in kilometers from the nearest all-weather road and the distance of the village to the township seat; and two measures of the size of the village – the village's population and the physical size of the village measured as the distance in kilometers between the furthest two hamlets); b) demand-side factors (including the number of collective enterprises; the share of households that are self-employed; the share of the labor force that is working as migrant workers; per capita land holdings to proxy for the importance of farming; and the share of cultivated land that is irrigated); and c) other factors (including the number of villagers that are in official positions in either the township or county government; five governance variables – a dummy variable that equals one if the village head turned over during the study period, the occupations of the village head and party secretary prior to taking office, and the level of education of the village head and party secretary; and per capita debt). All of the explanatory variables, when available, are for 1997. The mean, standard error and range of the main variables used in the regression analysis are in Appendix 6.2. Although we run the model for both the number of projects and the level of investment, because the results are robust, we report the results of the number of projects in the text (Table 6.4) and relegate the results for the regressions explaining the level of investment to the appendix (Appendix 6.3).

Although there are a number of exceptions, the results of the multivariate analysis of the determinants of public goods investment are mostly consistent with the descriptive statistics. For example, in the multivariate analysis we find supporting evidence for the demand-side hypotheses. In villages with more industrial and other commercial activity – that is those with collective enterprises and self-employed households – there is relatively more investment. However, in communities with more migrants, there is less investment. Hence, in the multivariate analysis, we find that in communities in which a larger part of the population has more local economic interests, there is more investment activity. It is possible that since attracting or making its own investment is costly in terms of time and capital that villages without close ties to the local economy (i.e. those with many migrants who live in communities far away from the home village) will not take steps to invest in public goods.

In addition to the demand-side hypotheses, a number of other results are consistent with the cross tabulation analysis (Table 6.4). For example, connections are important. In fact, in almost every one of the descriptive and multivariate exercises, villages with more *guanxi* in the township or county had high levels of public goods investments. Finally, we find that like the descriptive results, there is evidence of showcasing; we find the number of projects or the level of investment are inversely correlated with the distance of the village from the nearest all-weather road. Although it is unclear why, like the descriptive findings, we did not

*Table 6.4* Determinants of number of public goods projects between 1998 and 2003

| *Dependent variables:* | *Number of public goods projects* | |
|---|---|---|
| | *OLS* | *Tobit* |
| **Targeting factors** | | |
| Net per capita income, 1997 (yuan) | 4.10e-08<br>(0) | –0.00014<br>(1.22) |
| Net per capita income square, 1997 (yuan) | 1.66e-08<br>(0.7) | 0<br>(1.88)* |
| Percent of minority population | 0.002374<br>(0.79) | –0.00291<br>(1.86)* |
| Percent of hilly land over 25 degrees | 0.007085<br>(3.64)*** | 0.002949<br>(1.91)* |
| Distance from village committee to township seat (km) | 0.011216<br>(0.97) | –0.01641<br>(2.06)** |
| Distance from the village seat to the nearest road (km) | –0.01607<br>(3.81)*** | –0.00658<br>(1.96)* |
| Total population, 1997 (person) | 0.00021<br>(3.57)*** | 0.000271<br>(6.34)*** |
| Distance between two most distant small groups within this village (km) | 0.002905<br>(0.2) | 0.039351<br>(2.93)*** |
| **Demand side factors** | | |
| Number of collective enterprise | 0.107772<br>(2.75)*** | 0.074373<br>(2.67)*** |
| Percent of self-employed households | 0.026779<br>(3.28)*** | 0.019392<br>(3.65)*** |
| Percent of migrant labor | –0.00576<br>(1.48) | –0.00572<br>(1.96)* |
| Per capita land (mu) | –0.04014<br>(1.39) | –0.02637<br>(1.33) |
| Percent of effectively irrigated land | –0.00685<br>(3.95)*** | –0.00866<br>(6.66)*** |
| **Other factors** | | |
| Number of fellow villagers with township-above governments (person) | 0.030891<br>(4.12)*** | 0.020646<br>(3.94)*** |
| Village head turnover, 1998–2003, 1=yes, 0=no | 0.22298<br>(1.71)* | 0.102749<br>(0.97 |
| Village head occupation prior to office: 1=fulltime farmer, 0=not 1 | –0.21257<br>(1.88)* | –0.16451<br>(1.75)* |
| Schooling of village head (year) | 0.003529<br>(0.14) | –0.01813<br>(1.07) |

continued

*Table 6.4* (continued)

| *Dependent variable:* | *Number of public goods projects* | |
|---|---|---|
| | *OLS* | *Tobit* |
| Party secretary occupation prior to office: 1=fulltime farmer, 0=not 1 | –0.10934 (0.93) | –0.06384 (0.66) |
| Schooling of party secretary (year) | –0.01847 (0.77) | –0.01173 (0.72) |
| Per capita debt, 1997 (yuan) | 0.000162 (2.43)** | 0.00019 (1.80)* |
| Constant | 2.857202 (7.22)*** | 3.307571 (12.61)*** |
| Observations | 2324 | 2389 |
| R-squared | 0.12 | |

Notes.
1 Absolute value of t statistics in parentheses;
2 * significant at 10%; ** significant at 5%; *** significant at 1%

find many of the governance variables to be statistically significant. Two explanations are plausible. One is that since a large share of the village's investment is subsidized from above (or is initiated from above), the quality of the village's leadership does not matter. Alternatively, it could be that village leaders do not matter and that the power rests in the party secretary, and even in today's more market-oriented environment it may be that traditional ties to upper-level party officials (that are difficult to measure) matter more than whether or not village leaders have higher education.

A number of new results also appeared when using multivariate analysis, a fact that might mean that the more complicated relations were masked when using simple descriptive statistics (Table 6.4). For example, we find that large villages – those with larger populations – attract a greater number of public goods projects. We also find that villages with greater land per capita and those with a larger share of cultivated land that is irrigated have fewer investment projects. Apparently, China's industry-oriented fiscal and financial system (Wong 1997) also affects the intensity of investment.

## Determinants of funding from above and by the village

While the results in the previous section are interesting, one of the main conceptual problems with the determinants analysis of total investment is that the dependent variable (total investment) is actually the sum of two sources of investment being made by two entities – officials from above (subsidized investment) and village leaders (own investment). Each source of investment may have its own set of determinants. In fact, for a number of explanatory variables, it is possible that the expected sign in an equation explaining subsidized investment could be precisely the opposite of the expected sign in an equation explaining the village's own investment. As a consequence, it could be that these confounding effects are masking some important relationships in our data. Therefore, in this section we divide the explanatory variable into two parts – the proportion of subsidized investment and the proportion of own investment – and run two independent sets of regression analyses. However, because the coefficients of the two equations are the same except for their sign, we only report the analysis of the determinants of subsidized investment (Table 6.5).

In fact, when examining the determinants of the subsidized investment, the fit of the equation rises and the relationships between the proportion of investment and a number of the explanatory variables are sharper (Table 6.5). Moreover, the results can actually be interpreted in a way that provides a clear and mostly positive picture about the approach China's government is taking in its investment decisions. Specifically, in testing the proportion of funding from above, we find that public goods investments are being targeted to poor and minority villages. The results also show that officials are channelling funds to smaller, more remote and mountainous villages with little irrigated area. If truly representative of rural China in the late 1990s and the post 2000 period, then one interpretation of the findings is that officials have adopted a progressive or pro-poor, ethnically sensitive and environmentally oriented investment strategy. While we want to re-emphasize that our results suggest that China's rural leaders are moving in a direction that might help alleviate poverty, they do not tell us if enough in absolute terms is being invested. Comparative analysis suggests more is needed (CCICED 2004).

In contrast, there is a different profile of villages that are being asked to fund their own public goods investment. Specifically China's richer villages and those with a Han majority are being asked to fund public goods themselves. The same is true for villages that are closer to road networks and are located on more favorable land (e.g. land that is less sloped and more irrigated). Given these trends, one must question, however, the effect of rural tax reform policies; these contain various provisions making it more difficult for villages to raise funds from farm households to finance their own investments.

## Summary and conclusions

In this chapter we have used a new, nationally representative data set to create a profile of China's investment at the village level. In doing so, we have discovered that in recent years upper-level officials have begun to invest increasingly more in rural China. Moreover, unlike in earlier years, they are investing in public goods, frequently in projects that have both environmental and other spillovers. From this effort, there has been a rise in the number of investment projects, especially in roads and bridges, irrigation, drinking water, schools and environmental protection forests.

When assessing this effort, we also have discovered that at least in the case of funding directed from above, there is an effort to meet some of rural China's more pressing equity problems. While we do not know how investments were targeted

*Table 6.5* Determinants of subsidized public goods projects, 1998 and 2003

| *Dependent variables: proportion of subsidized investment in total investment* | *Coefficient* | *T-value* |
|---|---|---|
| **Targeting factors** | | |
| Net per capita income, 1997 (yuan) | 0.00159 | (0.45) |
| Net per capita income square, 1997 (yuan) | –0.00000 | (2.01)** |
| Percent of minority population | 0.17030 | (3.82)*** |
| Percent of hilly land over 25 degrees | 0.14374 | (3.33)*** |
| Distance from village committee to township seat (km) | –0.02133 | (0.07) |
| Distance from the village seat to the nearest road (km) | 0.20689 | (1.93)* |
| Total population, 1997 (person) | –0.00336 | (2.35)** |
| Distance between two most distant small groups within this village (km) | 0.46893 | (1.10) |
| **Demand side factors** | | |
| Number of collective enterprise | –1.09701 | (1.46) |
| Percent of self-employed households | –0.06310 | (0.44) |
| Percent of migrant labor | –0.07726 | (0.84) |
| Per capita land (mu) | –0.02811 | (0.05) |
| Percent of effectively irrigated land | –0.17261 | (4.13)*** |
| **Other factors** | | |
| Number of fellow villagers with township-above governments (person) | 0.53281 | (3.16)*** |
| Village head turnover, 1998–2003, 1=yes, 0=no | 6.31325 | (1.72)* |
| Village head occupation prior to office: 1=fulltime farmer, 0=not 1 | –2.62722 | (0.83) |
| Schooling of village head (year) | –0.30288 | (0.56) |
| Party secretary occupation prior to office: 1=fulltime farmer, 0=not 1 | 2.36733 | (0.72) |
| Schooling of party secretary (year) | –0.19654 | (0.38) |
| Per capita debt, 1997 (yuan) | –0.00157 | (1.03) |
| Constant | 60.79314 | (6.88)*** |
| Observations | | 2083 |
| R-squared | | 0.16 |

Notes:
1 Absolute value of t statistics in parentheses
2 * significant at 10%; ** significant at 5%; *** significant at 1%

in the past, according to our results we know that between 1998 and 2003, upper-level officials are focusing their efforts on poverty alleviation and are doing so in both minority and in environmentally sensitive areas. In fact, over all, China's investment into villages in poor, inland regions is now occurring at a higher rate and is growing faster than in richer areas. Our results show, however, that communities in better-off areas are making public goods investment themselves.

If this is true, then China's leaders should be praised for their efforts and encouraged to continue along the same path and expand future investment plans, though some problems such as showcasing still exist and should be taken into account by officials in their future work. During the 1980s and 1990s, it was shown that China was actually still taxing agriculture and the rural sector, although there were signs in the macro data that a turnaround was occurring. Our study suggests that indeed either the turnaround has actually occurred or that at least there is a shift from net taxation to net investment in rural China underway. Undoubtedly, given China's population size and land area, and the depth of poverty and backwardness in some regions, more is needed. However, at the very least, for perhaps the first time, it does appear as if the transformation to a more modern economic foundation is happening. Moreover, it appears as if China has now made a commitment to focus its resources on the development priorities that other more developed economies have found to be the key to successful development.

## APPENDIX

*Appendix 6.1* Relationship between number of and the level of total investment on public goods projects and village characteristics, 2003

| | | | | | |
|---|---|---|---|---|---|
| **1. Proportion of ethnic minority population** | **Category – Proportion of minority population quintiles** | | | | |
| | Bottom 20% | 2nd 20% | Mid 20% | 4th 20% | Top 20% |
| Number of projects | 2.9 | 3.1 | 3.4 | 3.6 | 3.3 |
| Investment (1000 yuan) | 209 | 254 | 228 | 266 | 236 |
| **2. Proportion of village land greater than 25 degrees** | **Category – Proportion of hilly land quintiles** | | | | |
| | 0 | 0–25% | 25–50% | 50–75% | >75% |
| Number of projects | 2.6 | 3.1 | 3.4 | 3.4 | 3.2 |
| Investment (1000 yuan) | 191 | 200 | 308 | 247 | 269 |
| **3. Distance of village seat to the nearest road** | **Category – Distance to nearest road quintiles** | | | | |
| | Bottom 20% | 2nd 20% | Mid 20% | 4th 20% | Top 20% |
| Number of projects | 3.0 | 3.0 | 2.9 | 2.9 | 2.9 |
| Investment (1000 yuan) | 291 | 223 | 184 | 194 | 202 |
| **4. Size of village** | **Category – Population quintiles** | | | | |
| | Bottom 20% | 2nd 20% | Mid 20% | 4th 20% | Top 20% |
| Number of projects | 2.8 | 2.8 | 2.9 | 3.2 | 3.2 |
| Investment (1000 yuan) | 186 | 195 | 223 | 252 | 401 |
| **5. Village collective enterprises** | **Category – Number of enterprises** | | | | |
| | 0 | 1 | 1–5 | 5–10 | >10 |
| Number of projects | 2.9 | 3.6 | 3.7 | 3.9 | 5.7 |
| Investment (1000 yuan) | 200 | 442 | 364 | 421 | 1125 |

| | | | | | |
|---|---|---|---|---|---|
| **6. Proportion of self-employed households as total village hhds** | **Category – Proportion of self-employed hhds quintiles** | | | | |
| | Bottom 20% | 2nd 20% | Mid 20% | 4th 20% | Top 20% |
| Number of projects | 2.8 | 2.9 | 3.2 | 3.2 | 3.8 |
| Investment (1000 yuan) | 161 | 220 | 241 | 339 | 346 |
| **7. Percentage of migrants as total village labor** | **Category – Percentage of migrant labor quintiles** | | | | |
| | Bottom 20% | 2nd 20% | Mid 20% | 4th 20% | Top 20% |
| Number of projects | 2.9 | 3.0 | 3.1 | 2.8 | 2.8 |
| Investment (1000 yuan) | 276 | 206 | 241 | 188 | 173 |
| **8. Per capita land** | **Category – Per capita land quintile** | | | | |
| | Bottom 20% | 2nd 20% | Mid 20% | 4th 20% | Top 20% |
| Number of projects | 3.4 | 3.0 | 2.8 | 2.8 | 2.8 |
| Investment (1000 yuan) | 369 | 230 | 183 | 172 | 182 |
| **9. Number of villagers working at township or county government** | **Category – Number of villagers** | | | | |
| | 0 | 1–3 | 3–10 | 10–20 | >20 |
| Number of projects | 2.7 | 2.9 | 3.1 | 3.5 | 3.9 |
| Investment (1000 yuan) | 141 | 249 | 234 | 303 | 464 |
| **10. Number of village head turnover between 1998 and 2003** | **Category – Number of turnover** | | | | |
| | None | At least one | | | |
| Number of projects | 2.7 | 3.0 | | | |
| Investment (1000 yuan) | 190 | 229 | | | |

Source: Authors' survey

*Appendix 6.2* Summary statistics of variables used in the regression

| Variable | *Obs* | *Mean* | *Std. Dev.* | *Min* | *Max* |
|---|---|---|---|---|---|
| **Project information** | | | | | |
| Total number of projects (including both public goods and development projects) | 2420 | 3.7 | 2.2 | 0 | 14 |
| Total number of public projects | 2420 | 3.2 | 1.8 | 0 | 13 |
| Number of subsidized investment projects | 2344 | 1.47 | 1.84 | 0 | 13 |
| Number of own investment projects | 2344 | 0.78 | 1.40 | 0 | 11 |
| **Targeting factors** | | | | | |
| Net per capita income (yuan) | 2420 | 1436 | 965 | 80 | 8000 |
| Percentage of minority population (%) | 2420 | 7.8 | 24.4 | 0 | 100 |
| Percentage of hilly land (%) | 2420 | 24.7 | 29.4 | 0 | 100 |
| Distance between village to town (km) | 2419 | 5.3 | 4.9 | 0 | 75 |
| Distance from village to nearest road (km) | 2420 | 6.1 | 11.0 | 0 | 110 |
| Total population | 2420 | 1435 | 1073 | 76 | 8700 |
| Distance between two furthest small groups (km) | 2420 | 2.4 | 2.6 | 0 | 30 |
| **Demand side factors** | | | | | |
| Number of village enterprises | 2420 | 0.3 | 1.4 | 0 | 45 |
| Percentage of self-employed households | 2420 | 4.0 | 6.9 | 0 | 85.2 |
| Percentage of migrant labor (%) | 2420 | 12.2 | 13.2 | 0 | 89.4 |
| Per capita land area (mu) | 2420 | 2.1 | 2.1 | 0.01 | 45.0 |
| Percentage of effectively irrigated land (mu) | 2420 | 42.8 | 38.9 | 0 | 100 |
| **Other factors** | | | | | |
| Number of villagers working at township | 2420 | 2.3 | 4.1 | 0 | 86 |
| Number of villagers working at county | 2420 | 2.7 | 4.8 | 0 | 45 |
| Village head's education | 2389 | 9.4 | 2.4 | 0 | 15 |
| Party secretary's education | 2381 | 9.7 | 2.5 | 0 | 15 |
| Per capita debt (yuan) | 2420 | 108 | 358 | 0 | 9474 |

*Appendix 6.3* Determinants of total investment in public goods projects at village level between 1998 and 2003

| | *Model (1) Provincial population weighted* | *Model (2) Regional population weighted* |
|---|---|---|
| **Targeting factors** | | |
| Net per capita income, 1997 (yuan) | –0.31774<br>(2.30)** | –0.33079<br>(2.24)** |
| Net per capita income square, 1997 (yuan) | 0.000094<br>(2.37)** | 0.000098<br>(2.34)** |
| Percentage of minority population | 0.448921<br>(1.11) | 0.499676<br>(1.17) |
| Percentage of hilly land over 25 degrees | 1.169004<br>(2.60)*** | 1.180395<br>(2.48)** |
| Distance from village committee to township seat | 0.677331<br>(0.46) | 0.479552<br>(0.32) |
| Distance from the village seat to the nearest road (km) | –3.5045<br>(3.14)*** | –3.05278<br>(2.74)*** |
| Total population, 1997 (person) | 0.112885<br>(6.31)*** | 0.113741<br>(6.22)*** |
| Distance between two most distant small groups within this village (km) | –3.27419<br>(0.76) | –1.36398<br>(0.26) |
| **Demand side factors** | | |
| Number of collective enterprise | 120.2922<br>(1.78)* | 128.8306<br>(1.76)* |
| Percentage of self-employed households | 0.190839<br>(0.1) | –0.93933<br>(0.43) |
| Percentage of migrant labor | –0.36961<br>(0.35) | –0.48361<br>(0.36) |
| Per capita land (mu) | 8.863307<br>(1.54) | 0.92482<br>(0.13) |
| Percentage of effectively irrigated land | –0.05513<br>(0.12) | –0.28039<br>(0.59) |
| **Other factors** | | |
| Number of fellow villagers with township-above governments (person) | 3.062545<br>(1.47) | 1.09036<br>(0.45) |
| Village head turnover, 1998–2003, 1=yes, 0=no | 21.83309<br>(0.66) | 16.53165<br>(0.48) |
| Village head occupation prior to office: 1=fulltime farmer, 0=not 1 | 8.214378<br>(0.29) | 0.296215<br>(0.01) |

continued

*Appendix 6.3* (continued)

| | *Model (1) Provincial population weighted* | *Model (2) Regional population weighted* |
|---|---|---|
| Schooling of village head (year) | –2.42564<br>(0.42) | 2.545216<br>(0.44) |
| Party secretary occupation prior to office: 1=fulltime farmer, 0=not 1 | –28.8258<br>(0.95) | –12.6718<br>(0.42) |
| Schooling of party secretary (year) | 2.324312<br>(0.49) | 2.585234<br>(0.6) |
| Per capita debt, 1997 (yuan) | 0.050688<br>(1.22) | 0.063311<br>(1.24) |
| Constant | 264.2339<br>(2.64)*** | 238.6537<br>(2.40)** |
| Observations | 2273 | 2273 |
| R-squared | 0.14 | 0.16 |

Notes:
1 Absolute value of t statistics in parentheses
2 * significant at 10%; ** significant at 5%; *** significant at 1%

## Notes

1 We would like to thank a number of people who have helped us in our efforts to design the survey form, collect and clean the data and develop the preliminary draft of this report. We above all thank the enumerators and supervisors who spent weeks in rural China collecting the data. A special thanks go to the two coordinators, Liu Haomiao and Li Qiang. Yang Xi has spent uncountable days entering and cleaning the data. We also received help during the design of the survey and training of the enumerators from Lin Yuxian, Tao Ran and Liu Jian. The ideas of Loren Brandt, Chen Jianbo and Achim Foch have helped at different times of the project. We want to acknowledge the financial assistance of the World Bank, the Ford Foundation, the Canadian International Development Agency, and National Natural Science Foundation of China (70225003) for financial assistance.

2 "A Quantitative Assessment of China's Poverty Status," Presentation in Workshop on "China Poverty Assessment Workshop," Beijing, 10 November 2005.

3 The sample villages come from six representative provinces. Jiangsu represents the eastern coastal areas (Jiangsu, Shandong, Shanghai, Zhejiang, Fujian and Guangdong); Sichuan represents the southwestern provinces (Sichuan, Guizhou and Yunnan) plus Guangxi; Shaanxi represents the provinces on the Loess Plateau (Shaanxi and Shanxi) and neighboring Inner Mongolia; Gansu represents the rest of the provinces in the northwest (Gansu, Ningxia; Qinghai and Xinjiang); Hebei represents the north and central provinces (Hebei; Henan; Anhui; Hubei; Jiangxi; and Hunan); and Jilin represents the northeastern provinces (Jilin, Liaoning and Heilongjiang). While we recognize that we have deviated from the standard definition of China's agroecological zones, the realities of survey work justified our compromises. Pre-tests in Guangdong demonstrated that data collection was extraordinarily expensive and the attrition rate

high. One of our funding agencies demanded that we choose at least two provinces in the northwest. Our budget did not allow us to add another central province (e.g. Hunan or Hubei) to the sample. The authors and several collaborators from inside and outside of China designed the sampling procedure and final survey instrument with the field work team, made up of the four authors and 30 graduate students and research fellows from Chinese and North American educational institutions (all with PRC citizenship and an average education level higher than a master's degree).

4 On average, the attrition rate was only 6 percent. In no case did we leave a township until at least 80 percent of the villages had been enumerated. In order to examine if the villages that were not enumerated (due to attrition) were systematically different from those that participated, we collected a set of variables about no-show villages from the township and ran a probit regression with the dependent variable represented as an indicator variable where the variable equaled one if the village did not come and zero otherwise. There were no variables that were significant. If a township had more than 25 villages, we randomly selected 25 of them. This affected fewer than five townships.

5 In calculating *all* public goods projects, we include investments made in electrical grid and telephone line upgrades. There were nearly 2,000 of these projects in our sample village between 1998 and 2003. In some sense, however, these projects are not run like the rest of the projects, either public goods investments or development projects. For example, in a vast majority of the electrical grid upgrading projects, the electrical company made all of the investment and did not include the village in the decision-making process. The cost of the project, according to our interviewees would be captured by higher electricity fees or increased electricity use. Given the different nature of these types of projects, in the rest of the chapter we do not include them in the analysis of public goods projects. Hence, this reduces the number of public goods projects from 7,950 to 5,975.

6 The number of projects was explained in note 4.

7 Grain for Green is a large national forestry program begun in 1999 that was designed to pay farmers to set aside cultivated land for the plantation of forest or grasslands. In total between 1999 and 2003, more than five million hectares nationally were converted from cultivated land to forests and grasslands (Xu and Cao 2002).

8 The absence of public investment into an activity, of course, does not mean that farm households do not have access to needed services. Private households may invest or otherwise provide their own services. For example, drinking water is provided as a public good in some villages while in villages without a publicly provided water system, households must expend capital and labor to secure their own drinking water.

9 Even though a village's own investment is theoretically supposed to be included in total spending on infrastructure (since formally it is paid for out of "self-raised funds"), according to our field work, the amount spent by villages on infrastructure is rarely reported or, at best, is reported only in fragmentary fashion.

10 Income could also be a demand-side factor. It is possible that as people get richer, they demand a better environment or an improved living standard that can be provided by public goods investments. When examining all public goods investments, we do not see evidence of this. However, when focusing on the propensity of villages to fund their own public goods, income is positively correlated and it may be that there is a demand-side explanation.

## References

CCICED (2004) "China's Rural Development in the 21st Century: Issues and Policy Challenges," Working Paper, Center for Chinese Agricultural Policy, Beijing: Chinese Academy of Science.

De Brauw, Alan, Huang Jikun, Rozelle, Scott, Zhang Linxiu and Zhang Yigang (2002) "China's Rural Labor Markets," *China Business Review*, March–April: 2–8.

Fan Shenggen, Zhang Linxiu and Zhang Xiaobo (2002) "Growth, Inequality, and Poverty in Rural China: The Role of Public Investments," IFPRI Research Report, 125.

FAO (Food and Agricultural Organization of the United Nations) (2002) "The State of Food Insecurity in the World 2001," Rome: FAO.

Fleisher, Belton and Yang, Dennis (2003) "China's Labor Markets," paper presented at Conference on China's Market Reforms, Stanford Center for International Development, Stanford University, 19–20 September.

Huang Jikun, Rozelle, Scott and Wang Honglin (2006) "Fostering or Stripping Rural China: Modernizing Agriculture and Rural to Urban Capital Flows," *Developing Economies*, 44 (1): 1–26.

Jin Songqing, Huang Jikun, Hu Ruifa and Rozelle, Scott (2002) "The Creation and Spread of Technology and Total Factor Productivity in China's Agriculture," *American Journal of Agricultural Economy*, 84 (4) (November): 916–39.

Khwaja, Asim Ijaz (2002) "Can Good Projects Succeed in Bad Communities? Collective Action in Public Goods Provision," Working Paper, Department of Economics: Harvard University.

McMillan, John (1997) "Markets in Transition," in D. Kreps and K. F. Wallis (eds.) *Advances in Economics and Econometrics: Theory and Applications*, vol. 2, Cambridge: Cambridge University Press, pp. 210–39.

Ministry of Communications (2000) "Investments in China's Rural Areas," Working Paper, Ministry of Communications, Beijing.

*Newsweek* (2005) "Does the Future Belong to China?" *Newsweek*, December 2005: 15–17.

Rozelle, Scott (1990) "Economics of Village Leaders in Rural China," unpublished Ph.D. Dissertation, Department of Agricultural Economics, Cornell University.

Timmer, Peter (1998) "The Agricultural Transformation," in Carl Eicher and John Staatz (eds.) *International Agricultural Development*, 3rd edn, Baltimore, MD: Johns Hopkins University Press, pp. 113–35.

Wong, Christine (ed.) (1997) *Financing Local Government in the People's Republic of China*, Oxford: Oxford University Press.

World Bank (2001) *The Alleviation of Poverty in China*, World Bank Report, Washington, DC: World Bank.

World Bank (2005) "A Better Investment Climate for Everyone," World Development Report 2005, Washington, DC: World Bank.

Xu Jintao and Yuying Cao (2002) "Efficiency and Sustainability of Converting Cropland to Forest and Grassland in the Western Region," Draft Report to CCICED Forest and Grassland Task Force.

# 7 Who receives subsidies?

## A look at the county level in two time periods[1]

*Victor Shih and Zhang Qi*

## Introduction

The 1994 tax reform brought about momentous changes to the Chinese tax system. Instead of individually negotiated tax contracts with the central government, local governments were forced to share lucrative categories of taxes, including value-added tax (VAT) and resource tax, with the central government. In the case of the VAT, the four layers of local government – provincial, prefectural/city, county, and township – together share only 25 percent of VAT intake (Brean 1998; Wong et al. 1995). To compensate for the sudden decrease in local income, the central government introduced a complicated transfer payment system. Whereas the pre-reform fiscal system only contained two main categories of transfer payments – fixed subsidies and earmarked subsidies – the 1994 reform saw the introduction of at least four new categories of subsidies.

This chapter first clarifies the characteristics of these various types of subsidies both before and after the 1994 tax reform. The heart of this chapter explores the determinants of subsidies allocation in both 1995 – just after the tax sharing reform – and in 2000. One clear, yet disturbing, finding from our analysis of county-level subsidies data is that the tax sharing system (TSS) shows a strong tendency to allocate resources away from poor counties to affluent counties in both 1995 and in 2000. Despite official rhetoric stating that the tax reform would increase the center's ability to allocate to poor regions, our data suggest the opposite. Second, we show a strong causal relationship between the number of fiscal dependents and subsidies allocation at the county level. This finding answers an important question concerning local finance: Why do local governments continue to expand despite the fact that they lack the revenue to pay for wages? Somewhat surprisingly our results reveal that expanding payroll constitutes a sure way of increasing subsidies remittance to the county. The following first provides an outline of the structure of state subsidies to the county level both before and after the 1994 tax reform, followed by a discussion of the data and methodology used in this chapter. Using regression analysis, the remainder of the chapter explores the various determinants of subsidies allocation in China.

## The structure of subsidies to county governments

In the economic literature on fiscal federalism, the central government ideally distributes transfers to local governments to enhance the overall welfare. In a welfare maximizing fiscal federal system, local governments would provide public goods that mainly benefit a given locality, while the central government would provide public goods that affect the entire country (Oates 1999). Because some public goods have spillovers, i.e. a welfare effect on neighboring localities, local governments under-provide them, thus diminishing overall welfare. For example, local governments might under-regulate clean air since they hope to free-ride on the clean air of neighboring regions. To encourage local governments to provide public goods with spillovers, the central government would provide them via fiscal transfers (Besley and Coate 1999).

Another goal of transfers is to effect a regional redistribution of fiscal resources. Although economically inefficient, equalizing transfers can ensure long-term political stability (Barro 1999; Smart 1998). Since the mid-1990s, the Chinese government has consistently claimed equalization as the main goal of concentrating fiscal resources at the center and redistributing them through subsidies. As a Ministry of Finance (MOF) decree states, "transfer payments are aimed at reversing the trend of increasing budgetary divergence between regions and at gradually effecting the equalization of local governments' ability to provide public services in order to realize the goal of comprehensively building the small prosperity society" (Ministry of Finance 2003a: 32–6).

Yet, transfers in China, even according to official policies, did not mainly aim at welfare maximization or at regional equality. Rather, official transfer policies both before and after the 1994 tax restructuring had the mixed objectives of appeasing vested interests, encouraging local investment, and redistributing fiscal capabilities across regions. Empirical findings presented in the latter part of this chapter reveal that transfers in reality were not equalizing on the whole.

Before the 1994 tax reform, subsidies to the county government broke down into fixed subsidies (*ding'e butie*) and earmarked subsidies (*zhuanxiang butie*). Fixed subsidies were the main mechanism whereby both central and provincial governments transferred money to poor and minority counties (Ahmad 1998; Park et al. 1996). At the local level, provinces negotiated with individual counties to determine the amount of fixed subsidies counties would receive over a given period of time. Counties, once they had agreed to an arrangement, could expect to receive this amount of subsidies automatically on a yearly basis (Park et al. 1996). Although originally equalizing in nature, fixed subsidies have become a mechanism for appeasing vested interests, since fixed subsidies do not change according to fluctuating economic circumstances but are provided on the basis of past subsidies level.

Earmarked subsidies, on the other hand, took the form of numerous individual grants from either the center or the provincial government to the county governments. These grants were designated for specific purposes, which ranged from construction, education, flood prevention to administration and even public security

(Ministry of Finance 2001b). Furthermore, these grants almost always require matching funds (*peitao zijin*) from the county government (Ahmad 1998; He 2003; Park et al. 1996). Application for earmarked grants typically entails an arduous two-step process, in which counties first receive the approval of the provincial financial department and other relevant provincial agencies, followed by a review by the MOF and relevant central agencies (Ministry of Finance 2001b).

Earmarked subsidies from the central state to local governments are by no means unique to China, and some earmarked grants encourage local governments to provide public goods with spillovers. Nonetheless, its overall orientation is clearly not toward welfare-maximization or equalization. First, the central and provincial governments continue to exercise highly discretionary and *ad hoc* control over earmarked subsidies (Wong 2005b). Besides providing funding to the stated purposes of these grants, the discretionary nature of earmarked subsidies also affords higher tiers of government an additional means of political control (Wedeman 1999). Furthermore, many of these grants prod local governments to provide public goods, which typically are provided by the central authorities in other countries (Mountfield and Wong 2005). Some earmarked grants even go toward resolving problems of national significance, such as bailing out distressed financial institutions to prevent bank runs (People's Bank of China and Ministry of Finance 2000). Moreover, the matching funds requirement furnishes affluent counties with a major advantage in winning earmarked subsidies. At the same time, earmarked grants which traditionally targeted disadvantaged populations in minority areas have faced continuous decline since the late 1980s (Wong 2003). The arduous application process also means that the right political connections can speed up the approval process considerably. Despite these drawbacks, Table 7.1 reveals that both in 1995 and in 2000, earmarked subsidies made up a large share of the total per capita subsidies in the average county.

The 1994 tax reform saw the introduction of a host of new subsidies categories at the county level. New categories of subsidies include tax rebate subsidies (*shuishou fanhuan butie*), original systems subsidies (*yuantizhi butie*) transfer payment subsidies (*zhuanyi zhifu butie*) bond issuance subsidies (*zengfa guozhai buzhu*) and wage increase subsidies (*zengfa gongzi buzhu*) (Budgetary Division of the Ministry of Finance 2001). After 1994, earmarked subsidies remained a major category of subsidies, while fixed subsidies were transformed into original system subsidies. According to a State Council document, original system subsidies were created to ensure that local governments continued to receive the same amount of subsidies as they had under the previous fiscal system (State Council 2003b). This category thus subsumed fixed subsidies and some items of earmarked subsidies (Lou 2002). As seen in Table 7.1, the two traditional categories of subsidies continued to make up the bulk of subsidies to the average county in both 1995 and 2000.

Among the new categories of transfers introduced in 1994, the tax rebate subsidies are transfers that a higher-tier government gives to the lower level after taxes have been successfully collected by the higher-tier government. Between the center and the provinces, the center distributed tax rebates to provinces according

*Table 7.1* Mean and standard deviation of per capita subsidies to counties in various categories, 1995 and 2000

| | *Mean 1995* | *SD 1995* | *Mean 2000* | *SD 2000* |
|---|---|---|---|---|
| Total subsidies | 42.96 | 41.87 | 40.14 | 47.54 |
| Fixed/original system subsidies | 20.24 | 34.08 | 14.08 | 19.14 |
| Earmarked subsidies | 10.49 | 13.34 | 14.3 | 19.7 |
| Tax rebate subsidies | 12.23 | 28.80 | 8.04 | 13.67 |
| Transfer payment subsidies | – | – | 3.67 | 6.6 |

Note: All figures denominated in Chinese *yuan*. Bond subsidies and wage subsidies are not included because these two subsidies only applied to a minority of counties

Source: Budgetary Division of the Ministry of Finance (2001)

to the loss in revenue suffered by the provinces after 1994 (World Bank 2002). The tax rebate is then set to increase annually based on the increase in VAT and consumption tax (*xiaofeishui*) collected in the province. Provincial governments, however, do not seem to follow any fixed formula in providing tax rebates to prefectures and counties.[2] Specifically, tax rebates grow at 0.3 times the growth rate of VAT and consumption tax collection *kept by the central government* (World Bank 2002).[3] By design, tax rebate transfers as a share of total VAT and consumption tax collection would shrink over time (World Bank 2002). By tying the growth of tax rebate transfers to the growth of local collection of VAT and consumption tax, richer counties with a more robust tax base would enjoy faster growth in tax rebates than poorer localities. Thus, a large element of the new transfer system is inherently regressive (World Bank 2002).

In 1995 another category of subsidies, transfer payment subsidies, was introduced to redress regional imbalance by implementing an objective formula for redistribution (Lou 2002).[4] Unlike the other categories of subsidies, which sought mostly to pay off vested interests, this new transfer aimed at redistributing tax capabilities across regions (Budgetary Division of the Ministry of Finance 2002). Instead of referring to “base figures” (*jishu*) to calculate transfer amounts, a complex system with numerous components was introduced to peg transfer payments. The overall aim was to truly effect equalization transfers in the fiscal system.

The basic concept behind transfer payment subsidies is that subsidies are distributed to localities where “standard expenses” (*biaozhun caizheng zhichu*) exceed “standard income” (*biaozhun caizheng shouru*) (Lou 2002).[5] In Anhui province, for example, standard income is a function of standard VAT collection, standard commercial tax collection, tax rebate subsidies, standard income and subsidies from penalties and fees, as well as fixed and earmarked payments to higher levels (Finance Department of Anhui Province 2000b). The “standard” tax collection figures are in turn the average of the “obligatory tax” (*yingshou shui*) and actual collection from the previous year. For example, standard VAT collection is calculated as follows:

$$\text{Standard VAT}_t = 0.5\ (\text{Obligatory VAT})_t + 0.5\ (\text{Actual VAT collection})_{t-1}$$

The obligatory VAT is, further, a function of industrial value added from the previous year multiplied by the effective tax rate. Approximately the same algorithm is used to calculate standard commercial tax (Finance Department of Anhui Province 2000b). "Standard" tax collection figures are used alongside actual collection figures in order to discourage local officials from under-collecting taxes in an attempt to boost subsidies in the subsequent year.

"Standard expenditure" is the sum of standard wage expenses, standard administrative expenses, agricultural expenses, and other expenses (World Bank 2002). The largest category on the expenditure side is of course wages, bonuses, and retirement benefits for fiscal dependents (*caizheng gongyang renkou*), which broadly include current state employees, teachers, decommissioned military officers, and government retirees. Fiscal dependent figures are not the actual number of current state employees, teachers, decommissioned military officers, and retirees in a given place, but the number of such personnel allowed by the state rosters offices (*bianzhi weiyuanhui*) at various levels.[6] Again, part of the equation to calculate standard expenditure is the "standard number of fiscal dependents." The standard number of fiscal dependents is the fitted value Y generated from a regression equation that takes into account population density, the number of township organizations, the number of primary and middle school students, and the number of health workers, among other variables (Finance Department of Anhui Province 2000b). By using standard expenditure and fiscal personnel figures, the central government discourages local officials from gaining the perverse incentive to expand the number of workers to obtain more subsidies. However, as the analysis below reveals, these efforts to control the number of fiscal dependents do not seem to be effective.

Clearly the Ministry of Finance went to great lengths to ensure that the transfer payment subsidies would go to truly needy localities and have an equalizing effect on fiscal capabilities. This system, however, still leaves some room for manipulation, especially by provincial governments. First, transfer payment subsidies to the counties involve a two-step process whereby the central government applies the standard calculations to determine transfer subsidies to the provinces and provinces apply essentially the same criteria to transfer to the counties (Finance Department of Anhui Province 2000b; Ministry of Finance 2003a). As is the case with all two-step transfers, the provinces can easily keep the lion's share of central transfers for provincial use. Even if provinces strictly apply the formulas, they can determine the overall amount to transfer to lower-level governments.

Furthermore, although the method of calculating various "standard" figures is known to both county and provincial officials, county officials only have data on their own county, not overall data from all the counties in a province. Since many "standard" figures are calculated on the basis of data aggregated from the other counties, provincial finance bureaux have an information advantage vis-à-vis the individual county governments. Finally, even if the transfer payment subsidies are given out strictly according to the formulas outlined above, Table 7.1 reveals that five years after its implementation, the formulaic transfer scheme remained a relatively small portion of the per capita subsidies received by the average county. Transfer payment subsidies did not appear to be an important element of the TSS and constituted only 3.1 percent of all central transfer payments in 2001 (World Bank 2002).

Besides these two major categories of new subsidies (tax rebate, transfer payment), bond subsidies and wage subsidies were also added on the county budgetary balance, but these two categories of subsidies only applied to a small number of counties in 2000. They essentially operated as another kind of earmarked transfers. In 1999, the central government ordered provincial governments to distribute additional wage subsidies to poor counties. Essentially, the higher share the wage bill took up in total county expenditure, the more wage subsidies a county received (Finance Department of Anhui Province 2000a). In subsequent years, however, wage subsidies became a significant category of transfers (Wong 2005a).

The 1994 tax reform greatly bolstered the fiscal clout of the central government. Examining the specific mechanisms of these subsidies, however, it remains doubtful that these new subsidies would effect a significant fiscal redistribution. By 2000, the center collected over half of all fiscal income, while it only spent one third of total government expenditure. In contrast, county and township government shared only 20 percent of total government collection. Yet, these grassroots levels of government were burdened with a disproportionate share of the expenditure needs (Mountfield and Wong 2005; Su 2003). Granted, with bolstered financial resources, the center can serve as the great equalizer and redistribute to needy localities. Yet, the analysis below reveals that subsidies allocation is probably not driven by this benign process.

## Data and methodology

The analysis below seeks to clarify the economic factors that drive the distribution of overall subsidies at the county level. Our data come from the *Statistical Material for Prefectures, Cities, and Counties Nationwide* (*Quanguo Dishixian Caizheng Tongji Ziliao*) published by the Ministry of Finance. This data-set covers county-level finance for every county-level administrative unit, including counties, county-level cities, and urban districts in 1995 and in 2000. We further enhance this data with economic reports and data on the poverty designation of counties (State Council Poverty Relief Leading Group 2003).[7] We chose to examine county-level data in these two years in order to gauge whether the TSS had succeeded in shifting the underlying logic of transfer payments in the first five years following its initial implementation.

We further cleaned the data by eliminating all county-level urban districts embedded in major cities. Ahmad's work on Beijing suggests that districts in large cities have much less fiscal independence than their county counterparts (Ahmad 1998). We do, however, include rural counties in directly administered cities, including Beijing, Shanghai, and Tianjin. The relationship between these municipal governments and their rural counties is akin to the relationship between provincial governments and counties. In any event, these minor adjustments are marginal, and we still have over 2,000 observations for each of the two years.[8]

With two years of data, we are left with two choices on how to approach our data analysis. First, we can combine the two years of data into a single data-set. This would allow us to take the first difference of both the dependent and the independent variables. Pooling the data from the two years, however, creates a serious problem: counties in China changed a great deal between 1995 and 2000. For some provinces or directly administered cities, the number of counties has actually shrunk by 50 percent. Even in primarily agrarian provinces like Anhui, the number of counties has decreased significantly. Only Xinjiang, Qinghai, Neimenggu, Hainan, and Liaoning had the same number of counties in 2000 as they did in 1995. The changing number of counties is only the first problem one encounters when comparing counties over time. Many counties merged with one another, split apart, were elevated to higher administrative status, expanded, or contracted in size. Without a better sense about how widespread these administrative changes actually were, it would be difficult to claim that counties in 1995 and 2000 are generally comparable. Given the comparability problem, we take a second, less optimal strategy of analyzing the 1995 and 2000 data separately. However, for the sake of robustness and to establish a firmer causal relationship, we do combine data from the two years in our last regression in order to instrumentalize variables in 1995.

Because the Ministry of Finance data provide only basic economic and demographic information about these counties, in addition to the fiscal variables, we mainly explore the impact of economic factors on subsidies distribution. More information is needed to construct a political-economy explanatory model. With the data at hand, however, we have more than enough information to find out whether subsidies are allocated to poor, needy counties.

We employ a gridlock approach in our empirical investigation. That is, we regress total subsidies for both 1995 and 2000 on a host of economic variables, including output per capita, fiscal shortfall, structure of the local economy, the State Council designation of a county, and the size of the fiscal dependents with and without provincial dummies. We estimate coefficients for both years in order to uncover any change in the correlation between various economic indicators and total subsidies between the two years. Second, we run the regressions both with and without provincial dummies because they represent two different approaches to understanding fiscal allocation. When the equation is estimated without provincial dummies, we examine how the fiscal system as a whole, including both central remittance to the provinces and provincial remittance to the counties, allocates subsidies. When we include provincial dummies, however, we examine how the fiscal system, when controlling for central remittance to the provinces and other provincial fixed effects, allocates subsidies. Another way to interpret our equation when provincial dummies are included is as illustrating how the average province allocates subsidies to the average county.

## Analysis and findings

The analysis below mainly aims at discovering whether "reversing the trend of increasing budgetary divergence" (Ministry of Finance 2003a) is indeed driving subsidies allocation in China both in 1995 and in 2000. If not, what other factors might be driving subsidies allocation? In our basic model, the dependent variable is total per capita subsidies received by a county in a given year, while the independent variables are county agricultural and industrial output, county fiscal shortfall, the ratio of agricultural output to total output at the county level, a dummy for nationally designated poverty counties, and the ratio of fiscal dependents to total population in a county.

Each of the explanatory variables constitutes a major algorithm whereby the fiscal system allocates subsidies to the counties. First, fiscal shortfall, or the difference between local collection and local spending, serves as an important control variable. Since counties are by law prohibited from running a deficit, provincial and central governments might just be sending funds to counties simply to prevent rampant deficits. After controlling for fiscal shortfall, we are more certain that money is transferred to a county net of the need to ensure budgetary balance in that locality. It is, however, important to note that allocating subsidies to deficit counties is not the same as allocating to poor counties, although the two phenomena are correlated.

If the fiscal system progressively allocates subsidies to poor places, then output per capita should be negatively correlated with subsidies per capita. On the other hand, it would not be surprising to find output per capita to be positively correlated with subsidies, since richer counties are more able to obtain earmarked subsidies due to their greater ability to meet matching funds requirements (Wong and West 1997). It is thus an important empirical question to uncover whether the TSS transfers progressively or regressively to counties.

In addition to output and fiscal balance, economic structure of the local economy can also play a role in determining transfers. In the progressive case, the higher the proportion of agricultural output, the more the center and the province would subsidize a county. However, as Fan points out, the reverse might well be true. Agrarian counties have less access to revenue streams from TVEs and thus less money available to pay for matching funds (Fan 1998). Moreover, over time, the relative difficulty of collecting revenue from the multitude of farming households might make local officials in agrarian counties increasingly predatory toward farmers, which further decreases an agrarian county's ability to provide for matching funds.

Finally, both Western and Chinese scholars point out that the ballooning of local fiscal personnel has rapidly increased local fiscal demand (Fan 1998; Park et al. 1996). Thus, if central and provincial governments are fearful of rampant wage arrears at the grassroots level, they would be inclined to increase subsidies with the surge in fiscal dependents. What remains unclear is the direction of causality between fiscal dependents and subsidies. According to Chinese accounts, a rising number of fiscal dependents leads to increases in government subsidies for several reasons. First, the central government raised wage standards for government employees, including teachers, several times since the mid-1990s (Wang 2002). This increased the local government budget's sensitivity to the rising number of employees. To compensate local governments for the increased expenses, the center allocated subsidies for the increased wage bill (Finance Department of Anhui Province 2000a). Second, with more and more functional bureaux being vertically managed by either the province or the central government, county-level bureaux, including tax bureaux, the administration for industry and commerce, and various product supervision bureaux, needed more specialized personnel and received grants from higher-level departments in the same functional system to fulfill these hiring demands (He 2003; Mertha 2005). Finally, county governments might simply be blackmailing higher levels with the possibility of rampant wage arrears and social stability. Given this perverse incentive, county governments would expand local fiscal dependents in the hope of attracting more central or provincial wage subsidies.

However, increasing subsidies might also be driving the growth of fiscal dependents. First, a surge in subsidies would allow local officials to hire more cadres to fill the ranks. With a higher number of employees, local officials can then ask central and provincial governments for more wage subsidies in subsequent years. Moreover, the increase in earmarked grants might also lead to higher numbers of fiscal dependents since earmarked grants at times demand specialized personnel, which forces the county to hire more people to administer the programs funded by these earmarked grants (Wang 2002). The last section of the chapter seeks to clarify the causation issue related to the size of fiscal dependents.

Subsidies (SUB) and output (OUTPUT) are recorded on a per capita basis and deflated by provincial level GDP deflator (1980=100). Fiscal shortfall (FISSHORT), which is the difference between local collection and local fiscal expenditure, is calculated as local collection-local expenditure/local collection. Strictly speaking, this variable records the fiscal balance at the county level, although with very few exceptions, counties generally run a pre-transfer deficit. The ratio of agricultural output to total output (ECONSTR) simply divides agricultural output by total output. The nationally designated poverty county dummy (NDP) records a one for every county designated by the State Council as especially needy (State Council Poverty Relief Leading Group 2003). Finally, the size of fiscal dependents (FISDEP) is the number of fiscal dependents per capita in the county.

These equations are estimated with generalized least-squares (GLS) because the assumption that counties are independent units of observations is unsustainable, thus causing a heteroskedasticity problem. Given this condition, estimation with ordinary least-squares (OLS) would produce inefficient estimates with high variance. GLS takes heteroskedasticity into account and produces more efficient estimators. Furthermore, the coefficients on Table 7.2 are recorded as standardized coefficients. Standardized coefficients inform the impact of a one-standard deviation shift in the independent variable on the dependent variable. Standardized coefficients are used in this case because the units of the independent variables are so different from each other. For example, because FISSHORT, ECONSTR, and

*Table 7.2* Effect of fiscal shortfall, output, economic structure, and fiscal dependents on total subsidies in 1995 and 2000

| | *1995 GLS* | *1995 GLS with fixed effects* | *2000 GLS* | *2000 GLS with fixed effects* |
|---|---|---|---|---|
| FISSHORT | –0.199*** | –0.119*** | –0.309*** | –0.187*** |
| OUTPUT | 0.211*** | 0.140*** | 0.138*** | 0.090*** |
| ECONSTR | 0.114*** | –0.051** | 0.182*** | 0.010 |
| FISDEP | 0.435*** | 0.324*** | 0.432*** | 0.352*** |
| NDP | –0.014 | 0.029** | 0.097*** | 0.098*** |
| Tianjin | | –0.086*** | | –0.119*** |
| Hebei | | –0.364*** | | –0.717*** |
| Shanxi | | –0.213*** | | –0.463*** |
| Inner Mongolia | | –0.133*** | | –0.364*** |
| Liaoning | | –0.101*** | | –0.276*** |
| Jilin | | –0.120*** | | –0.292*** |
| Heilongjiang | | –0.051* | | –0.250*** |
| Shanghai | | 0.012 | | –0.031*** |
| Jiangsu | | –0.246*** | | –0.512*** |
| Zhejiang | | –0.171*** | | –0.360*** |
| Anhui | | –0.387*** | | –0.541*** |
| Fujian | | –0.276*** | | –0.562*** |
| Jiangxi | | –0.299*** | | –0.457*** |
| Shandong | | –0.317*** | | –0.638*** |
| Henan | | –0.785*** | | –0.717*** |
| Hubei | | –0.277*** | | –0.477*** |
| Hunan | | –0.245*** | | –0.531*** |
| Guangdong | | –0.265*** | | –0.664*** |
| Guangxi | | –0.229*** | | –0.517*** |
| Sichuan | | –0.306*** | | –0.483*** |
| Guizhou | | –0.307*** | | –0.436*** |
| Yunnan | | –0.195*** | | –0.379*** |
| Shaanxi | | –0.244*** | | –0.503*** |
| Gansu | | –0.192*** | | –0.347*** |
| Qinghai | | –0.025 | | –0.133*** |
| Ningxia | | –0.045*** | | –0.148*** |
| Xinjiang | | –0.158*** | | –0.395*** |
| Hainan | | –0.105*** | | –0.213*** |
| Xizang | | –0.099*** | | –0.183*** |
| OBS | 2104 | | 1991 | 1991 |
| F Value | 63.87 | | 141.64 | 297.57 |
| Adj-R2 | 0.35 | | 0.46 | 0.79 |

Note:
The coefficients are reported as standardized coefficients. Standard errors are not reported because they are irrelevant in interpreting standardized coefficients.
*, **, *** indicate significance at 10%, 5%, 1% level respectively

FISDEP are all ratios, they can only fluctuate between zero and one. It would not make sense to interpret how much a one-unit shift in these variables would affect the dependent variable; that is impossible in the real world. Rather, it makes much more sense to ask how a one-standard deviation shift in these variables would affect the dependent variables.

The findings presented in Table 7.2 suggest some progressive and some regressive elements in the fiscal transfer system. They also reveal that the 1994 reform did not address the regressive nature of the transfer system which allocated more to richer, industrial counties and less to poor, agrarian counties. Finally, the clearest result from all four equations is that there is a high correlation between the size of a county's fiscal dependents and subsidies per capita, even when other economic characteristics are held constant. This relationship remains robust in both 1995 and 2000.

The coefficients of FISSHORT are consistently negative, suggesting that as a whole, counties with bigger fiscal shortfall received more transfer payments. This finding, however, does not mean that subsidies were allocated to poorer counties. It just means that subsidies tended to flow to counties with higher pre-transfer deficits. In fact, even affluent counties might suffer from high pre-transfer deficits. In our data-set, nearly 99 percent of counties in both 1995 and 2000 reported pre-transfer fiscal deficit. Moreover, provincial and central governments also provided deficit counties with more transfers as a matter of routine policy to constrain local-level government deficits. Provincial governments, in particular, might provide county governments with deficit reduction transfers in order to fulfill central demands to have essentially no deficit at the local level (Ministry of Finance 2001a). By including this variable in our equations, we can discern how higher tiers of government made transfers to the county net of the concern for maintaining the legally mandated budgetary balance. Of course, this concern for deficit reduction does not include latent deficit in the forms of debt and wage arrears.[9]

In terms of the most direct measure of economic well-being, per capita output (OUTPUT), the fiscal system as a whole, including both transfers from central to provincial and from provincial to county level, systematically allocated more money to richer counties in both 1995 and in 2000. Moreover, once provincial fixed effects are taken into account in the two years, the positive, systematic relationship remains, albeit with a lesser magnitude. The positive coefficients of output per capita in 1995 suggest that the fiscal system as a whole and the average province both allocated subsidies to richer counties. Similarly, in 2000, both the fiscal system as a whole and fiscal allocation in the average province remitted more subsidies to richer counties, all else being equal. In this respect, the post-1994 remittance system did not lead to a significantly less regressive transfer system. Granted, the coefficients for OUTPUT declined somewhat in 2000, but they remain positive and significant. In 1995, a standard deviation increase in county output per capita led to 0.21 yuan more in transfer per capita overall. In 2000, a one-standard deviation increase in per capita output brought the average county 0.138 yuan in additional subsidies per capita. For a county with a million people, a standard deviation increase in income would have brought an additional 210,000 yuan in transfers in 1995, while in 2000 it would have brought an additional 138,000 yuan in subsidies.

The coefficients of economic structure (ECONSTR) in 1995 suggest that the fiscal system as a whole was allocating more subsidies to agrarian counties. However, the average province transferred systematically less funds to the average counties. Clearly, central transfers to the provinces were responsible for much of the transfers received by agrarian counties, while at the provincial level rural counties were the subject of discrimination in receiving transfer payments. In 2000, while the system as a whole still transferred significantly more money to agrarian counties, the average province did not favor or discriminate against agrarian counties systematically. Again, this finding suggests that almost all of the subsidies allocated to agrarian counties stemmed from central policies to disburse subsidies to primarily agrarian provinces.

Preferential policies also extended systematically to nationally designated poverty counties (NDPs) in most of our equations, although the magnitude of the effect is surprisingly small. Although NDPs are designated by the State Council, our regression shows that the fiscal system as a whole did not systematically allocate more subsidies to NDPs in 1995. When central subsidies to the provinces and other provincial fixed effects are taken into account, however, the average province seemed to have allocated more funds to NDPs. In other words, special transfer payments to nationally designated poverty counties seemed primarily to be a provincial initiative in 1995. In 2000, however, nationally designated poverty counties received around 0.1 yuan extra subsidies per capita. This effect is robust both with and without provincial dummies, suggesting that both the central and provincial governments applied essentially the same algorithm in allocating to these counties. It is unclear whether this represents a progressive allocation of subsidies to truly needy counties, since the designation of NDP counties is a political process involving several central agencies, including the State Council Poverty Relief and Development Leading Group, the Ministry of Finance, and the State Planning Commission. Cadres in the Ministry of Finance freely admitted that counties with a high minority representation received special considerations for receiving NDP status (Agriculture Department of the Ministry of Finance 2002).

The strongest coefficient in this set of equations is the size of the fiscal personnel per capita (FISDEP). In both 1995 and 2000, both the GLS and fixed effect equations generate positive, significant coefficients for FISDEP. Moreover, the magnitude of this coefficient is larger than that of all the other variables, suggesting a strong correlation. In 1995, a county with one million residents received 435,000 yuan in additional subsidies for a standard deviation increase in fiscal dependents from the fiscal system as a whole and 324,000 yuan in additional subsidies from the average province. In 2000, a one-standard deviation increase in fiscal dependents in the same county drew an additional 430,000 yuan in subsidies from the fiscal system as a whole. Even controlling for provincial effect, the same one-million resident county obtained an additional 352,000 yuan in additional subsidies. More than the other factors in the equations, the size of fiscal dependents in a county is closely tied with the amount of subsidies received by the county. In the next section, we seek to clarify the causal relationship between fiscal dependents and subsidies allocation.

In general, the results presented in Table 7.2 do not suggest that concerns of economic equity underlie the allocation of subsidies to counties after the implementation of the TSS. Viewing our results alongside Wong and West's (1997) earlier findings, we come to the pessimistic conclusion that the Chinese fiscal system has allocated regressively away from poor localities for much of the reform. The TSS did not change the regressive nature of the fiscal system. Furthermore, although central policies effected substantial transfers to agrarian provinces, provinces themselves did not seem eager to undertake similar redistribution to agrarian counties. This speaks volumes to the urban bias at the provincial level. Although there was a tendency to allocate subsidies to deficit counties, deficit counties were not necessarily poor. Moreover, the tendency to allocate to deficit counties says more about provincial anxiety about explicit, local deficits than economic equity. Finally, fear of wage arrears and potential instability drove higher-tier governments to allocate subsidies based on the fiscal dependents in a county.

## Clarifying the causal role of fiscal dependents

Our preliminary investigation makes it clear that the size of fiscal dependents is strongly related to subsidies remittance. However, the direction of causality remains unclear. Theoretically, the causal arrow can go either way, from dependents to subsidies and vice versa. With this endogeneity problem, the estimated coefficients of the explanatory variables are no longer statistically consistent. Thus, this remains an issue to be settled with further statistical tests.

Fortunately, we have two years of data, which allows us to conduct a two-stage least squares estimation (2SLS). This procedure enables us to exogenize the main variable of interest, the size of the fiscal dependents, in estimating its effect on subsidies in 2000. The instruments should be exogenous and should be correlated with the main explanatory variable, which is FISDEP in 2000. Here, we use fiscal shortfall in 1995 (FISSHORT95) and fiscal dependents in 1995 (FISDEP95) as instruments to generate predicted values for fiscal dependents in 2000 (PFISDEP00).[10] By construction, since PFISDEP00 is predicted using variables from 1995, endogeneity is no longer a problem.The first-stage results are reported in Panel B of Table 7.3.

Because of the changing number of counties since 1995, combining the data from both years results in the deletion of a significant number of observations. We have to delete both abolished counties and newly created counties from our sample. However, given our need to clarify the causal relationship between fiscal dependents and subsidies, we are required to make this tradeoff. After combining data from the two years, we are left with a little under 1,800 observations. If jurisdiction changes were not an issue, we would have over 1,900 observations. Thus, combining the data from these two years results in the loss of 5 percent of our sample.

In our 2SLS estimation, we estimate essentially the same equations as we did on Table 7.2. In the second stage, the dependent variable is subsidies in 2000, while the independent variables are fiscal shortfall, per capita output, the NDP county dummy, and economic structure in 2000, as well as the predicted values of fiscal dependents in 2000. We also add a lag of the dependent variable, subsidies in 1995 (SUB95) in the equation. In Panel A of Table 7.3, we display the coefficients of the second-stage estimation.

When we use instrumental variables to estimate fiscal dependents in 2000, we find that most of the explanatory variables have the same impact on the dependent variables as they do on Table 7.2. Most significantly we find that fiscal dependents have the same, enormous impact on subsidies allocation. A standard deviation surge in fiscal dependents still brought around 0.45 yuan in per capita subsidies. Because we use the 2SLS procedure, we can say more confidently that the relationship between fiscal dependents and subsidies is a causal one. In other words, rising numbers of fiscal dependents indeed drove the allocation of subsidies at the county level. Politically, this suggests a curious process of subsidies remittance. While higher-level governments were less willing or unwilling to allocate subsidies based on criteria of income and structural inequality, they were more than willing to remit subsidies to county governments to pay for rising wage bills.

This phenomenon suggests three possible processes. First, provincial and central governments might be happy to increase subsidies to pay for new government workers in the various vertically integrated bureaucracies. Second, because grassroots government officials constitute the frontline in the state's daily struggle to regulate and to control society, both provincial and central governments are willing to bolster the capabilities of grassroots government. Indeed, the central government issued several decrees urging local governments to first pay for wage bills before considering construction (Ministry of Finance 2003b). As suggested earlier, central concern for local wage arrears leaves room for local governments to opportunistically bolster cadre ranks in order to blackmail provincial and central governments for more subsidies. However, doing so is not without cost, since central and local transfers are not sufficient for the entire wage bill. Local governments that expand fiscal dependents recklessly would receive more subsidies, but would face an even greater wage bill and higher deficits.

When we consider both local deficits and fiscal dependents, a coherent strategy of bargaining with, if not blackmailing, higher levels of government emerges. Although grassroots government officials are at the mercy of their superiors at the provincial and central level, they can threaten higher authorities with the prospects for social instability. Again, since the provincial government and the center need grassroots governments to handle most mandates (such as compulsory primary education) and the "dirty work" (such as birth control), grassroots governments can expand both fiscal personnel and expenditure opportunistically to wrest more subsidies from the provinces and from the center. Although this may lead to bigger fiscal shortfalls, our findings suggest that grassroots governments are willing to expand fiscal dependents and local fiscal shortfalls to obtain more subsidies.

## Conclusions and implications of recent changes

How the Chinese government distributes its subsidies has important implications both for future growth trajectory and for political stability in China. If the state

*Table 7.3* Effect of past subsidies, fiscal shortfall, output, economic structure, and fiscal dependents on total subsidies in 2000

| | *SLS without dummies* | *2SLS with dummies* |
|---|---|---|
| *Panel A* | | |
| SUB95 | 0.499*** | 0.499*** |
| FISSHORT00 | –0.156*** | –0.151*** |
| OUTPUT00 | 0.029* | 0.030*** |
| ECONSTR00 | 0.086*** | 0.026** |
| PFISDEP00 | 0.456*** | 0.290*** |
| NDP | 0.13*** | 0.085*** |
| Tianjin | | –0.080*** |
| Hebei | | –0.465*** |
| Shanxi | | –0.306*** |
| Inner Mongolia | | –0.256*** |
| Liaoning | | –0.199*** |
| Jilin | | –0.174*** |
| Heilongjiang | | –0.176*** |
| Shanghai | | –0.031*** |
| Jiangsu | | –0.343*** |
| Zhejiang | | –0.218*** |
| Anhui | | –0.302*** |
| Fujian | | –0.368*** |
| Jiangxi | | –0.258*** |
| Shandong | | –0.443*** |
| Henan | | –0.255*** |
| Hubei | | –0.280*** |
| Hunan | | –0.338*** |
| Guangdong | | –0.490*** |
| Guangxi | | –0.336*** |
| Sichuan | | –0.277*** |
| Guizhou | | –0.219*** |
| Yunnan | | –0.278*** |
| Shaanxi | | –0.247*** |
| Gansu | | –0.216*** |
| Qinghai | | –0.090*** |
| Ningxia | | –0.109*** |
| Xinjiang | | –0.295*** |
| Hainan | | –0.138*** |
| Xizang | | –0.159*** |
| OBS | 1798 | 1798 |
| F Value | 369.91 | 584.13 |
| Adj-R2 | 0.7 | 0.88 |
| *Panel B* | | |
| FISSHORT95 | 0.028** | –0.026** |
| FISDEP95 | 0.338*** | 0.415*** |
| Adj-$R^2$ | 0.34 | 0.49 |

Note:
The coefficients are reported as standardized coefficients. Standard errors are not reported because they are irrelevant in interpreting standardized coefficients.
*, **, *** indicate significance at 10%, 5%, 1% level respectively

actively undertakes to redistribute from richer regions to poorer regions, comparative research suggests that China would benefit from a higher likelihood of sustainable growth and political stability (Barro 1999; Easterly 2003).[11] Our findings, however, suggest that other factors underlie the distribution of subsidies in China. First, the pervasiveness of earmarked grants still provides more affluent localities with an advantage in applying for earmarked grants. Second, subsidies distribution seems to be driven by central and provincial efforts to prevent social instability and the collapse of grassroots governments. Instead of allocating to poor places, the central and provincial governments reward counties that most aggressively expand their personnel and expenditure. Over time, this allocation logic can only drive local governments to compete with each other to expand. Thus, a major reason why county-level dependents grew by an average of 4.5 percent between 1994 and 1999 is that local governments knew that they could benefit from central subsidies with an expanded workforce (Wang 2002).

In 2001 and 2002 further fiscal reform was carried out, which will have additional impact on the fiscal situation at the grassroots level. First, the past few years saw the expansion of the tax-for-fee reform (*feigaishui*), which seeks to replace the myriad fees at the local level with a standard agricultural tax (Gao 2002). Because many local governments at the county level or below had relied on fees for a large part of their expenditure, the tax-for-fee reform will significantly reduce their revenue sources. To compensate these local governments, the central government has once again concocted another scheme. As with transfer payment subsidies, the new tax-for-fee reform subsidies (*feishui gaige butie*) are calculated based on "standard expenditure" and the difference in pre- and post-reform revenue collection (Ministry of Finance 2003d).

Not only is local government completely at the mercy of "standard" estimates from the central government, they are also at the mercy of provincial governments, which distribute central and provincial transfers to the county and township governments (Ministry of Finance 2003c). Provincial governments are also supposed to provide a substantial share of the transfers to grassroots governments to support the reform (Ministry of Finance 2003c). Given our findings that provincial governments have a considerable urban bias, it remains unclear how much provincial governments will actually transfer to needy rural counties undergoing the tax-for-fees reform. Grassroots governments' only recourse may be to extract more subsidies from the center and the provinces by further expanding fiscal dependents and local deficits.

Another major recent development in the fiscal system is the tax sharing scheme for enterprise and personal income tax instituted in 2002. The tax sharing scheme in 1994 gave local governments exclusive claims over enterprise and personal income tax. However, with the rise of income tax, the central government doubtless wanted to secure a share of this dynamic income stream. Thus local governments were ordered to give 50 percent of the new increases in personal and enterprise income tax over to the central government in 2002 and 60 percent thereafter (Yang 2004: 80). Local governments, including provincial, city, and county-level governments, would share the remaining portion. As in 1994, this tax-sharing scheme will undoubtedly increase local governments' dependence on central subsidies. According to our findings, the strongest leverage local governments have to bargain for higher subsidies is an expanding workforce.

Due to central and provincial concerns for wage arrears and social instability, as well as their dependence on grassroots-level governments to implement various policies, provincial and central governments' commitment to freeze wage subsidies in accordance with "standard" expenditure lacks credibility. Thus, local governments opportunistically increase the size of the local workforce to blackmail higher levels of government for more subsidies. As a consequence, although the new tax sharing scheme and the tax-for-fees reform will decrease local revenue sources, local governments might have an even *higher* incentive to expand their workforce, since an expanding workforce and fiscal shortfall, rather than poverty, constitutes the surest way to increase subsidies allocation. As both Western and Chinese scholars have pointed out, the expansion of local government workforce produces undesirable consequences, from more fee collection, wage arrears, to even the disintegration of local level governments (Wong 1998; Yu 2003b). In other words, the expansion of local government only serves to increase the thirst and the capacities for rent-seeking at the grassroots level (Bernstein and Lu 2003; Yao and Yang 2003; Yu 2003a). While local officials everywhere are tempted to prey on the resources in their territories, Chinese officials are further free from bottom-up accountability mechanisms like elections.

## Notes

1 We gratefully acknowledge Liu Mingxing for generously providing the county-level data that made this study possible. We also would like to thank Zhang Xiaobo for the NDP county data. Last but not least, we are grateful to Christine Wong, Vivienne Shue and other members of the "Paying for Progress" Workshop for their invaluable comments.

2 From available regulations, it seems that provincial governments have the discretion to devise schemes for distributing tax-rebate subsidies to the prefectures and counties. See, for example, Henan People's Government (2004).

3 In the original State Council document issued in 1993, tax rebates are set to grow at 0.3 times the average national growth rate of VAT and consumption tax combined. However, the State Council modified the rule in 1994 to peg tax rebate increases to the growth in local VAT and consumption tax collection, not the national growth. Christine Wong at the World Bank then further found that in fact the MOF was only rebating the portion of the growth in VAT and consumption tax collection kept by the center. See State Council (2003a).

4 Lou Jiwei, the vice-minister of finance in that period, was likely a major champion of the transfer payment subsidies. In a speech given in January 2000, Lou praised the new system extensively for its scientific precision and criticized the old system of subsidies allocation for its arbitrary nature. See Lou (2002).

5 Besides this formula-based portion of the transfer payment subsidies, there is also a "priority" transfer category which provides transfers to poverty counties, minority counties, counties near border regions, counties affected by major dam projects, and counties in military restriction areas. The amount disbursed for priority transfers seems to be minimal. See Finance Department of Anhui Province (2000b).

6 For an excellent discussion of how rosters are set see Mertha (2005).
7 We would like to thank Dr. Zhang Xiaobo at the International Food Policy Research Institute for generously sharing the poverty county data with us.
8 A small number of these observations were dropped through list-wise deletion in our regressions due to missing information.
9 Bonuses and some categories of subsidies are not included in the official budget, even if bonuses at times make up a large portion of a government employee's salary. Salaries of employees not on the state roster are also not listed in the formal budget. See Gansu People's Government (2002).
10 These two variables are not the perfect instruments, since they are slightly correlated with the main dependent variable. However, they have the lowest correlation with the dependent variable out of all of the variables in our data-set.
11 Barro finds that inequality only retards growth at low levels of development.

## References

Agriculture Department of the Ministry of Finance (2002) "Zhongguo caizheng fupin zhengce: huigu, pingjia, he tiaozheng" (Chinese poverty relief policies: review, evaluation, and adjustments), *Zhongguo Caijing Xinxi Ziliao* (Material on Chinese Finance and Economic Information), 2003 (3).

Ahmad, Ehtisham (1998) "The Reform of the Fiscal Transfer System," in D. Brean (ed.) *Taxation in Modern China*, London: Routledge.

Barro, Robert J. (1999) "Inequality, Growth, and Investment," in NBER (ed.) *NBER Working Paper*, Cambridge, MA: National Bureau of Economic Research.

Bernstein, Thomas P. and Lü Xiabo (2003) *Taxation without Representation in Contemporary Rural China*, Cambridge, UK and New York: Cambridge University Press.

Besley, Timothy, and Coate, Stephen (1999) "Centralized versus Decentralized Provision of Local Public Goods: a Political Economy Analysis," NBER Working Paper 7084, Cambridge, MA: National Bureau of Economic Research.

Brean, Donald (1998) "Fiscal Reform in Modern China: An Overview," in D. Brean (ed.) *Taxation in Modern China*, London: Routledge.

Budgetary Division of the Ministry of Finance (2001) *Quanguo Dishixian Caizheng Tongji Ziliao* (Statistical Material for Prefectures, Cities, and Counties Nationwide), Beijing: China Fiscal Economic Publisher.

Budgetary Division of the Ministry of Finance (2002) *Guojia Yusuan Juesuan Jiyao* (A Collection of Documents for the State Budget and Final Budget), Beijing: China Finance and Economic Publisher.

Easterly, William (2003) "The Middle Class Consensus and Economic Development," *World Bank Staff Paper*, Washington, DC: World Bank.

Fan Gang (1998) "Market-oriented Economic Reform and the Growth of Off-budget Local Public Finance," in D. Brean (ed.) *Taxation in Modern China*, London: Routledge.

Finance Department of Anhui Province (2000a) "1999 nian Anhui sheng zengjia jiguan shiye danwei zaizhi zhigong gongzi he lituixiu renyuan lituixiu fei 2000 niandu sheng duixia zhuanyi zhifu banfa" (The method of disbursing transfer payments to lower levels to pay for the 1999 increase in wages and retirement benefits for government employees and retirees), Ministry of Finance (ed.), Beijing: Ministry of Finance.

Finance Department of Anhui Province (2000b) "2000 nian Anhui sheng duixia zhuanyi zhifu banfa" (Method of transfer payment from the Anhui provincial government to lower levels), Ministry of Finance (ed.), Beijing: Ministry of Finance.

Gansu People's Government (2002) "Guanyu quebao jiguan shiye danwei zhigong gongzi anshi zu'e fafang de tongzhi" (Notice concerning guaranteeing the timely payment of wages to government and business workers) in Beida Yinghua (ed.) *Zhongguo Falü Jiansuo Xitong* (China Legal Search System), Beijing: Beida Yinghua.

Gao Jianmin (2002) "Nongcun Shuifei gaige dui jichu jiaoyu caizheng de yingxiang" (The effect of the agriculture tax-fee reform on the budget for basic education), *Jiaoyu Pinglun* (Education Commentaries), 2002 (6).

He Chengjun (2003) "Xianxiang caizheng kunnan: xianzhuang, cheng'en, chulu" (The difficulties of county and township finance: current status, causes, and solutions), *Xianxiang Caizheng* (County, Village Finance), 2: 4–7.

Henan People's Government (2004) "Guanyu wanshan fenshuizhi caizheng guanli tizhi de tongzhi" (Notice concerning perfecting fiscal management system under the tax division sharing system), Shanghai Yuxi Shangwu Consulting, 1996; available online at <http://www.law999.net/law/doc/d013/1996/01/28/00117591.html> (accessed 13 September 2004).

Lou Jiwei (2002) "Shenhua shuishou gaige, qianghua caizheng guanli" (Deepen the reform of taxation; strengthen fiscal management), in Budgetary Division of the Ministry of Finance (ed.) *Guojia Yusuan Juesuan Jiyao* (A Collection of Documents Related to the State Budget and Final Budget), Beijing: China Finance and Economic Publisher.

Mertha, Andrew (2005) "China's 'Soft' Centralization: Shifting Tiao/Kuai Authority Relations Since 1998," *China Quarterly*, 184: 791–810.

Ministry of Finance (2001a) "Guanyu bianzhi 2000 nian zhongyang he difang caizheng juesuan cao'an de tongzhi" (Notice concerning drafting the 2000 central and local final budgetary account), in Office of the Ministry of Finance (ed.) *Caizheng Guizhang Zhidu Xuanbian* (A Collection of Finance Rules and Systems), Beijing: China Finance and Economic Publisher.

Ministry of Finance (2001b) "Zhongyang dui difang zhuanxiang bokuan guanli banfa" (Method of managing the disbursement of earmarked funds from the center to the local governments), in Office of the Ministry of Finance (ed.) *Caizheng Guizhang Zhidu Xuanbian* (A Collection of Finance Rules and Systems), Beijing: Finance and Economic Publisher.

Ministry of Finance (2003a) "2002 nian yibanxing caizheng zhuanyi zhifu banfa" (The method for regular transfer payments in 2002)," in Budgetary Division of the Ministry of Finance and Treasury Division of the Ministry of Finance (ed.) *Difang Caizheng Juesuan Wenjian Ziliao: 2002* (Documents and Information Concerning Local Final Budgetary Reporting), Beijing: China Finance and Economic Publisher.

Ministry of Finance (2003b) "Guanyu bianzhi 2002 nian zhongyang he difang caizheng juesuan (cao'an) de tongzhi" (Notice concerning drafting the 2002 central and local final budgetary report), in Budgetary Division of the Ministry of Finance and Treasury Division of the Ministry of Finance (ed.) *Difang Caizheng Juesuan Wenjian Ziliao: 2002* (Documents and Information Concerning Local Final Budgetary Reporting), Beijing: China Finance and Economic Publisher.

Ministry of Finance (2003c) "Guanyu xiada 2002 nian nongcun feishui gaige shidian xian (shi) zhongyang zhuanyi zhifu zijin de tongzhi" (Notice concerning disbursing central transfer payment to the counties (cities) for the 2002 tax-for-fees reform), in Budgetary Division of the Ministry of Finance and Treasury Division of the Ministry of Finance (ed.) *Difang Caizheng Juesuan Wenjian Ziliao: 2002* (Documents and Information

Concerning Local Final Budgetary Reporting), Beijing: China Finance and Economic Publisher.

Ministry of Finance (2003d) "Nongcun feishui gaige zhongyang dui difang zhuanyi zhifu zhanxing banfa" (Temporary method of central transfer payments to the local governments to help rural tax-for-fees reform), in Budgetary Division of the Ministry of Finance and Treasury Division of the Ministry of Finance (ed.) *Difang Caizheng Juesuan Wenjian Ziliao: 2002* (Documents and Information Concerning Local Final Budgetary Reporting), Beijing: China Finance and Economic Publisher.

Mountfield, Edward, and Wong, Christine (2005) "Public Expenditure on the Frontline: Towards Effective Management of Public Expenditure by Sub-national Governments in East Asia," in R. White and P. Smoke (eds.) *East Asia Decentralizes*, Washington, DC: World Bank.

Oates, Wallace E. (1999) "An Essay on Fiscal Federalism," *Journal of Economic Literature*, 37 (3): 1120–49.

Park, Albert, Rozelle, Scott, Wong, Christine and Ren Changqing (1996) "Distributional Consequences of Reforming Local Public Finance in China," *China Quarterly*, 147 (9): 751–78.

People's Bank of China, and Ministry of Finance (2000) "Difang zhengfu xiang zhongyang zhuanxiang jiekuan guanli guiding" (Regulations managing local earmarked loans from the central government), PBOC (ed.), Beijing: People's Bank of China.

Smart, Michael (1998) "Taxation and Deadweight Loss in a System of Intergovernmental Transfers," *Canadian Journal of Economics*, 31 (1): 189–206.

State Council (2003a) "Guanyu fenshui zhi caizheng guanli tizhi shuishou fanhuan gaiwei yu bendiqu zengzhishui he xiaofei shui zengzhang lu guagou de tongzhi" (Notice concerning linking the tax rebate under the tax division fiscal management system to the growth rate of regional value-added tax and consumption tax), in Budgetary Division of the Ministry of Finance and Treasury Division of the Ministry of Finance (ed.) *Difang Caizheng Juesuan Wenjian Ziliao: 2002* (Documents and Information Concerning Local Final Budgetary Reporting), Beijing: China Finance and Economic Publisher.

State Council (2003b) "Guanyu shixing fenshui zhi caizheng guangli tizhi de jueding" (Decision concerning the budgetary management system for the tax sharing system), in Budgetary Division of the Ministry of Finance and Treasury Division of the Ministry of Finance (ed.) *Difang Caizheng Juesuan Wenjian Ziliao: 2002* (Documents and Information Concerning Local Final Budgetary Reporting), Beijing: China Economic and Finance Publisher.

State Council Poverty Relief Leading Group (2003) *Zhongguo Nongcun Fupin Kaifa Gaiyao* (A Summary of Poverty Relief and Development in China), Beijing: China Finance and Economic Publisher.

Su Ming (2003) "Wuoguo xianji caizheng wenti de fenxi yu zhengce jainyi" (A policy analysis of the county-level fiscal problems and policy recommendations), *Xianxiang Caizheng* (County, Village Finance), 1: 4–5.

Wang Chaocai (2002) "Xianxiang zhengfu xianfa gongzi wenti yanjiu" (Studies of the problem of wage arrears in township and county governments), *Xiangzhen Caizheng* (Township Village Finance), 7.

Wedeman, Andrew (1999) "Agency and Fiscal Dependence in Central–Provincial Relations in China," *Journal of Contemporary China*, 8 (20): 103–22.

Wong, Christine (1998) "Fiscal Dualism in China: Gradualist Reform and the Growth of Off-budget Finance," in D. Brean (ed.) *Taxation in Modern China*, London: Routledge.

Wong, Christine (2003) "Ethnic Minority Regions and Fiscal Decentralization in China: The Promises and Reality of Asymmetric Treatment," in R. M. Bird and R. Ebel (eds.) *Subsidiarity and Solidarity: The Role of Intergovernmental Fiscal Relations in Maintaining an Effective State in Diverse Countries*, Washington, DC: World Bank.

Wong, Christine (2005a) "Can China Change Development Paradigm for the 21st Century," in Stiftung Wissenschaft und Politik (ed.) *SWP Working Paper*, Berlin: SWP.

Wong, Christine (2005b) "Public Sector Budget Management Issues in China," in OECD Public Governance Committee (ed.) *Working Party of Senior Budget Officials*, Paris: OECD.

Wong, Christine, Heady, Christopher and Woo Wing Thye (1995) *Fiscal Management and Economic Reform in the People's Republic of China*, Hong Kong: Oxford University Press.

Wong, Christine, and West, Lorraine (1997) "Equalization Issues," in C. Wong (ed.) *Financing Local Government in the People's Republic of China*, Hong Kong: Oxford University Press.

World Bank (2002) *National Development and Sub-national Finance* (Report No. 22951–CHA), World Bank (ed.), Washington, DC: World Bank.

Yang, Dali L. (2004) *Remaking the Chinese Leviathan: Market Transition and the Politics of Governance in China*, Stanford, CA: Stanford University Press.

Yao Yang, and Yang Lei (2003) "Zhidu gonggei shiheng he zhongguo caizheng fenquan de houguo" (The consequences of the institutional supply imbalance and fiscal federalism in China), *Zhanlue yu Guanli* (Strategy and Management), 3.

Yu Jianrong (2003a) "Nongcun hei'e shili he jiceng zhengquan tuihua" (Rural criminal forces and the retreat of the basic level government), *Zhanlue yu Guanli* (Strategy and Management), 5: 1–14.

Yu Jianrong (2003b) "Nongmin you zuzhi kangzheng ji qi zhengzhi fengxian" (Organized protests by peasants and the political risks), *Zhanlue yu Guanli* (Strategy and Management), 3: 1–16.

# 8 Local governance, policy mandates and fiscal reform in China[1]

*Liu Mingxing and Tao Ran*

## Introduction

The dilemmas of local governance in contemporary China have recently received a great deal of attention from both academics and policymakers. Many Chinese farmers, especially those in less developed regions, have been plagued by excessive tax burdens, insecure land property rights and intrusive local governments. It is widely agreed that the size of local governments is excessive and expanding too quickly; at the same time, local provision of public services frequently remains insufficient and of low quality. From the center's perspective, local government officials, in pursuit of their own interests, tend to ignore the demands of local people. However local officials, for their part, complain that higher levels of government, (especially the center) unduly monopolize fiscal resources. They argue that in many less developed regions the center has failed to provide fiscal transfers commensurate with ever-increasing local expenditure needs, thus creating local fiscal insolvency leading to chronic under-provision of public services.

Such differing governmental perspectives have generated differing analyses of and proposed solutions to China's current problems in delivering good standards of local governance to its people. On the one hand, the center understands that local government officials, who are appointed from above and lack accountability to local people, have a tendency to stray from good governance practices; on the other hand, fearing that uncontrolled elections could gravely weaken the center's ability to enforce its policies and even destroy the Party's power base, the center has no strong desire to promote popular elections at local levels. Instead it has tried to restrain local officials by issuing numerous policy documents designed to regulate local governments, requiring them to be more accountable to the center.

Can the center effectively improve local governance by issuing more policy documents and regulations? Many expert observers believe that such measures will not work because local bureaucrats can always manage to find ways to evade central regulations when they conflict with local vested interests. While not pretending to be completely innocent of all bad governance practices, local government officials still believe that they have many reasons to complain. Facing heavy expenditure responsibilities and a host of unfunded development mandates, local governments have no way to make ends meet except by drawing on extrabudgetary revenue sources obtained through fees levied on farmers and profits generated through the expropriation of farmers' land. Therefore, local officials, especially those in less developed regions, constantly seek changes in intergovernmental fiscal arrangements aimed at securing either larger fiscal transfers or higher shares of tax revenue.

This chapter is an attempt to approach these questions based on an analysis of China's local governance in the context of its central–local framework and decentralization experiences. The chapter is structured as follows: the second part explains central–local political and economic arrangements and presents a brief analysis of China's local government accountability in this context. Drawing on our fieldwork, the third part describes local governance heterogeneity across regions and links such heterogeneity to differentiated factor mobility and policy burdens across regions. In this part, we also quantitatively test three hypotheses that account for the mechanism, the time-series and the cross-sectional variations of rural tax burdens. The fourth part describes the recent policy changes bearing on central-local arrangements and local governance. We argue that more fiscal transfers to less developed regions, though necessary, would be far from adequate to solve the challenges local governments in China are currently facing. The final part concludes.

## An analysis of China's decentralization and local governance

### *Central-local framework*

China's present-day central-local framework is the product of incremental changes made over the past two decades of transition. Along with other important reforms in the agricultural and the state-owned industrial sectors which promote work incentives, fiscal and administrative decentralization was pushed forward in the early 1980s.[2] In a country as large as China, deregulation and economic liberalization had to be accompanied by a degree of fiscal and administrative decentralization, for without close coordination by local governments, the reform measures could not have been implemented. In the 1980s, therefore, local governments began assuming primary responsibility for local development. They took on a broad range of responsibilities which entailed the power to determine prices, approve or disapprove the creation of new firms, and make major investments with "self-raised funds" such as bank loans or local extra-budgetary funds (Oi 1995). In the 1980s, a fiscal contracting system characterized by "dividing revenue and expenditure with each level of government responsible for balancing its own budget" was introduced to ensure that there would be incentives for local governments to collect revenues. At the same time, control over expenditures was further decentralized and local governments assumed primary responsibility for providing education, health, housing, local infrastructure, and so forth (Wong 2000).

While China has made significant progress in economic liberalization, the highly centralized control of personnel has remained largely intact even to this day. Politically, China has maintained a centralized political system with the

Communist Party as the single ruling party and local officials appointed from above (World Bank 2002) Therefore, the concepts of "constitutional decentralization" or "political decentralization" that are prevalent in the experiences of many other liberalizing and decentralizing systems do not apply to China (Bardhan 2002). Neither do local governments in China hold any institutionalized rights to participate in central decision-making procedures; nor are there any widely accepted free elections at township levels, or indeed, at any other of the levels of government that stretch upward from the townships to Beijing.[3]

Political centralization does not mean that there has been no change in the political arena. China's reform of its personnel control system coincided with the beginning of its economic reforms. A crucial turnaround in personnel management has involved the wholesale change in the evaluation criteria for government officials. Political conformity that used to be the only important pre-reform criterion for promotion, gave way to economic performance and other competence-related indicators (Li and Zhou 2005). There has been a growing literature that emphasizes the role of political incentives or career concerns on the part of local officials in China.[4]

### *Economic recentralization after 1994*

In China, responsibility for government expenditures was decentralized to local governments even in the 1980s. But important new fiscal and tax reforms undertaken in 1994 and afterwards significantly re-centralized control over revenues, and this created large vertical imbalances that have not been offset by a sufficient quantity of equalizing transfers. Though total transfers were increased, much of that increase came from hundreds of types of earmarked grants allocated in an *ad hoc*, nontransparent fashion rather than from general-purpose equalizing transfers, which signals the center's obvious intention to retain control.[5] Therefore, the fiscal reforms since the mid-1990s, taken together, have imposed heavy fiscal burdens on local governments, especially those in rural areas and in the poor regions of the country.[6]

The expenditure responsibilities before and after 1994 were nominally unchanged with the sub-provincial levels (prefecture, county, and township) still facing the expenditure responsibilities that had been delegated to them through the decentralization of the 1980s. However, a critical difficulty arose with respect to the responsibility for maintaining the social safety net, and this was further aggravated by the large-scale restructuring taking place in China's state-owned sectors in the late 1990s. Many of the social service and social security responsibilities that used to be taken care of by state-owned enterprises were now passed to local governments without corresponding resources being set aside to meet these responsibilities.[7] Many local governments became insolvent and were in urgent need either of additional transfers or of a further rationalization of the intergovernmental fiscal system.

According to the World Bank (2002), nearly 70 percent of total public expenditure in China takes place at the sub-national (i.e. provincial, prefecture, county, and township) level, of which more than 55 percent is at sub-provincial levels. Problems are most acute at the county and township levels, which together provide the bulk of vital public services, including 70 percent of budgetary expenditures for education, and 55–60 percent of those for health. Cities at prefecture and county levels account for all local expenditures on unemployment insurance, social security, and welfare. However, due in part to high tax rebates which are given to relatively developed regions, and to higher-level government expenditures on capital construction undertaken since the middle of the 1990s to stimulate domestic demand, the actual fiscal situation faced by the localities has diverged sharply across regions. In richer regions, local governments, especially those at the county and township level, are generally able to provide decent public goods and services to residents and businesses, since they not only enjoy higher tax revenues coming from the development of non-agricultural sectors, but can draw on additional high income from the sale of rights to develop local land, and from certain profit remittances they receive from TVEs. By contrast, in less developed areas, most of which are located in inland China, local revenues must come mainly from agriculture, and are much more limited. In the absence of sufficient and dependable equalizing transfers from higher levels of government, local governments in less developed areas have frequently found themselves unable to pay their bills.

### *Political centralization and local government accountability*

Under a still-centralized political system with extensive expenditure decentralization but with little revenue decentralization, local government officials have tended to be more responsive to higher-level government policies than they are to local needs. These officials are, after all, controlled from above both by tight hierarchical personnel arrangements and by fiscal transfer arrangements.

The problem is further complicated and aggravated by the fact that all levels of government in China are growth-driven in nature. In China there is a set of performance indicators at all levels of local government that are used to evaluate local officials. The indicators usually include a number of economic targets such as the annual growth achieved in local GDP, the revenue collected and contributions to higher levels of the state, the volume of foreign investment attracted, as well as various "social" targets such as those for birth control, maintaining public security, raising school enrolments and so on. For example, throughout the 1980s and 1990s in agriculture-based regions, reaching the state grain procurement quota and implementing birth control policies were invariably two essential policy targets to be fulfilled at the township and village level (Edin 2003). Successfully reaching or exceeding the targets set up by higher-level governments is decisive for local officials seeking political promotion. In a process of political competition for promotion across all regions, local government officials understandably compete against each other to reach such policy targets.

In brief, the logic of local governance in a politically centralized system runs as follows: a system where all local leadership is appointed and monitored from above has to be kept because it is necessary for the Party to stay in power. Under continued political centralization, the policy targets of local governments are set from above since there is no election mechanism to reveal voters' preferences and thus to monitor local governments from below. Given that such policy targets must be implemented locally, the center has to monitor local leaders by stipulating policy targets and evaluating cadres in their performance on the basis of how well or poorly those policy targets are achieved.[8] To ensure that policy targets are met by local governments, the center either has to provide them with some financial support in the form of transfers, or it has to give them a certain autonomy in administrative methods and in taxation. In principle, the center could provide fiscal transfers to cover all the policy implementation costs. However, the financial and personnel costs of local policy implementation are not fully known to the upper-level government. The upper-level government, understanding its information disadvantage and that transfers alone would not be sufficient in inducing policy coordination, has to grant local governments a degree of autonomy in taxation (by, for example, turning a blind eye to illicit fee collections). However, once such autonomy is granted, local governments are able to take advantage of and draw on the legitimacy of higher levels of government to overcharge farmers and even engage in rent-seeking in the name of implementing upper-level policy. Under such circumstances, the center not only controls political appointments, but also has a strong incentive to control formal fiscal revenues while at the same time granting a degree of local informal fiscal autonomy. Therefore, controls on local cadres' careers, fiscal transfers, and a certain scope for local informal tax autonomy can all be used as carrots and sticks to induce better local coordination.

## Local governance heterogeneity, factor mobility and policy mandates

### *Heterogeneity in local governance practices*

Under the powerful influence of this general "logic" we also observe significant regional variations in local governance practices. In the more developed coastal regions, to a large extent, local governments have limited their predatory and regulatory roles and have been much quicker in readjusting their local policies. In wealthy Zhejiang province, for example, township governments have significantly changed their roles, lately emphasizing their provision of public services rather than their enforcement of administrative regulations. By setting up the so-called "Enterprise Service Centers" and "Agriculture Service Centers," township governments in the region have strengthened their roles in providing various public services to compete for industrial investment and promote agricultural development. Meanwhile, in many less developed regions, local governments tend to remain firmly engaged in implementing higher-level government policies so as to reach the policy mandates imposed from above.

The regional variation in governance practices can best be described by comparing the ranking of different policy mandates in local cadre evaluation.

Table 8.1 lists the top five tasks with the greatest weights in the evaluation of township cadres set by the county governments for 12 counties (or county-level districts) across nine provinces in China where the authors conducted surveys. We observe that fiscal revenue and tax collection targets are invariably important tasks to be fulfilled by township governments. In addition, birth control and public security targets are always policy mandates with veto-power for township governments.[9] However, there is also significant variation in the way these policy mandates are ranked by the county-level governments. In richer provinces such as Zhejiang and Fujian, evaluation of the implementation of central policies such as birth control and public security tends to be less important, while the policies initiated by county and municipal governments tend to be more important. These locally initiated policies usually focus on anti-corruption, environmental protection, urban infrastructure development, and local public service provision that are more closely related to building a climate conducive to investment in the locality. In contrast, the least developed regions of Gansu and Shaanxi attach much weight to state policies such as birth control, agricultural restructuring and compulsory education.[10] In the middle-income regions such as Sichuan, Henan, Hebei and Anhui which are agriculture-based provinces with fewer central transfers but heavier tax burdens and more serious conflicts between farmers and local cadres, the priority tasks for township governments are not only controlling birth and promoting agricultural restructuring, but also collecting taxes and preventing large-scale farmers' petitions and demonstrations.[11]

Administrative and fiscal arrangements also differ across regions. While in more developed regions, horizontal administration (or *kuaikuai*, or more decentralized administration) dominates, administration through line bureaux (or *tiaotiao*, or vertical, more centralized administration) is more common in less developed regions. Take Zhejiang, Hubei, and Gansu as examples. Before the rural tax reform in 2003, in the most developed province of Zhejiang, both the finance department and the land department were under the direct control of the township governments, while in the middle-income province of Hubei, township finance departments were under the control of township governments, but land departments were controlled by county land bureaux. The situation has recently been changed: with a tightening central policy on land management and the rural tax reform, Zhejiang's land departments at township level are now vertically administered with personnel and salaries directly controlled by county-level land bureaux. In Hubei, owing to the serious shortfalls at the county level, even finance departments are now vertically controlled by county finance bureaux. In the least developed province of Gansu, both land and finance departments at township levels were and still are vertically controlled directly by county bureaux to ensure tighter controls by upper-level governments. This is consistent with the regional patterns of county-township fiscal arrangements. In fiscal terms, township governments in relatively developed regions enjoy more fiscal autonomy and a higher marginal share in revenue. Township governments in Gansu province have no independent budgets.[12] Meanwhile in middle-income provinces such as Hunan and Anhui,[13] the most common fiscal arrangement is the so-called "Tax Sharing

*Table 8.1* Priority given to policy mandates in township cadre evaluation across regions

| *Rank*<br>*Locality* | *1* | *2* | *3* | *4* | *5* | *Targets with veto power* |
|---|---|---|---|---|---|---|
| Linxia county, Gansu province | Area of new terrace built | Agricultural tax and fiscal revenue | Birth control | Compulsory education | Number of new industrial enterprises | Birth control, public security |
| Binxian county, Shaanxi province | Agricultural restructuring | Fiscal revenue | Attracting outside investment | Per capita net income | Grain output | Birth control, public security, farmers' petition |
| Yantan district, Zigong city, Shichuan province | Fiscal revenue | Agricultural restructuring | Birth control | Per capita farmer's net income | GDP growth | Fiscal revenue, birth control, public security, working safety |
| Yuanyan county, Henan province | Industrialization level | Attracting outside investment | Upper level transfers | Birth control | Road construction | Road construction, farmers' petition, anti-corruption |
| Anyan county, Henan province | Birth control | Farmers' petition | Fiscal revenue | GDP growth | Number of labor migrating out | Birth control, public security, environment protection |
| Suning county, Hebei province | Upper level transfers and investment | Fiscal revenue | Grass-root party organization development | Farmers' petition | Birth control | Birth control, public security, working safety |

| | | | | | | |
|---|---|---|---|---|---|---|
| Qinyang county, Anhui province | Attracting outside investment | Fiscal revenue | Urban infrastructure development | Birth control | Public security | Birth control, public security |
| Xinhua county, Jiangsu province | GDP | Attracting outside investment | Fiscal revenue | Farmers' petition | Compulsory education | Attracting outside investment, birth control, farmers' petition, work safety, anti-corruption |
| Longhai county, Fujian province | Attracting outside investment | Fiscal revenue | Farmers' petition and public security | Grass-root party organization development | Urban and industrial development | |
| Changshan county, Zhejiang province | Attracting outside investment | Anti-corruption | Township leadership coordination | Fiscal revenue growth from industries | Farmers' petition | Birth control, public security |
| Xiucheng district, Jiangxin city, Zhejiang province | Attracting outside investment | Fiscal revenue from industries | Green agriculture | Urban development | Anti-corruption | |
| Linan county, Zhejiang province | Attracting outside investment | Number of industrial enterprises above scale | Fiscal revenue growth | Industrial growth | Urban and infrastructure development | Birth control, environmental protection, public security, attracting outside investment, corruption |

Note: In the table, the localities are arranged (from top to bottom), by local farmers' net income in ascending order

*Table 8.2* Priority given to policy mandates in village cadre evaluation across regions

| *Rank*<br>*Locality* | *1* | *2* | *3* | *4* | *5* | *Tasks with veto power* |
|---|---|---|---|---|---|---|
| Hanji township, Linxia county, Gansu province | Birth control | Agricultural tax | Public security | Road construction | Compulsory education | Birth control, public security |
| Yuanba township, Guangyuan, Sichuan province | Agricultural tax | Agricultural restructuring | Party organization development | Road construction | Grain output | Birth control, public security |
| Jinhe township, Guangyuan county, Sichuan province | Agricultural tax | Birth control | Public security | Party organization development | Working safety | Birth control, public security |
| Linyang township, Qingyang, county, Anhui province | Agricultural tax | Birth control | Public security | Party organization development | Village land management | Birth control, public security |
| Xinhuanlu township, Renqiu county, Hebei province | Agricultural restructuring | Agricultural tax | Public security | Party organization development | Birth control | Birth control, tax collection, farmers' petition, and anti-corruption |
| Diaoyu township, Xinhua county, Jiangsu province | New tax collection | Tax arrears collection | Village debt relief | Birth control | Farmers' petition | Tax collection, birth control, anti-corruption, farmers' petition |

| | | | | | | |
|---|---|---|---|---|---|---|
| Zhangtan township, Quzhou county, Zhejiang province | Industrial investment | Farmers' petition | Birth control | Village collective economy | Village administration | Birth control, public security, village administration, anti-corruption |
| Huibu township, Changshan county, Zhejiang province | Village planning | Farmers' petition | Agricultural restructuring | Birth control | Land management | Birth control, public security, working safety |
| Gaohong township, Linan county, Zhejiang province | Environment protection | Agricultural development | Birth control | Public security | Private enterprise development | Birth control, public security |

Note: In the table, the localities are arranged (from top to bottom) by local farmers' net income in ascending order.

System," in which, for any given tax, the township-level government usually delivers a certain benchmark amount to the county government, and then the additional revenue is shared by township and county. In the most developed regions such as Zhejiang, a different type of revenue sharing according to actually realized revenue is more common. Under this system, county-township governments do not share revenue by tax categories, but share according to the total tax revenue actually collected.[14] Though under such a system benchmark revenue or revenue quotas for major taxes are still imposed to ensure local delivery of taxes to the center, the revenue quotas to be submitted to upper levels usually constitute only a small share of total local revenue. This implies that township governments in more developed regions can reach their revenue quotas relatively easily and thus enjoy higher fiscal autonomy than those in less developed regions. The higher degree of administrative and fiscal decentralization means that in more developed regions local governments have both more incentives and higher capacities to serve local demands.

### *Factor mobility, policy burdens and local governance heterogeneity*

One important reason for interregional heterogeneity in local governance practices as well as in administrative and fiscal systems is variable actor mobility. In an industrializing country like China, interregional differences in levels of development contribute significantly to differences in local governance practices. In coastal regions where market-oriented industrialization started earlier, factor mobility is much higher and competition for investment and labor has begun to push local governments to deregulate and rescind various local policies that may restrict factor mobility or local competitiveness. To attract investment and increase the value of land (which is immobile but can be an important source of local extra-budgetary revenue), local governments in rapidly industrializing regions are keen to invest heavily in infrastructure development from local budgets and to establish industrial and commercial development parks offering preferential policies and tax breaks to investors. While in less developed regions with lower factor mobility (or where production factors, under market forces, are mostly moving out to other regions), competition for investment is less intense and local governments have a tendency to be more regulatory, or more predatory.[15]

However, we believe the factor mobility story cannot fully account for all the interregional heterogeneity in local governance in China. The particular growth-driven development strategy and the various policy mandates imposed from above have tended to produce even larger adverse impacts on less developed regions than would have been expected since the developed regions experience far less difficulty in meeting the policy mandates set by upper levels. For example, before the grain market liberalization in the early 2000s, state grain procurement quotas differed markedly across regions. The localities with higher per capita arable land (mainly more agriculture-based regions in inland China) usually had to fulfill heavier state grain procurement quotas.[16] In the late 1990s grain procurement quotas as a share of total grain output could be as high as 30–40 percent in the central province of Hunan and in Jilin, while they amounted to virtually zero in coastal provinces such as Zhejiang and Guangdong (Tao et al. 2004). As shown in our next section, the fact that rural tax burdens were heaviest in regions with high grain quotas is actually not a mere coincidence. It is precisely in these middle-income regions where there is relatively developed agriculture but a poorly developed industrial base, and where central transfers are scarce, that local governments directly tax farmers.

All in all, in more developed regions, the increasingly intensive interregional competition that has resulted from the much higher mobility of labor and capital, together with what are in effect proportionately lower policy burdens from above, have worked well to curb predatory and excessively regulatory government behavior and to make local government officials relatively adept at adjusting irrational policies to better meet local realities and relatively quick to compete in providing better services. However, in less developed regions, lower factor mobility, together with the relatively tougher-to-meet central development mandates and higher dependence on upper-level transfers work systematically to distort local government behavior and draw local governments in these regions into a style of political performance that caters to higher levels of government instead of local people and encourages unhealthy competition for upper-level transfers. Under heterogeneous policy burdens, yardstick competitions that involve comparing and evaluating local governance across regions become distorted. This means that competitions lose their effect in evaluating, controlling, and motivating cadres because everyone understands that policy mandates differ across localities and that the accomplishments of cadres in different localities cannot be simply measured with a single yardstick.

### *Policy mandates and rural informal taxation*

Policy mandates under central-local information asymmetry in implementation costs have also contributed to the perpetuation, even after the centralizing fiscal reforms of the mid-1990s, of what are effectively soft budget constraints on local governments. The issue of informal (i.e. illicit) fee collection by local authorities provides a good example. In the mid-1990s, excessive rural informal tax burdens became an increasingly serious problem in many agriculture-based regions in inland China where there were growing farmers' frustrations and complaints against local government predation (Bernstein 1999). As argued earlier, this phenomenon can in part be attributed to policy mandates having necessitated the granting of a degree of local tax autonomy. Since the financial and personnel costs of local policy implementation are not fully known to the upper-level government, the latter, understanding its information disadvantage and that transfers alone are not sufficient in inducing policy coordination, has to grant local governments some autonomy in taxation. The basic hypothesis here is:

> Hypothesis 1 "Policy mandates and rural informal taxation": other things being equal, the heavier the policy mandates from above, the higher the rural informal fees, including illegitimate local fundraising.

Starting from the 1990s, China has witnessed significant changes in the state grain procurement system. Further lifting of restrictions on grain trading and moves to commercialize the state grain trading system all led to a surge in market-oriented grain distribution and a gradual decline of state grain quotas (Sicular 1995; Rozelle 1996; Rozelle et al. 2000; de Brauw et al. 2004). The gradual erosion of state grain procurement quotas made it increasingly unlikely for township and village officials to deduct state agricultural tax and some of the local fees before paying farmers for their state grain quota deliveries. As a result, local officials now had to draw the state agricultural tax and fees directly out of farmers' pockets. This would significantly raise the costs of tax collection by increasing local cadres' administrative and personnel costs. In response, higher local fees had to be collected to compensate the revenue shortfalls.[17]

> Hypothesis 2.1 "Transition from low-cost taxation to high-cost taxation": other things being equal, the less likely it is that local officials can deduct state agriculture tax and local informal fees via the state grain procurement system, the higher their tax collection costs, thus the higher their local fee charges.

A further impact of agricultural liberalization was that it reduced both the quantity of the state grain quota as well as the grain market-procurement pricing margin. China's countryside in the 1990s also witnessed a fast price liberalization on all other major cash crops, sideline products, and on major agricultural inputs.[18] It used to be the case in the 1980s that local governments collected implicit taxes on crops such as grain (through over-procurement), cotton, rapeseed, sideline products such as cocoons and pigs, and agricultural inputs such as fertilizers and pesticides since they could control the transaction channels and prices. The gradual erosion of state grain procurement quotas, along with gradual erosion of regulations on cash crops and declining controls on transaction channels of major agricultural outputs and inputs, reduced the implicit taxes local governments could have access to, resulting in rising explicit taxes levied.

> Hypothesis 2.2 "Transition from implicit taxation to explicit taxation": other things being equal, the less local governments are able to levy implicit taxes (in the case of grain, through the price margin between the grain market price and the state procurement price), the more likely they are to turn to explicit fee charges.

Finally, the higher level of industrialization in some regions contributed to their lower levels of taxation. China's growth in the course of economic transition has been a spatially uneven process in which the coastal regions have been able to industrialize faster. This has been true also even for what were historically rural or agriculture-based localities. Rural counties in the coastal regions were able to achieve faster growth through booming TVEs, for example. Therefore, regions with faster industrialization opted to collect taxes on industrial firms. When grain sector marketization rendered direct tax deduction through the grain procurement system less likely and the cost of collecting taxes from individual rural households began to outweigh the resulting revenues generated, it became more cost-effective for local governments in more developed regions to forego such taxes and make up the lost revenue from industrial firms.

> Hypothesis 3 "Transition from agricultural tax to industrial tax": other things being equal, the higher the level of industrialization in the locality, the more likely local governments are to shift to industrial taxation, and the lower the direct tax burdens on individual farmers.

Using a large panel data set of over 6,000 rural households in 120 villages across 10 provinces from 1995 to 1999, we are able to account for the mechanism, the dynamics as well as the cross-sectional variation in rural explicit tax burdens within an integrated empirical framework.[19] Table 8.3 shows our quantitative results using fixed effect models that control both village and year dummies. The dependent variables represent different types of explicit informal rural tax burdens per capita for the $i^{th}$ household in $j^{th}$ village in year t. Specifically, $Hfeetotal_{ijt}$ is defined as total local fees per capita, $Hfee1_{ijt}$ is defined as the local fees legitimated by the state per capita, $Hfee2_{ijt}$ is defined as various local levies not legitimate but imposed by local government and village community organizations per capita. Therefore, *Hfeetotal*=*Hfee*1+*Hfee*2. We use the household-level tax variables as dependent variables, which enables us to use household land and labor variables that are important determinants of rural fee charges. We do not discuss the state agricultural tax here since this tax is a formal tax with state-defined rates rather than local fees that are more at the discretion of local officials.

Since state grain procurement was one of the major, though declining, policy mandates in rural China from the 1980s to 1990s, we use $Vgrainquota_{ijt}$, the per capita government grain procurement quota at village level as our policy mandate variable to test Hypothesis 1. Other independent variables include the implicit tax variable ($Pricemargin_{ijt}$), the ratio of grain market price to government procurement price at the village level minus one to test Hypothesis 2.2; and the industrialization variable (*Countyind*) represented by the share of industrial output in total output at the county level to test Hypothesis 3. To test Hypothesis 2.1, we include two variables as the proxies for the degree of non-availability of direct state agricultural tax deduction via state grain procurement. *Vnonde*1 represents the share of households in a village whose state agricultural tax cannot be fully deducted beforehand from their grain procurement payment. An alternative variable *Vnonde*2 is also used for robustness, which is a variable indicating the share of state agricultural tax in a village that cannot be deducted from grain quota payment.

Beside the village and year dummies, other control variables are also included. *Hlandpc* is the household-level arable land per capita. *Hlabshare* is the share of laborers as a share of household population, $Vsize_j$ is the total population of a village. $Vinc_{jt}$ is the average per capita net income in a village, and $Vpub_{jt}$ is the

*Table 8.3* Rural tax burden regressions, 1995–1999 (village and year dummies controlled)

| | *Regressions with Vnondesh*[a] | | | *Regressions with Vnondesh*[b] | | |
|---|---|---|---|---|---|---|
| | *Hfeetotal* | *Hfee*[b] | *Hfee*[c] | *Hfeetotal* | *Hfee*[b] | *Hfee*[c] |
| Vgrainquota | 0.115<br>(9.43)*** | 0.061<br>(9.49)*** | 0.054<br>(7.02)*** | 0.119<br>(8.20)*** | 0.032<br>(4.32)*** | 0.087<br>(8.70)*** |
| Vnondesh1 | 28.574<br>(13.49)*** | 17.812<br>(16.66)*** | 10.762<br>(7.71)*** | | | |
| Vnondesh2 | | | | 3.133<br>(6.83)*** | 0.311<br>(1.83)* | 2.822<br>(8.56)*** |
| Pricemargin | –5.021<br>(3.62)*** | –2.555<br>(3.44)*** | –2.466<br>(2.87)*** | –5.749<br>(4.09)*** | –3.174<br>(4.23)*** | –2.575<br>(2.91)*** |
| Countyind | –18.975<br>(4.72)*** | –1.091<br>( 0.49) | –17.884<br>(6.77)*** | –19.151<br>(4.68)*** | –1.28<br>(0.56) | –17.871<br>(6.67)*** |
| Hlandpc | 14.393<br>(23.50)*** | 8.053<br>(24.06)*** | 6.341<br>(18.65)*** | 13.977<br>(21.34)*** | 8.001<br>(22.03)*** | 5.976<br>(16.68)*** |
| Hlabshare | 13.967<br>(3.24)*** | 9.674<br>(3.56)*** | 4.293<br>(2.36)** | 14.541<br>(3.21)*** | 9.954<br>(3.58)*** | 4.588<br>(2.34)** |
| Vinc | 0.02<br>(5.92)*** | 0.01<br>(5.72)*** | 0.01<br>(4.20)*** | 0.019<br>(5.38)*** | 0.009<br>(5.24)*** | 0.01<br>(3.78)*** |
| Vsize | 0.005<br>(1.62] | 0.007<br>(3.21)*** | –0.002<br>(0.75) | –0.004<br>(1.16) | 0.001<br>(0.36) | –0.005<br>(2.08)** |
| Vpub | 3.94<br>(0.61) | 2.877<br>(0.77) | 1.063<br>(0.3) | 5.246<br>(0.81) | 2.01<br>(0.54) | 3.236<br>(0.9) |
| Constant | 65.343<br>(15.03)*** | 25.857<br>(10.41)*** | 39.486<br>(14.95)*** | 104.253<br>(20.87)*** | 38.853<br>(14.41)*** | 65.4<br>(19.37)*** |
| Obsers | 28819 | 28819 | 28819 | 28540 | 28540 | 28540 |
| R-squared | 0.56 | 0.64 | 0.38 | 0.56 | 0.63 | 0.38 |

Note:

a Robust t statistics in parentheses.

b * significant at 10%; ** significant at 5%; *** significant at 1%.

c All tax and income data are deflated into 1995 prices using the NSB provincial CPI.

share of collective economy in a village represented by the operating income for collective enterprise as a share of village gross operating income.

As Table 8.3 indicates, for regressions of different definitions of rural informal tax burdens, the coefficients for our policy mandate variable (*Vgrainquota*) are positive and significant at 1 percent level. The coefficients for the (non)-availability of direct tax deduction via state grain procurement (*Vnondesh*1 and *Vnondesh*2) are all positive and mostly significant at 1 percent level in Table 8.3. This supports our hypothesis 2.1 of "Transition from low-cost taxation to high-cost taxation." The coefficients for the implicit tax variable (*Pricemargin*) are all negative and significant for different definitions of local fees. This basically supports our Hypothesis 2.2 of "Transition from implicit taxation to explicit taxation." The coefficients for local industrialization (*Countyind*) are all negative and almost all statistically significant for *Hfeetotal* and *Hfee*2 at 1 percent level, but not for *Hfee*1. This means higher industrialization reduced local informal taxation mainly through its effects on *Hfee*2, the illegitimate fund-raising. This generally supports our Hypothesis 3 of "Transition from agricultural taxation to industrial taxation" in more industrialized regions.

## Fiscal reform and local governance

### *More fiscal transfers?*

By assuming that underdeveloped regions suffer from inadequate transfers, many analysts have argued that increasing transfers will have a salutary effect. But more careful studies have shown that the overall impact of intergovernmental transfers within the Chinese fiscal system is disequalizing – net of all effects, intergovernmental transfers tend to favor more developed provinces (World Bank 2002). Clearly, reliable levels of transfer should be made to poor localities that are otherwise genuinely starved of revenue. But higher transfers alone could hardly be expected to solve governance problems in such regions. If transfers are to be effective, they must include clear, credible, multi-year guidelines and commitments agreed between the center and local government. What have been the institutional obstacles that have prevented such a formula-based transfer mechanism from being established? And assuming that central transfers can be made to reach the people in greatest need, what might be the coordinated mechanism that would ensure such delivery?

As argued above, given lower factor mobility, and the existence of heavier policy burdens and higher dependence on upper level transfers, government accountability to the local constituency tends to be lower in less developed regions. Under these circumstances, enhancing transfers may only result in more political competition for the transfers, further expansion of local bureaucracies,[20] and rent-seeking behavior. Some good examples of this syndrome can be found in poverty alleviation projects. In China, one problem plaguing investment in poor areas is that subsidized loans and grant funds are often diverted to other uses before they can even reach the local people. In a study of the "Food for Work" (FFW) project in Guizhou and Sichuan provinces, Kang (1998) pointed out that some of the investments included in FFW in the 1990s had no direct relation to poverty reduction, and diversion of funds was a common practice. Such practices heavily dampened the effectiveness with which central poverty funds are used to the extent that Zhu and Jiang (1996) found that only through creative investment fund management, primarily dependent on keeping investment funds out of the fiscal system, could large investments be effectively made in remote rural areas. In the subsidized loan program, local officials have strong incentives to direct funds toward industrial projects, not only because they might generate more fiscal resources, but also because local officials face career evaluations in which TVE output and profit count as major indicators of successful performance even if they fail to contribute significantly to poverty alleviation (Morduch 2000). All such practices result in the leakage of benefits away from the poor and constitute a major constraint on the effectiveness of China's anti-poverty programs.

The diversion of transfers has not changed as much as might be hoped in recent years. Our field investigations in Gansu province in 2004 also found that after the rural tax reform, although the central government had significantly increased transfers for rural education, the local finance bureau retained almost all of the transfers for school operating expenditures and diverted them to other uses.[21] Therefore, increasing transfers alone may help to resolve resource problems, but without resolving incentive problems. Indeed, enhancing transfers may make incentive problems worse since local governments in the less developed regions have much stronger incentives now to plead poverty and to divert existing funds into other uses (so that the need for central government support becomes yet more obvious).

One important question pertains to why the center, with its greater resources after the 1994 fiscal reform, has not increased its equalizing general purpose transfers but has instead significantly increased earmarked transfers? The first answer to this question relates again to problems in local governance. The center knows that in lacking accountability to their people, local governments may easily divert general-purpose transfers to bureaucratic expansion and staff wages rather than to public goods and services that reach the villagers. Under these circumstances, earmarking the transfer and directing its use to designated purposes seems the only sensible alternative. However, given that funds are allocated from above and that the cadres' performance is evaluated by certain "core" indicators that are relatively easy to monitor, earmarking transfers inevitably distorts local incentives.[22]

Another problem with earmarked transfers lies in the arbitrary way in which transfer decisions are made, which has led to tactics of extensive negotiation and further rent-seeking by local authorities. Lack of rule-based formulae and transparency in transfers tends to systematically distort local incentives and draw local governments in poor regions into unhealthy competition for more transfers and political performance that caters to higher levels rather than local residents. In the end, these transfers are usually channeled into poorly targeted patronage-type programs that provide grants too small and dispersed to meet basic needs in poorer regions. One example of this is also to be found in the evolution of the poverty alleviation programs now carried out across China. In these programs the political competition for attaining "poverty county" status was fierce (Park et al. 2002).

### *Decentralization or re-centralization?*

Recent years have seen a trend toward a re-centralization of powers in the areas of both fiscal and administrative reform. On the fiscal front, the center has begun to claim a share of the personal and enterprise income taxes that used to belong exclusively to localities. In 2002 the central government also initiated the rural tax reform that aims to remove all local fee charges and replace them with land-based agricultural taxes and fiscal transfers from upper-level governments.

Centralizing administrative measures have also been introduced. The most striking examples are in rural land requisitions and arable land protection. Responding to protests by farmers about the inadequacy of the compensation for requisitioned land, the center sent out many policy documents to local governments requiring them to constrain their abusive land-requisitioning practices and increase compensation to farmers. The center also plans to centralize the power to requisition land to the provincial and central level by establishing a vertically controlled land management system with tighter land supply quotas and stronger supervision. Such measures reflect the center's intention of limiting transgressions in granting arable land use rights, illicit expropriations of arable land and actions damaging to arable land management. Starting in 2005, numerous development zones have had to be removed and national inspection teams have been sent out. A newly promulgated Party document has declared that China intends to establish and implement the most rigorous arable land protection system in the world to ensure farmers' rights and national food security (State Council 2004).

Broadly speaking then, instead of decentralizing controls further, the center has lately sought to centralize fiscal and administrative power. Considering some of the very serious problems that have prevailed in rural taxation and in land requisitioning, and the social unrest and political instability that have ensued, it is understandable that the center has chosen to implement such policies. But it is dubious as to whether these new measures will bring the desired results. In general, in the absence of free elections and meaningful local participation, local governments inevitably lack genuine accountability and the center has to step in to heavily regulate local government behavior, directly dictating what shall be done and what cannot be done. Once local governments are deprived of most of their fiscal and administrative autonomy, the only choice for the center is to keep control in its own hands and provide transfers. While these transfers embody central policy intentions, they not only entail significant costs in dampening local initiatives to mobilize resources and cater to local needs, they may also easily lead to the further expansion of the local bureaucracy and to rent-seeking.

In recent years local governments in some agricultural regions have responded to the rural tax reforms with various countermeasures to cushion the negative fiscal impacts. During our recent visit to a county in Hunan,[23] we found that local leaders had significantly raised the "permanent agricultural output from unit of land" on which the agricultural tax is based to compensate for the center's having required the agricultural tax rate to be set at 7 percent and its having removed all fee charges. At the same time, a local fee levy for "flood control" was significantly raised. As another example, in our recent field survey in Northern Jiangsu,[24] we found that though the agricultural tax and fees that used to be the main local revenue source had been gradually phased out after the rural tax reform, other forms of charges such as those for vehicle plates, marriage certificates, and administrative fees for land turnover contracts had increased significantly. Although in some regions cutting redundant staff from government administration and public services has begun in response to the "hunger therapy" that has followed the rural tax reform, such downsizing has been very difficult to implement in practice.[25]

Another and perhaps more profound issue hampering the rural tax reform and fiscal centralization is that local governments are now increasingly dependent on higher-level government transfers. The problem lies not so much in whether the center can provide sufficient transfers, but in whether such gap-filling transfers will discourage local resource mobilization and give perverse signals of a "soft budget constraint" to local governments. If local finance and fiscal authority are de-linked from local governments' service provisioning responsibilities and functions, then local officials will have little incentive to effectively provide public goods and services because a higher share of fiscal resources would come from transfers that would better reflect upper-level policy intentions. Therefore, expenditure decentralization without corresponding local tax powers will not engender the tax competition that drives the revenue-maximizing local governments, nor will it promote local government's incentives to serve the real needs of local populations. On the contrary, decentralization funded by "common pool" resources like grants and revenue-sharing might have the opposite effect. By severing the link between taxes and benefits, mere expenditure decentralization might turn the public sector's resources to uses of little relevance to local needs.

A similar logic applies to the recent reform of land administration. Even if the centralizing policy measures can limit abusive land requisitions in the short term, it will not work well in the long term since monitoring costs will be very high and local governments will be able to find ways to evade upper-level regulations. More importantly, given that the center has limited information about local land demands, defining local land quotas in a centralized manner will seriously limit local government capacity to attract investment and may be harmful to local development and to the nation's industrialization and urbanization. In more developed regions such as Zhejiang and Jiangsu where the authors recently carried out fieldwork and interviews, such constraining effects have quickly emerged and have meant that local governments have been forced to break the investment contracts signed with foreign investors because the center has significantly reduced local land use quotas.[26] Moreover, a centralized land management system in which a land market cannot develop means that there is no institutional guarantee for the protection of farmers' interests since the prices of their land are still to be decided by upper-level government instead of being revealed by the market mechanism.

This is despite the fact that the center has instructed local governments to increase the compensation paid to dispossessed farmers.

## Conclusion

The current fiscal system in China has significantly impaired the capacity of local governments in less developed regions to provide decent public goods and services. Matching actual local fiscal needs with more equalizing transfers is therefore necessary to ensure equity in public service access across regions. However, owing to the lack of government accountability to the local population under the current centralized political system, increasing transfers alone cannot guarantee better local government efficiency and public service provisioning. If free local-level elections are not achievable in the short run, improving local governance in China at the current stage requires a fundamental change of the current "growth-centered" development strategy that imposes policy burdens and various development mandates from the center. It also requires a thorough reform of the current cadre evaluation system which is characterized by performance contracts that directly target local economic growth and fiscal revenue. Instead of trying to create economic growth itself, what the local government should be doing is finding ways to provide public goods and services that may, in the long run, promote economic growth. Only when unreasonable policy burdens are downgraded and cadre evaluation criteria are reoriented to providing public goods that are more closely related to local needs can the conditions for downsizing excessive local bureaucracies be created and the role of healthy regional competition be strengthened to contain local misbehavior. Otherwise the alternative can only be further administrative and fiscal centralization, which in turn may bring yet more distortions in local government behavior. In the long run, good governance will be the outcome of a decentralized administrative and fiscal system which includes a sound intergovernmental fiscal arrangement; wider local political participation, and free competitive elections of local officials (supported by information revealed through yardstick comparisons); and still stronger factor mobility across regions.

## Notes

1 Part of the material in this section is based on the authors' field work in 2003 and 2004 for an ongoing project "Rural Taxation, Policy Burdens and Local Governance in China" funded by the Ford Foundation and China National Science Foundation (project number 70303011). Liu Mingxing also wants to thank the China National Science Foundation (project number 70433002) for financial support. The authors carried out field work at the village, township and county level in the eastern provinces of Jiangsu, Zhejiang and Hebei, the central provinces of Anhui and Hunan, and the western provinces of Shaanxi and Gansu. The authors would like to thank Professor Vivienne Shue, Christine Wong, Rachel Murphy, and Kun-chin Lin for helpful comments. The usual disclaimer applies.

2 In fact, the process of devolving economic authority to local governments began much earlier, even in the 1960s and 1970s (Wong 1986). During the planned economy period there were cycles of centralization and decentralization, and so the fiscal

decentralization in the 1980s was largely a matter of catching up with the decentralization in other economic controls (Lin et al. forthcoming).

3 Although grassroots (village-level) elections have been taking place quite extensively across the country since the late 1980s, the elected village committees are conceived of as community organizations, rather than as units of state administration. These grassroots leadership selections do not qualify, therefore, as elections to local-state governmental offices (Zhang et al. 2004).

4 According to this view, the readiness of the Chinese central government to reward and punish local officials on the basis of their economic performance motivates them to promote the local economy (Blanchard and Shleifer 2001). The reward and punishment mechanisms are made possible within the multidivisional-form (M-form) structure of the Chinese economic system, which allows yardstick competition among local officials (Qian and Xu 1993; Qian and Weingast 1996).

5 After the 1994 fiscal reform, the center has gained a great deal of allocative control. However, a large share of central revenues is returned to the localities through tax rebates and earmarked transfers (which tend to be disequalizing) instead of general-purpose transfers (which can be equalizing). Tax receipts accrue to the center before rebates are made, allowing the center to withhold funds if local governments fail to comply with central policies. Furthermore, the center's allocative flexibility has been increasing over time as the share of tax rebates has fallen in total transfers. However, the center has not increased the share of formula-driven equalizing general-purpose transfers, but has instead significantly increased its earmarked transfers, which is a relatively discretionary subset of intergovernmental transfers (Wong 2000; World Bank 2002).

6 For more information about fiscal reforms since 1994 see Chapter 1 by Wong in this volume.

7 An important dimension of administrative decentralization in the 1980s and early 1990s was that more state-owned enterprises came under the control of local governments at provincial, municipality and county levels. Since state-owned enterprises usually provided a wide range of social services to their employees, such as education, health care, and pensions, more local government ownership of state-owned enterprises has naturally meant that local governments began to shoulder the primary and ultimate responsibilities for these expenditures which continued to have a very significant impact on patterns of local public finance into the 1990s.

8 Some scholars have vividly described the current arrangement as a "pressure imposing system" (Rong et al. 1998), under which all local government and Party agencies and cadres, from county to village level, face constant pressures from above to perform according to higher-level policy. As a result, local cadres are enmeshed in meetings, documents, reports, receiving visitors, and passing various inspections from above. However, since these policy targets are set from above, it is highly likely that they are not consistent with local needs because of the high transaction costs of catering to local preferences by the center, such as the costs in gathering local information. To meet all their targets, local officials have a tendency to fabricate statistics on economic growth and government revenues, exaggerate farmers' income growth and under-report rural tax burdens. Either showcase projects (such as the more visible roads or expensive education and health care facilities) top the local government agenda, or already excessive local fee charges on farmers are increased yet again to meet financial needs.

9 Veto power implies that if township leaders fail to attain these targets, this would cancel out all their other positive work performance, however successful, in the comprehensive evaluation at the end of the year (Edin 2003).

10 Our field investigations in some industrialized counties in Zhejiang show that although birth control and compulsory education are still important in cadre evaluations, the targets are set at levels that are relatively easy to reach in almost all townships so that, in the final evaluation, they do not make a difference. However, what really matters in these regions is usually whether the townships fulfill the targets set on land

development, environmental protection and outside investment (authors' interview in Linan county and Shaoxin county, Zhejiang province May, 2004).

11 In China, farmers' petitions usually take the form of lodging collective complaints at a higher level of government. In the late 1990s and early 2000s, heavy tax burdens in China's agriculture-based regions led to a rising frequency of collective complaints. Since maintaining social stability (or public security) has been a "hard" target that must be met in almost all regions, cadres' annual assessments (which affect salary and promotion) may be downgraded if too many complaints are filed in a locality (O'Brien and Li 1995).

12 Authors' interview in Linan county and Shaoxin county, Zhejiang province May 2004.

13 Authors' interviews in Yuanjiang county, Changde city Hunan province January, 2004 and authors' interviews in Qingyang county, Anhui province, April 2004.

14 Authors' interviews in Hezheng county and Linxia county, Gansu province, November 2004.

15 Although the less developed regions have also witnessed significant increases in infrastructure investment in recent years, most of this investment has come from earmarked transfers from the provincial and central levels of government, rather than from local budgets.

16 A second example of regional heterogeneity in policy enforcement lies in the center's birth control policy. Alhough the center calls for a relatively homogeneous birth control policy across the country, in less developed areas where income is lower, non-agricultural employment more limited and females less well-educated, farmers on average strongly prefer to have more children than those in richer regions. Therefore, poorer regions face greater difficulties in fulfilling the birth quota set by the center, and this leads to demand for higher administrative and personnel resources to enforce birth control policy in less developed regions. Further examples can be found in the implementation of the center's nine-year compulsory education policy. For more on the relatively high costs of education in poorer regions and villages, see Chapter 4 by Rachel Murphy in this volume.

17 Compared to previous direct deduction of taxes and some fees via the state grain procurement system, the work of collecting explicit taxes from individual rural households is much more demanding. Anecdotal evidence also suggests that in many less developed regions, a vicious cycle emerged: local governments had to recruit more staff, both formally and informally, to ensure tax collection; higher tax revenues then had to be used to support an enlarging local bureaucracy. This in turn led to even higher tax collections and larger local bureaucracy (Chen 2003; Yep 2004).

18 For example, in the case of fertilizer, Ye and Rozelle (1994) show that after an early attempt at market liberalization in 1986 and 1987, perceived instability in the rural economy in 1988 led to sharp retrenchments. Only in the early 1990s did agricultural officials once again remove the controls on fertilizer marketing and begin to encourage private trade.

19 The data used for our analyses are the product of annual household surveys conducted by the Survey Department of the Research Center on the Rural Economy (RCRE) in Beijing. Household-level surveys from over 120 villages across 10 provinces (Anhui, Gansu, Henan, Hunan, Jilin, Shanxi, Sichuan, Guangdong, Jiangsu, and Zhejiang) are matched with corresponding village-level and county-level data.

20 See further Chapter 7 by Shih and Zhang in this volume.

21 Authors' interviews in Hezheng county and Linxia county, Gansu province, November 2004.

22 For instance, in China's anti-poverty programs, local governments have a tendency to focus more on projects that can reduce poverty headcounts quickly but ignore the poorest people most in need. Since local officials are evaluated in no small part on the basis of concrete targets such as the number of poor that have been lifted out of poverty, officials have an incentive to direct the funds to the better-off poor households or areas

with better location and better natural resources so that project costs can be lower and the expected success rate higher (Zhu and Jiang 1996).

23 Authors' interviews in Yuanjiang county, Hunan province, December 2003

24 Authors' interviews in Taichang county, Jiangsu province, September 2004.

25 The progress of government downsizing is related to job opportunities outside the administrative sector and the wage premiums in government sectors. In Jiangsu province, some local cadres have left their official jobs for better jobs in the private sector, while in Gansu we found that there has been a significant increase in the numbers of both teaching and administrative staff at local public schools after the upper level governments required a timely and full delivery of school salaries. Even in Jiangsu, however, most cadres are still able to stay in their posts and receive 70 percent of their salaries.

26 Authors' interviews in Linan county and Shaoxin county, Zhejiang province May 2004 and interviews in Wuzhong county and Taichang city, Jiangsu province, August 2004.

## References

Bardhan, Pranab (2002) "Decentralization and Governance in Development," *Journal of Economic Perspectives*, Fall 16 (4): 185–206.

Bernstein, T. (1999) "Farmer Discontent and Regime Responses," in Merle Goldman and Roderick MacFarquhar (eds.) *The Paradox of China's Post-Mao Reforms*, Cambridge, MA: Harvard University Press, pp. 195–219.

Blanchard, Olivier and Shleifer, Andrei (2001) "Federalism With and Without Political Centralization: China Versus Russia," IMF Staff Papers, International Monetary Fund, 48 (4): 8.

Chen Xiwen (2003) *A Study On China's County and Township Public Finance and Farmer Income Growth*, Shangxi: Shangxi Economic Press.

De Brauw, A., Huang, J. and Rozelle, S. (2004) "The Sequencing of Reform Policies in China's Agricultural Transition," *Economics of Transition* (September), 12 (3): 427.

Edin, Maria (2003) "State Capacity and Local Agent Control in China: CCP Cadre Management from a Township Perspective," *China Quarterly*, 173 (March): 35–52.

Kang Xiaoguang (1998) "The Commentary on China's Poverty Alleviation," Paper prepared for UNDP, Research Center for Eco-Environmental Sciences, Chinese Academy of Sciences.

Li Honglin and Zhou Li-An (2005) "Political Turnover and Economic Performance: The Incentive Role of Personnel Control," *China Journal of Public Economics*, 89: 1743–62.

Lin Yifu, Tao Ran and Liu Mingxing (forthcoming 2006) "Decentralization and Local Governance in China's Economic Transition," in Pranab Bardhan and Dilip Mookherjee (eds.) *Decentralization to Local Governments in Developing Countries: A Comparative Perspective*, Michigan: MIT Press.

Morduch, Jonathan (2000) "Reforming Poverty Alleviation Strategy," in Anne Krueger (ed.) *Economic Policy Reform: The Second Stage*, Chicago, IL: University of Chicago Press.

Oi, Jean (1995) "The Role of Local State in China's Transitional Economy," *China Quarterly*, 144, Special Issue: China's Transitional Economy: 1132–49.

O'Brien, Kevin and Li Lianjiang (1995) "The Politics of Lodging Complaints in Rural China," *China Quarterly*, 143 (September): 756–83.

Park, Albert, Wang Sangui, and Wu Guobao (2002) "Regional Poverty Targeting in China," *Journal of Public Economics*, 86: 123–53.

Qian Yingyi and Weingast, B. (1996) "China's Transition to Markets: Market-Preserving Federalism, Chinese Style," *Journal of Policy Reform*, 1: 149–85.

Qian Yingyi and Xu Chenggang (1993) "Why China's Economic Reforms Differ: The M-Form Hierarchy and Entry/Expansion of the Non-State Sector," *Economics of Transition* (June), 1 (2): 135–70.

Rong Jinben, Cui Zhiyuan et al. (1998) "From a Pressure Imposing System to a Democratic Cooperation System: The Political Reform at County and Township Level" (in Chinese), Beijing: Chinese Press of Translating and Editing.

Rozelle, S. (1996) "Gradual Reform and Institutional Development: The Keys to Success of China's Rural Reforms," in Barry Naughton (ed.) *Economic Reform in China: Lessons for Economics in Transition*, Ann Arbor: University of Michigan Press, Chapter 7.

Rozelle, S., Park, A., Jin, H. and Huang, J. (2000) "Bureaucrat to Entrepreneur: the Changing Role of the State in China's Grain Economy," *Economic Development and Cultural Change*, 48 (2): 227–52.

Sicular, T. (1995) "Redefining State, Plan, and Market: China's Reforms in Agricultural Commerce," *China Quarterly*, 144: 1020–46.

State Council (2004) "Policy Directives to Promote Farmers' Income," Beijing: State Council (February), 8.

Tao Ran, Lin Yifu, Liu Mingxing and Zhang Qi (2004) "Rural Taxation and Government Regulation in China," *Agricultural Economics*, 31: 161–8.

Wong, Christine (1986) "Ownership and Control in Chinese Industry: The Maoist Legacy and Prospects for the 1980s," in Joint Economic Committee, US Congress, *China's Economy Looks Toward the Year 2000*, Washington, DC: USGPO, pp. 571–603.

Wong, Christine (2000) "Central-Local Relations Revisited: The 1994 Tax Sharing Reform and Public Expenditure Management in China," *China Perspective*, 31 (September–October): 52–63.

World Bank (2002) *China National Development and Sub-national Finance: A Review of Provincial Expenditures*, Washington, DC: World Bank.

Yep, R. (2004) "Can 'Tax-for-Fee' Reform Reduce Rural Tension in China? The Process, Progress and Limitations," *The China Quarterly*, 177: 42–70.

Ye Qiaolun and Rozelle, Scott (1994) "Fertilizer Policy in China's Reforming Economy," *Canadian Journal of Agricultural Economics* (July), 42: 191–208.

Zhang Xiaobo, Fan Shenggen, Zhang Linxiu and Huang Jikun (2004) "Local Governance and Public Goods Provision in Rural China," *Journal of Public Economics*, 2857–871.

Zhu Ling and Jiang Zhongyi (1996) *Public Works and Poverty Alleviation in Rural China*, New York: Nova Science Publishers.

# Index

Note: *italic* page numbers denote references to figures/tables.

For Product Safety Concerns and Information please contact our EU representative GPSR@taylorandfrancis.com
Taylor & Francis Verlag GmbH, Kaufingerstraße 24, 80331 München, Germany

www.ingramcontent.com/pod-product-compliance
Ingram Content Group UK Ltd.
Pitfield, Milton Keynes, MK11 3LW, UK
UKHW020202200926
475702UK00004B/584
*9780415422543*